Let's Talk
About Relationships
CASES IN STUDY
SECOND EDITION

Let's Talk About Relationships

CASES IN STUDY

SECOND EDITION

Thomas L. Veenendall
Montclair State University

Marjorie C. Feinstein
College of St. Elizabeth

WAVELAND
PRESS, INC.

Prospect Heights, Illinois

Consulting Editor

Robert E. Denton, Jr.

Photo Credits:

Alison Pederson pp. xvi, 24, 148, 178, 278, 318, 346

Thomas L. Veenendall pp. 70, 118, 206, 253

For information about this book, write or call:
    Waveland Press, Inc.
    P.O. Box 400
    Prospect Heights, Illinois 60070
    (847) 634-0081

Copyright © 1996, 1990 by Waveland Press, Inc.

ISBN 0-88133-864-8

Printed in the United States of America

7   6   5   4   3   2

Dedication

This book is dedicated by Marji to Norman, Samantha, and Jeffrey. Tom dedicates this book to his very special friends, Kurt, Tom, David, and Henry, and to those teachers in his life who have revealed to him at least a glimpse of the truth: Marianne W., Bernie S., Gerald J., Alyce T., Christopher S., and Louise H.

About the Authors

Thomas L. Veenendall is program coordinator and professor of communication studies at Montclair State University in Upper Montclair, New Jersey, where he has taught for fifteen years. He has authored or co-authored eleven textbooks and instructor's manuals focusing on effective communication. A past president of the Eastern Communication Association, Dr. Veenendall has been recognized as an Outstanding Alumna in Communication of Michigan State University and is a recipient of the Eastern Communication Association Teaching Excellence Award. He received his doctorate from the University of Denver in 1982, his M.A. from Western Michigan University, and his B.A. from Michigan State University. During his twenty-five years in education, his teaching and research interests have included interpersonal and nonverbal communication, public relations and desktop publishing, and applied communication.

Marjorie C. Feinstein is program director and assistant professor of communication at the College of Saint Elizabeth in Morristown, New Jersey, where she has taught for three years. She received her B.A. from Emerson College, her M.A. from Montclair State University, and her doctorate will be granted from New York University. She has taught a variety of communication and theatre courses over the past twenty-two years, with recent research and publication projects in interpersonal communication, conflict management, and experiential learning. In addition to her education work, she is directly involved in the development and implementation of the communication major at the college of Saint Elizabeth where she is a frequent facilitator for faculty development and instructional practice programs. During her professional career, she remains active in communal fund-raising efforts while maintaining a fulfilling family life with her husband, Norman, and children, Samantha and Jeffrey.

Preface

As authors, we have been very pleased with the response to the first edition of *Let's Talk About Relationships: Cases in Study*. With this revision we have been equally challenged by suggestions and reviews from many of you to produce an improved second edition. We are satisfied that we have met that challenge and we are excited to share our efforts with you.

Revisions and Additions

This book is about the process of creating, developing, changing, and improving relationships of all types. The experiential approach used in the development of the chapters continues to prove to us that an interactive methodology works best, especially for interpersonal communication. We have refined, enhanced, and expanded our original concept of this book through a complete revision of all chapters, the addition of mini-cases or situations presented within the text, the revision or replacement of 27 cases, and the addition of 14 new cases and 3 new chapters.

Chapter 1 is a new introductory chapter which consolidates theories on the process of interpersonal communication, some of which were previously in the chapter on perception and meaning. Two other new chapters (chapters 13 and 14) were added to incorporate coverage of the characteristics of relationships and communication competence, respectively. All other chapters were updated, revised, and developed as appropriate to growing interests and research in interpersonal communication effectiveness.

One of the new features of the book is the incorporation of mini-cases or "situations" presented within the text designed to provide instant examples or illustrations for the major concepts included in each chapter. Some are actual cases written in dialogue and others are descriptive situations or scenes. Both are designed to provide short, poignant, applicable examples of target terms or core concepts. This new feature integrates an additional experiential dimension into the text of each chapter.

The chapter headings and subheadings have been carefully revised, reorganized, and reworded to establish a clear outline of the core concepts covered in each chapter.

Special Features

The original and continued special features of this book include target terms for each chapter, case studies written in dialogue to be used as experiential vehicles for discussion of these target terms, and the condensed summary of theories and concepts in each chapter.

The first feature we have continued in this revision is the use of target terms introduced at the beginning of each chapter. The highly positive feedback we received from both students and instructors encouraged us to continue their use and refine their application. Each target term is defined in the glossary and listed in the term index. This should assist students in discovering, locating, and clarifying target term meanings. These target terms are also used at the beginning of each case to provide a focus for a discussion and/or analysis of each case.

The primary special feature of this book is the inclusion of sixty-one case studies written in dialogue. These case studies are focused to the target terms and the core concepts in each chapter. You will find that these case studies work well in establishing the connection between the theories and concepts to the practical, interpersonal communication strategies.

The final special feature of this book is the use of condensed coverage of theories and concepts in the chapter texts. Students and instructors have commented on the ease with which the material can be absorbed because of its simplicity and focused format. Each chapter is a summary of the major interpersonal communication theories and concepts, which allows instructors and students to quickly grasp the main ideas. The chapters are short, easy to read, and thorough.

Theme

The development of this book was based on the concept that you cannot change other people, you can only change yourself. This idea presents itself through many avenues in the book as a self-awareness process that seeks to provide multiple strategy choices for interpersonal communication competence and effectiveness. If we are not aware of our problems and issues, we cannot correct them. If we become aware of them, we need methods to deal with them. This book seeks to provide a repertoire of strategies which can be applied to various situations. To select the strategy, first ask "what is the desired outcome?'' If we want a person to know that we feel a certain way, we might select one strategy. If we do not care enough about the relationship to expend the energy necessary to deal with the problem, we would select another strategy. If the relationship is important to us, we would select yet another strategy. Therefore, the theme of having a flexible approach to selecting the strategy that might work best in any given situation is the goal of this book. This theme is the connecting link that holds this book together—from the target terms for each chapter to the reflective responses for each case.

Organization

The book is organized into fourteen chapters which include topics that are the key variables in the study of interpersonal communication. Each chapter begins with a list of target terms which are covered in that chapter and a list of core concepts developed in that chapter followed by a short and focused chapter summary of theories and concepts. There is an overview at the beginning of each chapter and a summary at the end of each chapter with a complete reference list. Each chapter includes four to six cases complete with target terms, preview notes, and case participant descriptions. Each case also includes case concerns (questions about the case) and reflective responses (questions for application).

Acknowledgments

Revising a book on relationships is only possible when this act is built on the wisdom, support, and care of many people. We are greatly appreciative of our colleagues, families, friends, and each other, all of whom have added a wealth of knowledge to this project through countless hours of understanding and encouragement.

We offer special gratitude to the staff at Waveland Press and especially to Carol and Neil Rowe. Carol and Neil provided their expertise and insight in all areas of textbook publication. A special note of tribute goes to Carol for her meticulous editing.

To students and colleagues at Montclair State University and the College of Saint Elizabeth, we voice our appreciation of their concern about our efforts in writing. The following Montclair State University students outdid themselves in their efforts to make this second edition a book of which we all could be proud. Maria DaSilva meticulously edited the many drafts of this revision and helped to make the text accurate and precise. To Brian Vigorito, for the endless hours of outlining, desktop publishing (for the Instructor's Manual), and editing to make things just right, we offer sincere and heartfelt thanks. To Dawn Bognar, for completing the indices and glossary, we say thanks for your efficiency and accuracy. To Alison Pederson, who shot many of the new photographs for the book, we offer a special note of appreciation and admiration for your professionalism. Thanks also to Linda Greenberg, who so diligently proofed and edited early drafts. Special thanks to Sister Jacqueline Burns, Laura Winters, and Johanna Glazewski at the College of Saint Elizabeth for providing a rich, supportive, academic environment for writing and research of this type.

To our families, for their love and support in understanding our needs, thanks go to Vi and Neal Veenendall, Shirley and Sidney Feinstein, and Adele and Victor Chalfin. Special attention must be given to the all too frequently requested understanding of Samantha and Jeffrey, Marji's children.

To special friends, we offer a sincere personal note of gratitude. Donald Battjes, Jr. provided a comfortable space for Tom in which to write and constant moral support through countless revisions; Henry Blumenkranz released tension and stress through therapeutic massage. Marji thanks everyone who graciously made concessions when time was at a premium.

Finally, we both acknowledge the enrichment we provided for each other, without which this revision could not have been completed.

Thomas L. Veenendall
Marjorie C. Feinstein

Contents

10   Power   231

11   Dealing with Conflict   255

12   Relationship Stages   279

1
Chapter

The Interpersonal Communication Process

Specific Goals for Understanding Chapter One

TargetTerms

- consensual validation
- SMCR model of communication
- F.O.R. (frame of reference)
- conveyor-belt theory of communication
- bull's-eye theory of communication
- transactional communication
- noise
- nonverbal channels
- the types of communication
- communication
- communication axioms
- communication functions

CoreConcepts

1 the need and desire to be understood by other human beings
2 the process of communication including the creation and transfer of meaning
3 the definition of communication and its types
4 the factors that influence and create barriers for the process of communication such as the axioms and functions

1

"But you just don't understand . . ."

Overview

To be understood, by at least one other person, is one of the strongest desires human beings have, and this need can only be satisfied through the process of communication. When people do not understand us, we feel alone, threatened and frustrated. As human beings we have an innate need to be understood by others. When we do not feel that we have this understanding, the feeling of being misunderstood can drive us crazy. We begin to feel as though no one understands who we are and what we mean. Feeling understood by others is a vital, inborn human need which is based on our ability to communicate clearly and effectively.

As senders, we think what we say is perfectly clear; as receivers, we think we understand exactly what the sender meant. But we have all had the experience—probably too many times—when we were not understood by another person or when we got the wrong idea from a message someone sent to us. This frustration is compounded by the fact that many times we assume we are understood when in fact we are not. Alternatively, perhaps we acted as the faulty receiver and misunderstood someone else's message unknowingly.

These "communication breakdowns" (as they are sometimes called) or this less than effective communication process can result from a lack of understanding of the process of communication and the way meaning is transferred from one person to another. The anxiety produced by this miscommunication, however, can be most aggravating—we really need and want to be understood by other human beings. This strong desire is a primary motivator to investigate how this process called communication actually works.

In this chapter, we will investigate the transfer of meaning from one person to another and the factors that influence that process. We will explore the need and desire to be understood, the process of creating and transferring meaning through the actual process of communication, the factors that influence that process, and, overall, some of the barriers to accurate and effective communication. In doing so we will discover the basic communication axioms and functions.

The Need to be Understood

Harry Stack Sullivan (1953, p. 224) is one of the many theorists who states that the strongest desire in human beings is to be understood— by at least one other person. The search for mutual agreement pervades our journey through interpersonal relationship territory and is usually referred to as **consensual validation** (Sullivan, 1953). Although the technical definition of consensual validation relates to Sullivan's therapeutic work with mental patients, we can use this term to refer to the need to receive confirmation of our perceptions. This need usually manifests itself in statements such as "That was a great movie, wasn't it?"

Sullivan maintains that without the understanding of at least one other person, we can develop symptoms of anxiety, stress, and feelings of alienation. Sometimes we say, "But, you just don't understand." We feel as though we will go "crazy" if we do not find someone to understand what we mean. Sometimes we really want more than understanding; we want agreement. The ability to distinguish the difference between understanding and agreement is an important one if we are to achieve satisfaction from our interactions. No matter which need is surfacing—the need to be understood or the need to be agreed with—the need is strong and it is satisfied only by other people through interpersonal communication.

What Do You Think?

Terry: I'm so upset. Everything is going wrong today.

Kim: Don't get so bent out of shape. Things can't be that bad.

Terry: My car was broken into; they smashed my window, broke the door lock, and took my radio—all in broad daylight in the parking lot at work!

Kim: Well, it's not the end of the world. I've had worse happen. One time . . .

Terry: Oh, never mind. Just forget I said anything. You just don't understand.

What does Terry want from Kim? What feeling is Terry experiencing? Why?

The Process of Communication: Characteristics & Models

Meeting the need to be understood is accomplished only through effective communication processes; Sullivan (1953) adds the twin goals of personal satisfaction and security without fear and anxiety.

Understanding the process of communication can assist in accomplishing these goals. David Berlo (1960) provides us with a basic **model of communication—the SMCR**—that involves a **source** or sender (S) who sends a **message** (M) through various **channels** (C) to a **receiver** (R) who then provides feedback (see chapter 3) to the sender as the process begins again. Berlo was the first theorist to add the feedback loop to this process and to maintain that it was, in fact, a continuous, circular process, not a linear progression with a beginning and an end.

Figure 1.1: The Berlo Model of Communication

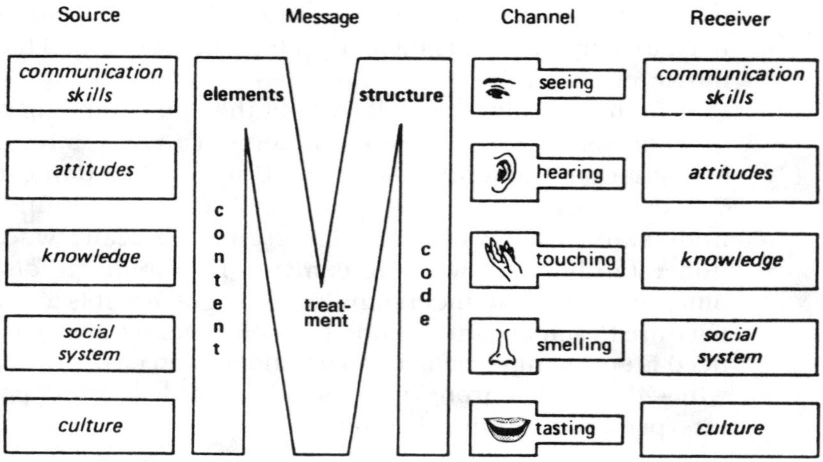

Diagram from *The Process of Communication: An Introduction to Theory and Practice* by David K. Berlo. Copyright © 1960 by Holt, Rinehart and Winston, Inc. Reprinted by permission.

According to Berlo's model, our communication is influenced by each of the following, in terms of the sender and the receiver:

- the **frame of reference** or **F.O.R.** of the sender and the receiver (communication skills; beliefs, attitudes and values; general knowledge and information; our social system; our culture)
- the way the **message** is formulated (elements, content, treatment, structure, code)
- the **channel** used (seeing, hearing, touching, smelling, tasting)

Understanding each of these influences can increase the clarity in message dissemination.

Source and Receiver F.O.R.

We are, of course, most influenced by our own frame of reference (F.O.R.) and the dissimilarities of others' frames of reference. You may enjoy and relax to classical music, while I find it very annoying. This difference in F.O.R. may impact the way we communicate. Frame of reference can be defined as our picture of the world which has been influenced by everything we have ever seen or done. Instinctively, we think that all frames of reference match and that ours is the same as our friends. We tend to think, "Doesn't everyone see it this way?"

Well, the answer is "no." Everyone actually sees and interprets things very differently. This faulty reasoning of thinking everyone sees things the way we do causes us to assume that others understand our meaning which then absolves us from any responsibility beyond sending the message. If we say to a friend, "I'll meet you at the haunted house," and our friend is unaware that the house on the corner of Fifth and Elmwood is "labelled" the haunted house, then our friend will not know where to meet us. The frames of reference are different, and misunderstanding is the result. Taking into account that our friend is new in the neighborhood, we could make our message more clear by saying, "I'll meet you at what we call the haunted house—the one on the corner of Fifth and Elmwood. Do you know where that is?" This message acknowledges the differences in frames of reference and takes responsibility for clear, transactional message dissemination by asking for feedback (Myers and Myers, 1992, p. 23).

Using the "**conveyor-belt theory**"[1] of communication removes the necessity of us providing or allowing feedback and makes the communication process very one-sided (Berlo, 1960). Gail E. Myers and Michele Tolela Myers refer to this type of communication as the "**bull's-eye theory** . . . a one-way act like shooting an arrow into a target" (1992, p. 23). These two theories do not work; they are based on the philosophy that the sender need only create and send a message; after that, it's the receiver's problem. These two theories absolve the sender from any responsibility in communicating the meaning of the intended message and assume that everyone has the same frame of reference. Once we identify and accept that **everyone** has a *different* frame of reference, we can then begin to accommodate these differences in message creation, take responsibility for the messages we send, and process our messages through a **transactional communication** process as described by Berlo (1960).[2] A transactional view of communication reveals that communicators normally send and receive messages simultaneously and suggests that this process is more like a motion picture than a set of still photographs (Adler, Rosenfeld, and Towne, 1992). Richard L. Weaver (1993, p. 50) explains that transactional communication emphasizes that who people are (with reference to others) is a result of the communication events—the transactions—in which they are involved. In other words, transactional communication involves the interaction of the sender *and* the receiver in the exchange of information—it is NOT a one-way channel; rather, it is shared participation in the process with equal responsibility for understanding the message.

What Do You Think?

Boss: OK, first take this package over to shipping, then clean up the lunch room, and then repaint the lines on the floor. See me when you're done.

Worker: OK. What color . . .

Boss: Make sure you get done today. We don't have time to waste around here. Any questions? (*the Boss walks away without looking at the worker or waiting for questions*)

Worker: Yeah, I . . .

LATER THAT DAY

Boss: Shipping said they don't have that package yet. What happened? And—good grief, I can't believe you painted the lines red. They're supposed to be white. Didn't you hear what I said?

Worker: Yes, but . . .

Boss: No buts about it. Now do it over.

What theory of communication does this scene illustrate? What needs to happen for more effective communication to occur?

The communication abilities and skills that we have will greatly influence our effectiveness as communicators—whether we are sending or receiving a message. We have to know our audience before we can formulate our message so it is aimed at the frames of reference of audience members. Poor articulation or other weak vocal aspects (variety, stress, volume, pitch) can make a message imperceptible. These communication skills and competencies affect our sending and receiving of messages.

Message clarity is also affected greatly by our insecurities and uncertainties—or our attitudes about ourselves, about others, and about events and objects. If we are unsure about an idea or a piece of information, the message we send will not be clear. A low self-concept also can create low-level message clarity. When we are unsure or uncertain about ourselves or something else, we are unclear. Thus, the way we perceive ourselves significantly affects how we communicate.

Our general knowledge about a subject affects our ability to communicate clearly and accurately. As a communication professor, if I had to present a lecture on chemistry, my lack of knowledge about chemistry would greatly impede my ability to send a message to you with any sense of clarity. Is your knowledge of sports greater than your friend's? Do you get frustrated when you try to communicate about that subject? Basically, we can not talk about information we do not know—at least not clearly and intelligently.

The social system in which we live and the cultural heritage through which we are raised will greatly influence the way we communicate. If you were raised in New York City and I was raised in Indiana, the values of our respective social systems can be quite different. If you were raised in an Italian family and I was raised in a Dutch family, the way we handle conflict can be quite different. In these cases and other similar social system and cultural heritage examples, we can see that our frame of reference is formulated differently, which in turn affects the way we communicate. Communication skills, self-concept, general knowledge about a subject and individual frames of reference influence the way we send and receive messages.

What Do You Think?

Terry: I can't wait to buy a new car. This one is almost three years old.

Kim: Why? I think this one is great. You can give it to me if you want to get rid of it.

Terry: But it's so old. I need a new one. The seats are worn and dirty, the paint is scratched, and it has almost 50,000 miles on it. Time to get a new one.

Kim: We always kept our cars for 8–10 years—you know, until they wore out. It seems like such a waste to get a new one to replace this perfectly good car.

Terry: Well, I guess we do things differently in my family.

What factors of the F.O.R. are causing the differences here? Why do Terry and Kim see things so differently? Where do their frames of reference differ?

Message Creation

The way we put the **message** together before we send it has great impact on the outcome of the communication. The message can be affected by the content (the words we choose), the elements (verbal and nonverbal aspects), the treatment (written or oral forms), the structure (grammar and syntax), and the code (the language used). The most obvious example of this part of Berlo's model is the language we speak. If you and I speak different languages, we will have difficulty understanding each other. If you speak French and I attempt to speak to you in French, we will do better in communicating. Closer to home is the example of speaking the same language (English) but using provincial expressions which again can reduce clarity. For example, if I order a "soda" in Michigan, I would get soda water, ice cream, and flavoring. If I order a "soda" in New Jersey, I would probably get Coca Cola or be asked which flavor. If our vocabulary is weak, we will not be able to select the most appropriate words to express our meaning. Also, using slang words or obscenities can change the way our message is received. Proficiency in language use increases our communication effectiveness in creating a clearer message.

What Do You Think?

Kim: Can you put that thing over there, please?
Kelly: Sure.
Kim: Oh, no. I meant over there, not here.
Kelly: Oh, I see.
Kim: No, put it vertically, not horizontally.
Kelly: OK.
Kim: No, I mean the other way.

Why was Kim's message confusing to Kelly? How can Kim make the message clearer?

Channel

Finally, the **channels** used in the communication process involve one or more of our five senses: hearing, seeing, touching/feeling, smelling, and tasting. In the normal communication process, we primarily use sound and sight for the sending and receiving of verbal (and nonverbal) messages. If we talk too softly, our receiver may ask us to repeat ourselves. If the receiver is hearing impaired, our message may be only partially heard and/or misunderstood. If our receivers are poor listeners, they may delete, distort or add to our message.

Distortion or "noise" can affect the various channels. **Noise**, any interference in the communication process, can be physical or psychological. For example, being tired or hungry can affect the receiver's listening ability. A noisy radiator can interrupt a teacher's answer. Worrying about a test you will have in the next class will impede your listening ability in this one. So, clearing the channels of all distortions or imperfections can increase the chances of the message getting through clearly to the receiver.

What Do You Think?

Kelly: (*entering class with Kim*) Wow, I'm really surprised that we're having a test today.
Kim: WHAT?! You're kidding, right?
Kelly: No, weren't you here yesterday?
Kim: Of course I was. I sat right next to you.
Kelly: Well, didn't you hear Dr. Graham announce about the test for today?
Kim: I guess not.
Kelly: Well, what happened? Weren't you listening?
Kim: Well, I thought I was. I've just had so much on my mind lately. My parents are getting a divorce and I'm right in the middle of it.

Why was Kim's channel blocked? What kind of noise kept Kim from hearing the announcement about the test?

Nonverbal Channels

Not all communication is verbal. As communicators, we realize that the wink of an eye or a lilt of one's voice can clearly express what a person is trying to convey. There are many **nonverbal channels** such as proxemics (space), chronemics (time), haptics (touch), oculesics (eye gaze), facial expressions, kinesics (body language), paralinguistics (the sound or tone of the voice), environmental factors (weather, color, objects, design), and dress and adornment (clothing, make-up, jewelry) which have an effect on the way we communicate and how we are understood. While researchers have focused an enormous amount of attention on the power of nonverbal communication, we wish to add that when analyzing interpersonal communication, we must always remember to consider how the nonverbal aspects of communication affect our message sending and receiving.

When deciding the meaning of messages you receive, the nonverbal component is a big consideration. The nonverbal elements listed above each individually and collectively influence the verbal content of the message. In order to decipher the total meaning of the message, the verbal content and the nonverbal implications need to be considered together in a total "message picture." For example, if I say, "Paul, would you please close the door" in an authoritative, angry voice, the message Paul will receive is one of demand, requirement and control. I can make it sound like I have power over Paul to shut the door and that if he doesn't do what I ask, he will be in trouble. However, I can also say "Paul, would you please close the door" in a friendly, requesting voice. This time Paul would probably still close the door but might feel more equal, friendly and respectful than before. The nonverbal element of the message can have a very strong impact on the actual verbal content, and it is important when analyzing the cases in this book to consider this impact. (See "Further Reading" at the end of this chapter for references containing more information on nonverbal communication.)

Definitions

Frank E.X. Dance (1970) reviewed ninety-five definitions of communication and was unable to come up with a comprehensive definition. According to Dance, "No one of the 95 definitions reviewed, adequately covers the entire range of behaviors studied" by communication scholars (pp. 201–210). Since that time, many other definitions of communication and interpersonal communication have emerged. B. A. Fisher (1978) maintains that the process of human communication in all its forms is seen differently by different theorists depending upon their theoretical perspective and the particular element(s) of communication on which they are focusing.

First, we need to identify the various **types of communication**. Although all forms of communication follow some basic patterns, there are distinct differences in the various types of communication in which we participate. Frank Dance and Carl Larson (1972) identify the different types or levels of human communication as follows:

- **intrapersonal**—communicating with oneself
- **interpersonal**—communicating with one or more people face-to-face with the possibility of immediate feedback
- **public**—one person communicating to many with delayed feedback

Joseph A. DeVito (1994, p. 6) adds four more areas or types of communication to help us understand how human communication is categorized:

- **small group**—communication with a small group of three or more persons
- **organizational**—communication within a formal organization
- **intercultural**—communication between persons of different cultures
- **mass**—communication addressed to an extremely large audience, mediated by audio and/or visual means

These types of communication are both additive and reciprocal. The levels are additive in that what we learn in intrapersonal communication is a foundation for developing effective interpersonal communication, and our effectiveness in interpersonal communication can build confidence for effective public speaking. All the levels are reciprocal in that they also all affect each other. So, even though we may define the various types differently and make certain distinctions between the types, they are also integrated in such a way that they are difficult to isolate precisely. As we write about interpersonal communication in this book, we will also be learning about the basic process of communication, and the various other types of communication will infiltrate our discussions. Lines are drawn between the types of communication primarily for the sake of studying them and to identify specific characteristics which assume greater or lesser importance depending on the context in which the communication takes place.

Communication can be defined as the process of transmitting and interpreting messages (Weaver, 1993). Weaver goes on to define **interpersonal communication** as involving at least two people providing feedback, not necessarily face-to-face nor intentional; producing some effect which is affected by the context and noise; and exhibiting verbal and/or nonverbal behavior (Weaver, 1993, pp. 19–20). Daniel J. Canary and Michael J. Cody (1994) define interpersonal communication as "the exchange of symbols used to achieve interpersonal goals" (p. 28). A broader way of defining the process of communication and also identifying what happens during interpersonal communication is the definition given by Ronald B. Adler and

Neil Towne (1993). "Communication is a continuous, transactional process involving participants who occupy different but overlapping environments and create a relationship by simultaneously sending and receiving messages, many of which are distorted by external, physiological, and psychological noise" (Adler and Towne, 1993, pp. 14–15).

Communication Axioms

There are several **communication axioms** and postulates that define what communication is and how it operates. Axioms are generalized truths or characteristic statements of a process. These characteristics distinguish some important principles of the communication process and will help us better understand how it works (Barnlund, 1962; Watzlawick, Beavin, and Jackson, 1967):

- **we cannot NOT communicate**—everything we say and do sends a message
- **communication can be intentional or unintentional**—messages can be planned and sent on purpose or they can be unplanned and spontaneous
- **communication is circular**—this is the I-talk, you-listen, you-talk, I-listen cycle
- **communication is transactional**—meaning is transmitted through interaction
- **communication is dynamic**—each person brings his/her own personality into the process
- **communication is unrepeatable**—no communication is ever the same twice
- **communication is irreversible**—communicated messages cannot be erased
- **communication is an evolution of meaning**—meanings are in people not in words
- **communication is complex**—because humans are involved, communication is not scientific but includes many uncontrolled variables
- **communication will not solve all problems**—sometimes talking things out will not solve the problem because the differences in values may still exist
- **communication is not a natural ability**—the skills of effectiveness must be practiced
- **more communication is not always better**—we do not have to say everything we think and feel; sometimes not saying anything is better because we tend to say too much

There are additional communication axioms specifically for interpersonal communication:

- interpersonal communication involves **a process of adjustment**
- interpersonal communication involves **a content and relationship dimension**
- interpersonal communication involves **metacommunication** (talking about the communication process)
- interpersonal communication involves **at least two people providing feedback, producing some effect, and need not be face-to-face**

Understanding how the process of communication occurs can help us understand how to improve our communication effectiveness. Our communication patterns may fall victim to various communication barriers when we ignore one of the axioms; if we become aware of these barriers and how to avoid them, we can alleviate them and begin our path toward more effective communication encounters.

What Do You Think?

Teacher: OK, now, these are the requirements for the term paper: 5–6 pages, typed, with at least 6–8 outside sources and topics must be approved by me by Friday.

Student #1: I thought you said last week that the paper had to be 6–8 pages. Which is correct?

Teacher: Oh, yes. It's 6–8 pages with 5–6 outside sources. And the paper must be on computer or any word processor.

Student #2: You already approved my topic; may I go ahead with my research?

Teacher: Sure. Just turn it in to me again on Friday to be sure.

END OF SEMESTER, LAST CLASS PERIOD

Student #3: Here's my term paper.

Teacher: But it's only 5 pages.

Student #3: But you said, 5–6 pages with 3–4 sources. That's what I did.

Where is the confusion here? Which axioms of communication are illustrated with this scene?

Functions of Communication

Communication serves many functions which characterize the reasons we communicate. Through communication, we satisfy many basic needs which help us to operate in the complex information age. Adler and Towne (1993) report that the **functions of communication** include:

- **satisfying our physical needs**
- **identifying our needs to ourselves and others**
- **providing for our social interaction needs**
- **providing for our practical needs for information**

Rudolph F. Verderber (1993) explains the reasons we communicate in a slightly different way:

- **to meet needs**
- **to enhance our sense of self**
- **to develop relationships**
- **to fulfill social obligations**
- **to exchange information**
- **to influence each other**

On a lighter note, Dance and Larson (1976) include what we as graduate students affectionately called "linking, stinking (the use of communication to control) and thinking" or more specifically, connecting with other human beings, controlling or regulating human behavior, and developing our higher method of thinking and reasoning.

All of these functions of communication are motivators for us to participate in this complex process we call communication. We use communication to achieve many goals, not the least of which is to relate to other human beings to fulfill various needs. Interpersonal communication defines, maintains, and changes our self-concept and our relationships. Avoiding communication inhibits not only our socialization process but also impedes our personal development as human beings. Communication plays a major role in our lives and the better we understand how it operates, the more success we can achieve.

Summary

As human beings we have a high need for acceptance and validation evidenced in our struggle with self and others in our development as people. Understanding the process of communication including the transfer of meaning and the factors that influence this process will assist us in developing more effective communication styles. By understanding the characteristics of communication and specifically of interpersonal communication, we come closer to becoming the best communicators possible. Applying the axioms and utilizing the functions of communication can improve our approach to interpersonal effectiveness.

Notes

[1] The term "conveyor-belt theory" refers to the view of the communication process as one-way, similar to the "bull's-eye theory" (Myers and Myers, 1992, p. 23). The sender views his/her job as sending a message only, without any additional responsibility; this type of person neither endorses nor understands the necessity of feedback (Berlo, 1960).

[2] The term "transactional communication" refers to the view of the communication process which implies "interdependency and mutual reciprocal causality between sender and receiver (Myers and Myers, 1992, p. 24).

References

Adler, Ronald B., Lawrence B. Rosenfeld, and Neil Towne. *Interplay: The Process of Interpersonal Communication*, 5th ed. New York: Holt, Rinehart and Winston, 1992.

Adler, Ronald B. and Neil Towne. *Looking Out, Looking In*, 7th ed. New York: Holt, Rinehart and Winston, 1993.

Barnlund, Dean C. "Toward a Meaning-Centered Philosophy of Communication." *Journal of Communication*, 12, no. 4, (1962):202–203.

Berlo, David. *The Process of Communication*. New York: Holt, Rinehart and Winston, 1960.

Canary, Daniel J. and Michael J. Cody. *Interpersonal Communication: A Goals Based Approach*. New York: St. Martin's Press, 1994.

Dance, Frank E.X. and Carl E. Larson. The "Concept" of Communication. *Journal of Communication*, 20, (1970):201–210.

_____. *Speech Communication: Concepts and Behavior*. New York: Holt, Rinehart and Winston, 1972.

_____. *The Functions of Human Communication: A Theoretical Approach*. New York: Holt, Rinehart and Winston, 1976.

DeVito, Joseph A. *Human Communication*, 6th ed. New York: HarperCollins, 1994.

Fisher, B. Aubrey. *Perspectives on Human Communication*. New York: Macmillan, 1978.

Myers, Gail E., and Michele Tolela Myers. *The Dynamics of Human Communication: A Laboratory Approach*, 6th ed. New York: McGraw-Hill, 1992.

Sullivan, Harry Stack. *The Interpersonal Theory of Psychiatry*. New York: Norton, 1953.

Verderber, Rudolph F. *Communicate!*, 7th ed. Belmont, CA: Wadsworth, 1993.

Watzlawick, Paul, Janet Helmich Beavin, and Don D. Jackson. *Pragmatics of Human Communication: A Study of Interaction Patterns, Pathologies, and Paradoxes*. New York: W. W. Norton, 1967.

Weaver, Richard L., II. *Understanding Interpersonal Communication*, 6th ed. Glenview, IL: Scott, Foresman, 1993.

Further Reading

Knapp, Mark. *Essentials of Nonverbal Communication*. New York: Holt, Rinehart and Winston, 1980.

Leathers, Dale. *Successful Nonverbal Communication: Principles and Applications*, 2nd ed. New York: Macmillan, 1992.

Case 1

TargetTerms

- communication is irreversible (axioms)
- the functions of communication
- consensual validation

PreviewNotes

Did you ever wish you hadn't said something? This case illustrates that issue.

CaseParticipants

Jon—a friend of Karen's
Karen—a friend of Jon's

"Uh-oh! Something tells me I shouldn't have said that!"

Karen has just left the hairdresser after cutting her long hair quite short when she runs into her friend Jon who is about to sit down in a nearby coffee shop. Although Karen appears to be quite pleased with her new haircut, she is eager to hear her friend's response to her new "do." As Jon motions her to come and join him, he says:

Jon: What've you been up to? You look tired.

Karen: Well, you're right. I just had my hair cut and it feels like I've been there all day.

Jon: So, that's what's different about you.

Karen: C'mon, what do you think?

Jon: Truth?

Karen: Of course I want the truth.

Jon: (*sincerely*) Well, it's really short and it makes you look a lot older.

Karen: Well, thanks a lot!

Jon: No, I didn't mean that. What I meant is that you look so much more sophisticated than you did before. More business-like, more . . .

Karen: You're drowning in it!
Jon: No, really, I do like it.
Karen: Then, why didn't you say so when I sat down?
Jon: Because, to be honest, I didn't even notice that you looked different.
Karen: Great—just what I wanted to hear! (*She walks away feeling depressed and rejected.*)

CaseConcerns

Discussing the Case

1. Which communication axioms or postulates are at work in this case? Explain your answer.
2. Do you suppose Jon could have or might have given more consensual validation to his friend Karen. Explain your reasoning.
3. What is Karen communicating as her most pressing need when she sees Jon? Did she clearly express this need?
4. Is the communication that has taken place in this case reversible? If so, how can the transaction that has taken place be reversed?
5. How does the way Karen perceives herself reflect itself in the way she communicates? Do you feel that the way you personally feel about yourself at a given time affects the way you communicate to others?

ReflectiveResponses

Processing the Learning

1. How would you respond to significant others in your life who have changed their looks to a style you feel is counterproductive?
2. When communicating with others, do you consider how you might consensually validate the other person or do you focus on the message you are sending? Is it possible to do both when communicating in your personal, academic and/or professional life?
3. How do you feel when you request information from another and you receive an unexpected response? Do you feel that one of the functions of communication is to be honest?

Case 2

TargetTerms

- F.O.R. (frame of reference)
- transactional communication
- noise
- need to be understood

PreviewNotes

Sometimes communication is more difficult when the frames of reference are too different

CaseParticipants

Jan—Marlene's mother who is forty-something
Marlene—Jan's teenage daughter

"Stop playing that song!"

During a long three-hour drive Jan and Marlene find that they have a great deal to learn about each other's taste in music. While both Marlene and Jan want to control their respective "station hopping," the two learn about the differences in their frames of reference.

Marlene: Are we there yet?

Jan: If you don't stop blaring that music, we won't make the next mile. How can you listen to that garbage? I'm getting such a headache.

Marlene: Hey, Mom, listening to your "lite" music could put you to sleep—and we'll never get there, anyway.

Jan: Not so funny! I'm the Mom and this is my car. So just change the station, please.

Marlene: Wait a sec. How about listening to one of my more mellow tapes?

Jan: I give in. Start playing. I'll give you one more chance.

Marlene: Good. But, even when I played the other tape, I don't think that you listened to the lyrics. Did you know that the song we're listening to is about Eric Clapton's very young son who died.

Jan: Really? (*She makes an effort to hear the words and starts to actually smile while driving*.) So—now it makes sense—that's why he keeps repeating "Will you know my name when I see you in heaven?"

Marlene: The words are really sad, Mom.

Jan: Shhh—I'm trying to listen. The song is getting to me.

Marlene: Now that you've made the effort to listen to my music, I'll keep my mouth shut for one minute of your "Lite FM."

Jan: Hearing you say that made it worth my while to try to understand your music. Now, how would you like to listen to the mid-afternoon opera program? I read in the paper today that the featured music is from "La Boheme." Now, there's a sad story for you . . .

Marlene: (*with a broad smile*) Ummm . . . I may be getting a little tired!

CaseConcerns

1. What are some of the influences of Marlene's frame of reference? Of Jan's?

2. Do you believe that Marlene will make a responsible attempt to listen to the mid-afternoon opera program? Why or why not?

3. Briefly explain how transactional communication is taking place between Marlene and Jan.

4. Since the way we put a message together has an impact on the outcome of the communication, discuss whether or not you feel that Jan was able to effectively verbally communicate to her daughter. Do the same with Marlene. Would you want to change the way the two communicated to enhance the outcome of their exchange. If so, what would you have them say?

5. Discuss the impact here of the need to be understood.

ReflectiveResponses

1. Relate an experience in your life where you tried to reap the benefit of understanding a new idea or way of doing something. What were some of the influences that caused you to see something in a different way? Did this affect the way in which you communicated?

2. Can you think of an incident in your life where you seemed to shut off understanding someone else's frame of reference. What were the circumstances, and do you still feel at this time that you were justified in your original position? If not, why in retrospect are you now able to change your communication behavior?

Case 3

TargetTerms

- functions of communication
- consensual validation

PreviewNotes

Communication functions help to develop and support a relationship through consensual validation.

CaseParticipants

Jack—Jill's husband of 20 years who is celebrating one of his mid-life birthdays

Jill—Jack's wife who takes him out to dinner for his birthday

"Birthday blues"

The setting of this scene is an outdoor cafe on a breezy summer night in a trendy spot of any city. This particular night is a major feast for "people-watching." After ordering their dinner, Jack is especially quiet as Jill says:

Jill: How's it feel to be approaching your next century of life?

Jack: (*very sarcastically*) Thanks for the reminder. I don't need this tonight.

Jill: (*sensitively*) A little touchy, aren't you? Wanna leave?

Jack: (*looking around at all of the sights in the street*) No, it's not you, it's me. I hate birthdays.

Jill: Why?

Jack: They make me feel old. And depressed. And unspecial.

Jill: Nice birthday list! Why so sad?

Jack: I just don't think that I did anything of value this year. Like we wanted to get away for awhile and we didn't. I wanted to upscale my office and I couldn't. There's a million things that I didn't do.

Jill: So, you didn't do them. There's always next year.

Jack: I know you're right, but just look at all of these people in the street. They look happier than me and it's *my* birthday.

Jill: Honey, why don't you just get a can of worms and start munching away. (*She notices that he is beginning to smile.*) Well, *I* think that you're the best.

Jack: Do you really mean that?

Jill: Sure, I do. Think about how wonderful our lives are and the wonderful success you've had. (*She points to a homeless person begging for money.*) Then, there are those who don't have such opportunities—it does put things in perspective.

Jack: How do you always know how to make me feel appreciated?

Jill: Women's intuition?

Jack: Whatever. You do it well. Thanks, honey.

CaseConcerns

1. What function of communication does Jill fulfill for Jack in this case?

2. Identify the use of consensual validation in this case.

3. Describe the language each uses to communicate his or her needs to the other in this case. What type of impact does the choice of words have on the communication that takes place between the two.

ReflectiveResponses

1. Describe why you might use certain channels of communication in your involvements with others. For example, when might a letter be appropriate to express yourself? When might a telephone conversation be more appropriate than a person-to-person meeting?

2. How do you communicate your needs to significant others in your life? Think about how you may communicate your feelings and wishes to different people. Is there a difference in the way you communicate to a male or female friend? A parent? A husband, wife or lover? A professor? A therapist? Others? To what do you attribute the similarities or differences in your messages?

3. Do you believe that communication is a natural ability? Support your answer as best you can with ideas from this chapter as well as from your personal experience.

4. Explain what is meant by the statement, "All communication is in some sense ambiguous and can be subject to differing interpretations and meanings."

Case 4

TargetTerms

- chronemics (nonverbal channels)
- communication axioms
- F.O.R. (frame of reference)

PreviewNotes

Timing can greatly affect the communication process and even change the message.

CaseParticipants

Victor—managing partner of a legal firm who is demanding of his office staff

Ella—secretary, en route to a surprise party for her sister which begins promptly at 6:00 P.M., on a Friday late afternoon.

"Oh . . . and just before you go . . ."

Anxious to be on time for her sister's surprise party, Ella is hurriedly, but carefully, checking over her desk while preparing to leave. As she looks up, she sees Mr. Jimenez approach her with an urgent look on his face. The following exchange takes place in a small business office at 5:22 P.M., on a Friday late afternoon.

Victor: Oh, there you are—good—you're still here. I just got the final draft of that buy-sell agreement in and it needs to be Fed Ex'ed no later than 7:00 P.M. Do me a favor, will you, and do a search on the file.

Ella: I was just about to . . .

Victor: Do a search on the file?

Ella: No, actually I was getting ready to leave.

Victor: I know, I know, but this is really important.

Ella: Really, what would you have done if I had left—which I was just about to do.

Victor: But, you didn't—we're wasting time—so let's get going.

Ella: But—

Victor: Listen, I'll make it worth your while.

Ella: It's not that. I even stayed later tonight to clean up all these files—but I really can't stay any longer.

Victor: Are you telling me that you can't help me out this once. I mean, really, Ella, I wouldn't ask you if I didn't think that this was really important. The client is counting on us. (*He looks at her with a rather helpless face.*)

Ella: I wish I didn't have these plans, but I do.

Victor: And I wish I didn't have this deadline, but I do.

Ella: It's my sister's surprise party—and I'm already under the wire in getting there on time.

Victor: So, a few minutes here or there won't matter, will it? C'mon, I really need your help.

Ella: I guess there's no choice, is there? (*Reluctantly, she begins to turn on the computer while internally bursting at the seams.*)

CaseConcerns

1. How does timing affect the communication that takes place in this case? Do you believe that the communication exchange would be altered in this case if the time of day or the day of the week were different? Why or why not?

2. One of the issues in this case is on the content and relationship dimensions in communication. Describe what you perceive to be the relationship and the content dimensions in this case.

3. There are two perspectives working in this conflict situation. One of the considerations is from the point of view of the secretary while another perspective is from the point of view of the boss. Consider how you would answer the following questions as the character in the case. a) Victor, why didn't you warn Ella about the possibility of working late on the contract? b) Ella, why didn't you tell your boss how much being on time to the party meant to you? Do you feel that you could have told him about the party earlier?

4. How do you feel now that Ella has consented to stay later and finish the document? Do you believe that her decision to stay later will have an influence on future dealings that Ella and Victor have with each other? How so?

ReflectiveResponses

1. Do you think about timing when you communicate with another person? Can you relate an incident in your life when you did not consider timing when talking to someone? What was the effect on your communication exchange?

2
Chapter

Self-Concept

Specific Goals for Understanding Chapter Two

TargetTerms

- mirror image
- looking-glass self
- self-concept
- barriers to growth
- locus of control
- perceived self
- ideal self
- imagined self
- real self
- self-honesty
- co-dependency
- shoulding

CoreConcepts

1   the nature of our self-concept
2   the effects of the self-concept on our interpersonal interactions
3   the process of growth and development of our self-concept
4   barriers to the growth and development of the self-concept
5   how to change your self-concept

"I've gotta be me . . ."

Overview

We cannot talk about relationships without first talking about the self. As humans, we are unique, complicated individuals, each with our own picture of the world. This frame of reference is ours and ours alone—no one else in the entire universe shares our personal frame of reference. While we do have many commonalities with many different people, we are still completely and wholly unique in our individual perceptions. This uniqueness and our picture of this uniqueness is called our self-concept, which emerges out of one's interactions with significant others (Mead, 1934). A mental motion picture is developed as we proceed through this self-discovery process which creates a constantly changing image of the "self" playing in our heads. This self-concept, then, is what influences everything we say and do.

In this chapter we will discover the influence of the self-concept on our relationships. We will explore the nature of the self-concept, the effects of the self-concept on interpersonal interactions, the ways in which the self-concept grows and develops, the major influences on the self-concept, the barriers the self-concept must face, and how the self-concept changes.

Self-Concept Defined

Self-concept can be defined in many ways. Ronald Adler and Neil Towne maintain that is "a relatively stable set of perceptions you hold of yourself" (1993, p. 40). They argue that even though the self-concept frequently changes, it is more useful to think about the self-concept as a single entity that is roughly consistent over time. Charles Brown and Paul Keller (1979) see the self-concept "in motion" and refer to it as a motion picture that plays in our head—the picture of a person in process (p. 29). Philip Emmert and Victoria Emmert add more to the definition describing it as "the aggregate of those physical, social, and psychological perceptions of ourselves that we have derived from our experiences and interactions with others" (1984, p. 58).

The self-concept is said to emerge from the mirror image we see of ourselves in others and from our looking-glass self reflected when exploring our personal world through self-contemplation and discovery (Cooley, 1956). The **mirror image** is the picture we get of who we are from significant others and our **looking-glass self** is the picture we get from our own perceptions and reflections. Simply stated, the self-concept is the image we hold of ourselves including: physical features, emotional states, talents, likes, dislikes, values, roles, and needs (Adler, Rosenfeld, and Towne, 1992, p. 27). It includes multiple images and multiple selves all blending together to form a unique personality with a unique frame of reference, all of which affect the way we communicate.

The Effects of Self-Concept on Interpersonal Interactions

Together, all these perceptions we have of ourselves affect our interpersonal transactions. While discovering who we are and focusing the mental picture, we discover complex, life-long processes that strongly affect the communication process. The self-concept has a tremendously strong impact on the way we communicate. For example, if we are unsure of ourselves in the sport of tennis, when we are involved in tennis, the way we talk, the words we choose, the way we stand, and the way we actually play will be affected by this insecurity. When we are confident about the material on a test, we answer the questions with self-assurance and conviction. The reverse can be true for both of these cases. How we view ourselves—our self-concept—greatly influences the choices we make (either consciously or unconsciously) in the communication process. Thus, "the self is created and maintained through interpersonal transactions" (Smith and Williamson, 1985, p. 130). This means that we are influenced by those with whom we relate and how they react to us.

However, sometimes there is a conflict in our mind between searching for the self and forming relationships; these two processes sometimes clash because of our opposing goals. This is how it works. During the self-discovery process, we meet other people with whom we form various types of relationships. This necessary and valuable process of relationship formation both interferes with and assists in our quest for self-awareness. While we are trying to discover who we are, we are simultaneously trying to form relationships with others who also want to know about us and themselves. Forming relationships interferes by forcing us to communicate information we are unsure of to others in order to develop relationships for which we are not ready. Also, it interferes by requiring us to self-disclose before we have processed the thoughts thoroughly in our minds. How can we tell somebody else who we are when we are not sure about the information ourselves?

The dichotomy is that this process also helps us learn about ourselves, so the process assists in our quest for self-awareness through the "mirror image" reflected from others or the "looking-glass self" which allows us to "see" who we are. Our self-concept is not created in a vacuum; it is developed through our perceptions of what others think about us. However, when we are unsure about who we are or our mental image of "self" is unclear, relating to others is more difficult. This paradox multiplies if the number of relationships increase (which is what usually happens) and the self-awareness process is slow or dormant (which can easily happen because of our resistance to change and/or fear of finding out something about ourselves that we do not want to know).

Thus, we can see two primary connections between the self-concept and its interrelationship with the communication process. First, C. H. Cooley claims that nothing is known about the self except through the "looking-glass self" obtained from interaction with others (1956). This concept maintains that the self-concept develops only through communication with others (verbal and/or nonverbal). Second, self-knowledge is a function of self-disclosure. It is through the disclosure of information to others that we learn about ourselves (Jourard, 1971). Consequently, the creation, development, and maintenance of the self-concept depends on human interaction.

What Do You Think?

Mom: Why so down?
 Son: Oh—just nothing and everything.
Mom: Can I help?
 Son: No, there's really nothing specific.
Mom: How about that big math test you had last week? How did you do?
 Son: Oh, that—uh, not too well, I . . .
Mom: It can't be that bad. I bet you got an "A"—you're always so good in math.
 Son: Mom—just leave me alone, will you?! Just mind your own business!

How do you communicate in situations such as this? How does your self-concept affect the way you communicate?

Growth and Development of the Self-Concept

Just as the environmental conditions affect the growth of a plant, the development of the self-concept in a human being is affected by the socialization and enculturalization process. Plants cannot grow without water, sunlight, and the proper temperature. A plant will grow differently if insufficient sunlight is available for long periods of time. The plant may still be alive but will probably be dormant, limp, or disfigured. Too much water will affect the roots of the plant and high temperatures will make most plants wither and even die.

The self-concept is very similar in that it requires certain "nutrients" in order to be healthy and strong; it is influenced by many outside factors. Influences such as parents, school (teachers and peers), friends, and life's experiences act as nutrients to the self-concept and introduce outside stimuli that affect its growth. The self-concept is also influenced by our interpersonal needs, values, and satisfying (or unsatisfying) relationships—all greatly affecting the "life" of the self-concept.

Our communication behavior is the outward, verbal manifestation of our developing self-concept. We talk the way we do as a result of the combined influences we have received. All of these influences act as motivators to our communication behavior. For example, all human beings have needs that motivate our behaviors (Maslow, 1970). One of these needs is our need for self-esteem. If our self-esteem need is not met, for example, by accomplishments in our career, that need for personal power will be fulfilled in other ways. Another example concerns the values we learn (mainly from our parents), which also motivate our behaviors (Rokeach, 1968). If we become friends with "the wrong crowd" (according to Mother), our values may change to those of our new friends. Consequently, our view of the value of honesty may be reversed and our character marred. (Mother already knew this!) A third example is the influence self-disclosure has on our communication patterns (Jourard, 1971; Powell, 1969). Sharing who we are with others is frightening, because we are unsure how they will perceive us. So, quite often we use a facade in self-disclosure to protect ourselves from imagined harm. Thus, growth and development of things (plants or people) are influenced by many outside forces, all of which play an important part in creating who we are. Our job is to come to know and understand these influences and, in the process, come to know ourselves better as a result. Then, and only then, can we become better communicators.

Barriers to the Growth and Development of the Self-Concept

There are also certain barriers, or things that we view as deficiencies in the self-concept, that impair or impede the communication process and the growth of the self-concept. Some general **barriers to growth** include: 1) physical image, 2) intelligence, 3) the social self, and 4) the moral/ethical self. If we think we are fat, we develop a negative self-concept in a society where "thin is in!" If we are told when we are young that we are no good and that we can never do anything right, we develop a negative self-concept about our abilities and our intelligence. Not fitting in with the "in" crowd can create a feeling of alienation for our social self. Being made to follow rigid and unreasonable rules can challenge and confuse the moral or ethical self.

With these and other barriers present, relating to others can become confusing and frustrating. Our attitudes about ourselves can get in the way of effective communicating when those attitudes are unhealthy or nonsupportive of our self-concept. We end up not saying what we mean, and we communicate from a place of insecurity which can manifest itself in sarcasm or superiority. Our verbal and nonverbal communication behaviors become incongruent. Such ambiguous communication is confusing, and others may find it difficult to relate to us—leading to frustration for all parties involved.

Locus of Control: Victimization or Personal Power

One of the ramifications of these barriers is that we create a view in our minds of where the power or control in our life lies—outside of us or within us. This perception of our personal power refers to the concept of **locus of control**—a person's orientation toward the sources of rewards for his or her actions (McCroskey, Richmond, and Stewart, 1986, p. 114). The choice between two perceptions establishes the individual's orientation. A person with an **interior locus of control** perceives that "reward for actions follows from their own behavior" (1986, p. 114). They believe that they are responsible for their own actions and that the results accomplished or rewards received can be attributed to their own behavior choices. A person with an **exterior locus of control** perceives that "reward for actions stems from outside forces" (1986, p. 114). They believe that luck, chance, and other people are responsible for the things that happen to them and that they have no power or control over what rewards or consequences occur in their lives. Person A feels "in charge" of life and actions, while person B feels like a victim who is under the power of fate and other people.

This view of our self-concept, again, greatly influences how we interact with others. It decides if we have a "poor me" attitude or an "isn't life great" perspective. Person A will communicate clear, direct, honest messages without fear of incrimination or punishment; person B will communicate unclear, indirect, and unsure messages exuding insecurity and uncertainty while relying on luck or other outside forces for help.

What Do You Think?

Terry loves to go out and have fun. Kim and Kelly call frequently to ask Terry to join them. Terry usually goes along, hoping for a fun time but always comes home bored and frustrated. Terry feels this same way at work.

Where is Terry's locus of control and why?

Perceived Self vs. Ideal Self: Who Am I?

Another consequence of the barriers we create to the development of the self-concept is what Carl Rogers (1972) calls the "perceived vs. the ideal self." Rogers (1972) states that a healthy correlation between the two is most desirable, but that normally we tend to have false perceptions of our "perceived self" and seldom very realistic visions of the "ideal self." The **perceived self** tends to come from other people's perceptions while the **ideal self** tends to come from our inner being. However, when given a choice, we gravitate toward our ideal self and seek to change other peoples' perceptions of the presently perceived self. For example, if our parents perceive us as strong in business skills (because we "should" be), but we dislike business classes and detailed financial work, a conflict develops between the picture of the perceived self presented by our parents and the picture of our ideal self presented by our inner wisdom. Sometimes we follow other peoples' perceptions of who we are (or who they want us to be), but eventually, Rogers (1972) says, we will gravitate toward the ideal self and become who we really want to be.

Another way to describe this scenario would be to use the words "**imagined vs. real self**." Here, we can develop either an "imagined" image of our self-concept (one which is housed in self-deceit, ignorance, and fantasy) or a "real" image of our self-concept (one which is housed in reality and honesty). Obviously, the "real" image is healthy and the "imagined" image is detrimental to our self-concept. For example, if our life's goal is to become a musician, but our parents will not pay for our education unless we study something "practical," we might pursue a major in business to please our parents. This "imagined" image of the self that we are living out is not true to who and what we really are—the "real self." Although we may enter a business career, chances are that eventually we will either make a drastic change by becoming a member of a rock group, or we will gradually ease into a career in the field of music (perhaps even using our acquired business skills). In this context, Rogers (1972) believes that the true "real self" or the "ideal self" we have been seeking will emerge eventually, even if stifled temporarily. Conversely, when someone else sees a different "self" for us than we do, and we accept their version (either through force or ignorance), the "real self" is prostituted for their "imagined," imposed version. We may do this to please others and end up becoming someone we do not know or like. Developing a realistic perception of the self is the most healthy path and allows the emergence of the "real self" or "ideal self." In the end, we have to become who we really are and no one has the right to impose a different version.

What Do You Think?

Jim knew he was gay for a long time but was afraid to tell anyone, especially his parents; so he pretended to be straight and tried to fit in. His parents always talked negatively about homosexuality so he tried to live up to their perceived image of him. His dreams were of a place where he could be himself and not carry around this burden of being his parents' imposed version of their son. After graduation from high school, Jim moved to a big city.

Why did Jim move? Describe Jim's real or ideal self. Describe the perceived or imagined self imposed on Jim.

Self-Honesty: Facing Our Truth

Another major barrier to the development of a healthy self-concept is the lack of **self-honesty**, which is simply being willing to tell yourself the truth about who you are. It is very easy to lie to oneself. As the saying goes, you can justify anything if you talk about it long enough. What this means from a communication perspective is that we can convince ourselves that something is true about ourselves to avoid the pain of it not being true. A typical result of this problem is when males treat illness as a masculine weakness and say things like, "Oh no, I'm not sick. I'll be alright. It's nothing. I can handle it." Through denial and self-deceit, we can create dangerous situations for ourselves. This barrier is not only harmful to the effective development of the self-concept; it is also detrimental to effective interpersonal communication. If we cannot be honest with ourselves, how can we be honest with anyone else? Even though it may be painful to know the truth about how others perceive us, this knowledge is vital in the process of self-discovery and growth. While one person's opinion is not necessarily the impetus for personal change, we might want to consider feedback from others if it becomes consistent in nature or we are treated the same way by many people. Even though it is hard to acknowledge that we may have faults, to face the truth is always the best policy. As the saying goes, the truth will set you free—but first it may make you go through hell.

What Do You Think?

Betty, recently divorced, was having trouble at work. In her managerial position, Betty was constantly receiving negative feedback from her employees. She could not understand why. She thought she gave very clear directions and was very consistent in carrying out the rules she had created. She ran a tight ship. Her supervisor even told her that she was abrasive during her recent evaluation. Betty was frustrated because she thought she was doing a good job and others around her were telling her different information. Even her children were giving her a hard time lately.

What is wrong? What "truth" is Betty missing about herself? Why might she be unable to see this "truth"? How is this problem affecting her communication with others?

Co-dependency: Where Did I Go?

A popular contemporary buzz word is the term co-dependent. Originally coined by Alcoholics Anonymous, co-dependency meant trying to help an alcoholic, but doing exactly the wrong things which actually supported his or her habit. The co-dependent then becomes part of the problem and is just as dependent upon the alcohol (or in this case, the alcoholic) as the alcoholic. Typically co-dependents use language like "if you really loved me you would . . ." or "come on, just this one time." **Co-dependency** in relationships is basically the same thing—giving up part of who we are to "help" someone, although that person does not respect us and manipulates us into performing unhealthy behaviors. When the "help" offered or requested supports an unhealthy behavior (any type of addiction—alcohol, drugs, food, sex, gambling, physical or mental abuse), it becomes a co-dependent behavior.

Melody Beattie (1987), author of the ground-breaking book, *Co-dependent No More*, maintains that we are all co-dependent to some degree. Her twelve or more pages of co-dependent behaviors could convince anyone that his or her behaviors are co-dependent. Unfortunately, we can identify with many of these unhealthy behaviors because we were taught as we grew up that performing some of these types of behaviors meant that we were "nice" people. Basically, co-dependent behaviors are doing things we do not really want to do so that the other person will like or love us—or at least not be mad at us. We falsely confuse this with love and being a "nice" person. Beattie maintains that whenever we give up any part of who we are or what we stand for, we start down the road of co-dependence—sometimes never to return. Every time someone is allowed to tread on our co-dependent, low self-concept, a little piece of who we are falls away—until nothing is left and we feel no sense of self. While this may sound somewhat extreme, consider the millions of women who finally give up everything in order to regain a sense of self after years of verbal (and perhaps physical) abuse and self-concept "treading." Clearly, we can begin to realize the impact of co-dependency on our interpersonal communication.

Love is not about giving up who we are. Love is about being the best person we can be through creating, developing, maintaining, and changing our self-concept through healthy interpersonal relationships. Giving up who we are or allowing our self-concept to be "tread upon" is never healthy nor productive. Developing a healthy self-concept is not selfish or egocentric; it is a gift to ourselves first and then to others. Then and only then can we offer effective communication in developing a healthy relationship with others.

What Do You Think?

Kim's best friend Terry has a problem which is fast becoming Kim's problem, too. Terry constantly asks Kim to do things—errands, favors. Although Kim does not mind helping most of the time, Terry seems to be shirking responsibilities more and more, and getting Kim to do things that Terry could easily do. Kim is now becoming resentful, but does not dare to say "no" to Terry for fear of losing the friendship.

What would you do? What would you say to maintain your own identity and avoid becoming co-dependent?

Changing the Self-Concept

The possibility of changing the self-concept always exists. If something in our life is not working, we are the only ones who can do something about the problem. While the concept of change is often frightening, it can also be helpful and healthy. Even though we have this little voice inside that tells us not to change because everything is all right the way it is, that voice acts as a mechanism to maintain balance. It is usually easier to keep things the same; we do not need to find the energy it takes to rethink, revamp, and reorganize our lives. However, if we keep running into similar problems throughout our lives, that should be a clue that we might need to change our approach.

There are many "self-help" paperbacks that proclaim the need to generate positive self-concept through positive change. *Pulling Your Own Strings*, by Wayne Dyer (1979) is one good example. Dyer suggests that we give up the victim role and take charge of our lives. He refers to the process of victimizing ourselves as **shoulding** on ourselves—telling ourselves that we HAVE to do something or being dominated by guilt, rules, and "shoulds" that we receive from parents, friends, society, and culture. The dangerous part is that we could (and probably do) "should" on others (usually under the guise of helping). Sometimes when people "should" on us a lot, we end up doing it to others just for the sake of revenge and self-survival. For example, see if you do this to others or if others do this to you.

What Do You Think?

Your best friend is in love with a person who is taking advantage of him or her. You think he or she is being a fool to stay in this relationship. You want to help by telling him or her what he or she should do so he or she does not get hurt.

Is this "shoulding" or "helping"? Why do we feel it necessary to say anything at all? Why do we feel responsible for other peoples' business? Is it any business of ours? Why might we try to control this situation?

Dyer (1979) maintains, as do many other theorists, that we have the ability to control who we are through self-assertiveness and the building of positive self-esteem. Like Dyer, most theorists maintain that the way to achieve effective communication and a healthy self-concept is by loving ourselves, accepting ourselves exactly as we are, and not criticizing ourselves for "bad" behaviors. Finally, remember that **we can only change ourselves, we cannot change another person**. With this focus, our growth will be positive, the self-concept will be healthy, and our communication interactions more effective.

Summary

The self-concept is a complicated motion picture that changes as we grow and change. It is strongly influenced by the socialization process and certain barriers that we encounter and create. A healthy self-concept is needed to allow clear and effective communication. The self-concept, whether healthy or not, influences the process of communication. In order to have productive communication, we need to remember we can only change ourselves; we cannot change another person.

References

Adler, Ronald B., Lawrence B. Rosenfeld, and Neil Towne. *Interplay: The Process of Interpersonal Communication*, 5th ed. New York: Holt, Rinehart and Winston, 1992.

Adler, Ronald B. and Neil Towne. *Looking Out, Looking In*, 7th ed. New York: Holt, Rinehart and Winston, 1993.

Beattie, Melody. *Co-dependent No More*. New York: HarperCollins, 1987.

Brown, Charles T. and Paul W. Keller. *Monologue to Dialogue: An Exploration of Interpersonal Communication*, 2nd ed. Englewood Cliffs, NJ: Prentice-Hall, 1979.

Cooley, Charles. *Human Nature and the Social Order*. Homewood, IL: The Free Press, 1956.

Dyer, Wayne. *Pulling Your Own Strings*. New York: Avon, 1979.

Emmert, Philip and Victoria J. Lukasko Emmert. *Interpersonal Communication*, 3rd ed. Dubuque, IA: Wm. C. Brown Publishers, 1984.

Hay, Louise L. *You Can Heal Your Life*. Santa Monica, CA: Hay House, 1986.

Jourard, Sidney. *The Transparent Self*, rev. ed. New York: Van Nostrand Reinhold, 1971.

Maslow, Abraham. *Motivation and Personality*. New York: HarperCollins, 1970.

McCroskey, James C., Virginia P. Richmond, and Robert A. Stewart. *One on One: The Foundations of Interpersonal Communication*. Englewood Cliffs, NJ: Prentice-Hall, 1986.

Mead, G. H. *Mind, Self, and Society*. Chicago: University of Chicago Press, 1934.

Powell, John S.J. *Why Am I Afraid to Tell You Who I Am?* Niles, IL: Argus Communications, 1969.

Rogers, Carl R. *On Becoming A Person*. Boston: Houghton Mifflin, 1972.

Rokeach, Milton. *Beliefs, Attitudes and Values*. San Francisco: Jossey-Bass, 1968.

Smith, Dennis R. and L. Keith Williamson. *Interpersonal Communication: Roles, Rules, Strategies, and Games*, 3rd ed. Dubuque, IA: Wm. C. Brown, 1985.

Case 5

TargetTerms

- victim role
- shoulding
- self-love
- self-honesty
- imagined versus real self
- self-concept growth barriers
- locus of control

PreviewNotes

This case describes a person with a very low self-concept who continually creates barriers restricting growth and development.

CaseParticipants

Arlene Lowell—pretty and exuberant; athletic; enjoys getting involved in the various activities of the university that she attends; has a tendency to be involved in the problems of others

Sarah Pollack—attends the same university as Arlene; has a propensity to constantly downgrade herself for a variety of reasons

"Easy for you to say!"

Arlene and Sarah share adjoining rooms in a dormitory suite at their school. Deciding to "burn the midnight oil," Arlene begrudgingly stays in one Saturday night to complete the final copy of a research paper. That same night also finds Sarah studying, but only for lack of other plans. Nothing is pressing; nothing ever seems to be with Sarah. It is out of total boredom that she tiptoes into Arlene's room and says:

Sarah: Sorry to bother you. I was just going to the basement to get something to eat. Want anything?

Arlene: No, but thanks anyway.

Sarah: Sure?

Arlene: Sure—I was just getting into this—

Sarah: Looks like you're working really hard tonight. I haven't heard a sound from this room all night. I'm always amazed at how well you get it all together.

Arlene: Me! Yeah, sure! This is only my four hundredth copy of the same page. Don't believe what you think you see. I'm as far away from getting it together as anyone can possibly imagine. If you could only hear my "screaming" inside. The paper's due Monday.

Sarah: How can you be so loose? I'd be frantic if I had just started a term paper that's due in twenty-four hours! I really envy you. You do everything so nonchalantly. I wish I could be like that.

Arlene: No you don't—I'm crazed and have only myself to blame. I waited and unfortunately, now I'm paying the price.

Sarah: That's what I mean. You kind of roll with whatever punches you get. Me—well, I get so hung up in the crazies of school, that I don't get to enjoy it here.

Arlene: Well, then, that's simple. Stop worrying!

Sarah: Easy for you to say. You're the one who has the dates and the grades. You always look as if you can go out—on fifteen seconds notice! How would you know what it's like to be me? I feel like an outcast.

Arlene: I'd say that you were feeling a little sorry for yourself tonight.

Sarah: Why should you be different from everyone else? Although, I did think you were a little different than the rest of them.

Arlene: Honestly, I didn't mean anything by that. Really! Anyhow, how'd we get into this at eleven-forty-five on a Saturday night?

Sarah: Just what I thought! You couldn't care less either.

Arlene: Look, if I don't like who I am, I better damn well do something about it. Know why? Because, no one, but no one is going to do it for me.

Sarah: That can work for you because you have all the basics which I lack.

Arlene: Like what?

Sarah: Looks?

Arlene: That's not all there is to being content.

Sarah: It sure helps.

Arlene: So, why don't you try to do something about it and quit complaining!

Sarah: Like what? Plastic surgery?! Oh, I should have known better; I never should have bothered you! (*She starts out of the room.*)

Arlene: Why are you *so down* on yourself?

Sarah: Got any better ideas?

Arlene: Do you want to hear? (*Sarah nods resentfully.*) O.K.—you just tell me when to stop.

Sarah: How bad is this going to be?

Arlene: Stop being so defensive; start living your own life with only *you* deciding what you should do.

Sarah: I don't trust myself to do that.

Arlene: There's only one person who can make you what you want to be—
and it's certainly not me.
Sarah: I don't really need to be lectured. I feel lousy enough.
Arlene: You came to me, Sarah.
Sarah: I didn't "come" to you. I only asked you if you were hungry.

CaseConcerns

1. Arlene's self-concept was not a major focus in this case. By drawing inferences from the information presented, how would you describe Arlene's view of herself.

2. Sarah communicates in a way that is indicative of how she feels about herself. How would you describe those feelings? What does this say about her self-concept and its impact on the way she communicates?

3. What difficulties does this case present concerning forming a relationship when the self-concept is still developing? If we are constantly growing and changing, how does this alter relationship development?

4. What are some of the barriers that could possibly impair the development of relationships of your own? In thinking about this issue, "call up" some of your own personal concerns that clearly affect the way in which you interact with people?

5. How would Wayne Dyer's theory of victimization explain Sarah's self-concept? What would he say she is doing to herself and how would he suggest that she free herself from this pattern?

6. Analyze Sarah's self-concept with Carl Roger's imagined versus real self-concept.

ReflectiveResponses

1. It is late on Saturday night. You're alone in your dorm room or apartment typing a last minute paper. Sarah (or her prototype) comes to you and asks if you are also hungry. The conversation makes a similar turn. How do you respond?

2. When someone has an extremely low self-concept is there anything that can be done to bring it to a higher level? Can a significant other change another's feeling about himself or herself or must it come from within the person?

Case 6

TargetTerms

- co-dependency
- locus of control

PreviewNotes

Giving up who we are and being overly involved with another person creates co-dependency

CaseParticipants

Randy—Mike's roommate
Mike—Randy's roommate

"Please . . ."

The following telephone conversation occurs between Randy and Mike during one late afternoon.

Mike: What time will you be home tonight?

Randy: I'm working late at the office.

Mike: Again? You've been doing this to me a lot. What'll I do for dinner?

Randy: Fix it yourself. It's all in the refrig.

Mike: I can't. I don't know how. It's no fun to eat alone anyway.

Randy: How many times have we gone through this?

Mike: Ah, come on . . .

Randy: I've got to work.

Mike: I'll come to your office and we'll go to dinner after you're finished.

Randy: I can't work with you here and you know it.

Mike: I don't want to be alone again tonight. Come on, do it for me.

Randy: Turn on some TV. Listen, I've got to get off the phone now.

Mike: Don't go. Tell me again, what's in the refrigerator. If you really cared, you'd be home with me.

Randy: There's some chicken, a salad, some leftover pasta.

Mike: You know—I'll wait for you to come home. It'll be easier. I miss you. I don't like to be alone.

CaseConcerns

1. Why do you suppose Mike is so concerned about being alone?
2. What kinds of words does he use to convey his reliance on his roommate?
3. If you were Randy, would you come home earlier? If not, what would you say to your friend to communicate your real feelings?
4. How is co-dependency an issue in the communication that takes place in this case?

ReflectiveResponses

1. Has there been a time in your life when co-dependent behavior was evidenced? Do you believe that you recognized the tendency toward unhealthy behavior at the time?
2. In your estimation, what is the difference between being a nice person to a significant other and supporting his or her co-dependent behavior?

Case 7

TargetTerms

- perceived vs. ideal self
- self honesty

PreviewNotes

How we perceive others may not be how they perceive themselves. This perceptual inaccuracy causes communication problems.

CaseParticipants

Brad Sanford—a 24-year-old gay man who lives at home and works in retail
Esther Sanford—Brad's 55-year-old mother

"Who's fooling whom?"

There seems to be constant bickering at the Sanford residence. Brad's mom seems to question everything he does and never misses a chance to offer her opinion.

Brad: See you later.

Mom: Where are you going?

Brad: Out.

Mom: I know, out, but where? And who are you going with? Is it that Jeff person again?

Brad: Mom! Come on! You drive me crazy with your questions. I'm 24 years old. Do you have to know everything? And, what's wrong with Jeff?

Mom: I just want to know what you're doing and where you're going, that's all. Is that so bad? I don't like Jeff. He's, he's . . . gay.

Brad: So what?

Mom: You're not like that and he's a bad influence.

Brad: Mom, how many times have I told you that I *am* gay and Jeff is a good friend.

Mom: No, you're not gay. If you were, you wouldn't have girlfriends like Janice and Sally. Someday you'll find the right girl and give up this crazy phase.

Brad: Mom, this is not a phase. Being gay is not something you give up or even choose. It's something you're born with—it's not a choice.

Mom: There you go again, blaming me. It's all my fault.

Brad: Oh, Mom. I wish I could make you understand that I am gay and it's *not* your fault. I love you. Don't you understand that?

Mom: I know. And someday you'll get married and give me beautiful grandchildren. I just know it.

CaseConcerns

1. What is Brad's perceived self? What is Brad's ideal self? Why are they different?

2. Where does Brad's ideal self originate?

3. How can he change his perceived self?

4. What is Esther's perceived self? How does this affect her communication with Brad?

5. Is Brad being honest with himself? Is Brad disclosing his self-honesty to his mother? What happens when we are not honest with ourselves?

6. Describe Esther's reception of her son's honesty. Why can't she accept his honesty?

ReflectiveResponses

1. How does your perceived self affect the way you communicate?

2. Mark Knapp has offered us different versions of self-perception that have an effect on the way we communicate. Consider the following:

   I am who I think I am
   I am who you think I am
   I am who I think you think I am
   I am who you think I think I am

   Analyze your self-concept in view of these statements.

Case 8

TargetTerms

- locus of control
- perceived versus ideal self
- co-dependency
- self-desire for self-esteem
- shoulding

PreviewNotes

This case illustrates the strong need for self-esteem in developing your own self-concept. We also discover some barriers in accomplishing this goal.

CaseParticipants

Deborah Parnell—regally attractive and independent 52-year-old, mother of two grown children who has been married for 27 years. She is employed as a broadcaster for a local independent station. Recently, she initiated a marital separation which amazed her circle of friends.

Lydia Rosner—conservatively well dressed and fashionable 50-year-old; self employed as an interior designer, married, actively involved mother of three; past college roommate of Deborah.

"It's my turn . . ."

The following exchange occurs after Deborah decides to separate. At a private lunch date, the two women seem to be at opposite ends of a spectrum as Deborah elaborates about her circumstances.

Deborah: And, so, I know that it's what's best.

Lydia: I can't believe that I'm listening to this. Do you realize what you're doing—not only to yourself, but to your family.

Deborah: Why is it that I have to constantly explain myself to everyone—especially you of all people.

Lydia: Please—I'm not sure how to ask this . . .

Deborah: What is it?

Lydia: (*hesitant*) Well, this is certainly not to be taken in the wrong context, but, are you involved with someone else—I mean . . . is there someone?

Deborah: Lydia, you've crossed a very important boundary in our relationship—my privacy. I really thought that you would allow me the venting of my feelings, rather than exploiting me about them.

Lydia: Now, let's not get so huffy about this. I'm here and I'll always be here for you because I care. I'm just trying to understand. And, furthermore, you still haven't answered my question.

Deborah: What do you want to hear me say? (*increasing sarcasm*) Just let me know. Is there any one answer that will give you more pleasure than another? (*and louder*) That he is a clone of Richard Gere or Tom Cruise, or that he is fifteen years my junior and cherishes the ground that I walk on? The honest to goodness truth is that there is no one . . . I wish there were.

Lydia: What's going on with you? Why all this change at this stage of your life? You're supposed to be winding down now; instead, you're shifting gears.

Deborah: For twenty-seven years, I was always Mrs. David Parnell, wonderful wife of the super engineering whiz—never Deborah—for whatever she may have made of herself. David never even acknowledged my successes. The fact remains that I am someone, and now it's my turn.

Lydia: Have you ever mentioned this to him?

Deborah: Oh, we've rehashed this issue a thousand times if not more. He makes me feel guilty for having to work late; I never have any indication of his hours from day to day. I love my work, Lydia! I've paid my dues to get where I am and it's now my turn—time just for me. There were twenty-six years in our married life where I gave every part of me to please David and everyone else and I'm sick of it.

Lydia: I suppose what I am really wondering is whether or not it is reconcilable?

Deborah: I've been trying to make it all better for the last few years thinking that the kids would suffer if we couldn't make it work. Now there are no excuses . . . the kids are making their own lives, and now it's time for Mom to make hers.

CaseConcerns

1. Why should this case be included in a chapter entitled, "I Gotta Be Me"?

2. What is Deborah's "real" image of herself? How does that differ from her "imagined" image of herself? Consider the same questions for Lydia.

3. What is the difference between Lydia's self-concept (of herself) and that which is perceived about Lydia by Deborah?

4. Do you feel that Lydia has previously pleased or appeased others through an imposed version of what she has wanted them to feel about her? Does this type of situation ever happen to you personally in relationships? Do you do this to others or do others do this to you? Why do you suppose we act in this way?

5. Wayne Dyer talks about "shoulding" in his book, *Pulling Your Own Strings*. Does this concept interfere in the communication process illustrated in this case. How?

6. How would you have ended this case? By relating to one of the theories in this chapter, create a new ending to Lydia and Deborah's lunch date. After you have written the dialogue for your imagined culminating scene, briefly tell how your end result touches upon one or any of the concepts discussed within the chapter.

7. Do you feel that Deborah was co-dependent upon David in her entire marriage? To what extent do you believe all couples in relationships should be dependent upon each other? Explain how you may have developed your thinking about the issue of co-dependence in intimate relationships.

ReflectiveResponses

1. Has there been a time in your life when you wanted to just be "you" and everyone else seemed to want you to be one of "them"? If applicable, how did this make you feel? Does your self-concept have an effect on the way you communicate with others?

2. How do you personally feel about pressing a significant other about an important decision? Do you have any feelings (or rules?) about sharing very personal information about yourself with special people in your life. What have you done in the past if another person did not appear to accept what you were sharing about yourself? Did your response affect future communication with the other person?

3
Chapter

Perception

Specific Goals for Understanding Chapter Three

TargetTerms

- perception
- frame of reference (F.O.R.)
- perceptual framework
- principle of consistency
- selective exposure
- selective attention
- selective perception
- selective retention
- attribution
- perceptual checking
- semantic differential
- punctuation of communication events

CoreConcepts

1 the impact of the perceptual process on communication
2 defense mechanisms and protective filters that affect our communication
3 increasing the accuracy of our perceptual interpretations

"But I thought you meant . . ."

Overview

Did you ever have an argument with a friend only to realize later that you were not even arguing about the same thing—that your perceptions of the event or issue were quite different? We say to the person the next day, "but I thought you meant . . ." This is a common occurrence. Because of differing perceptions or interpretations of an event or issue, our communications can become cross-wired or confused. These problems are inherent in all relationships because of individual perceptual differences.

These perceptual differences can be visual or verbal in nature. We have all had the experience of witnessing an accident only to hear reports that were quite different from our own. We have all experienced an argument as described above caused by differences in perception. When others perceive our behaviors or our messages differently than we intend, it can be one of the most frustrating experiences we can have. To have someone else not understand us the way we want to be understood can even be painful. One of the biggest lessons of life—and one that can really open our eyes—is to realize that everyone does not see things the same way we do. As we learned in chapter 1, every frame of reference is unique. No matter how well we know someone or how important that person is to us there are no guarantees that our perceptions will match. To understand the process of perception and the way that it impacts on our communication transactions is a big step toward more effective communication.

In chapter 1, we investigated the transfer of meaning from one person to another. We will now investigate the influence of our individual perceptions on that transfer process, the impact of the perceptual process on communication, and certain perceptual defense mechanisms and protective filters that affect our communication. Finally, we will explore several methods with which to improve our perceptual accuracy.

Perception Defined

The way we attach meaning to word symbols is directly influenced by the way we perceive things. **Perception** can be defined as the process of becoming aware of objects and events from our senses (DeVito, 1995, p. 46) and our own frame of reference (F.O.R.). The way in which we communicate those perceptions is the basis for the development of meaning. This meaning is then transferred from one person to another through the process of communication, as discussed in chapter 1. Individual perceptions are quite important in the overall process of communication because they influence the way we behave and the way we send and receive messages. We have *visual* perceptions of objects and events, and we have *perceptual* interpretations of events, objects, and messages. Both can be troublesome to our communication and can reduce the accuracy and efficiency of our interactions.

What Do You Think?

Stare at the triangle below for three seconds. Then close your book. Write down what the phrase said on a sheet of paper.

Were you accurate? If not, why not?

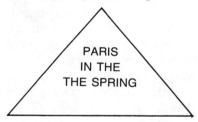

The Impact of the Perceptual Process on Communication

Our frame of reference also can be referred to as our **perceptual framework**—that which we create from our awareness of objects and events as perceived from the senses. The three key principles of the **perception process** are presented in Karl Albrecht's *Brain Power*:

- **recognition**—deciding which stimuli deserve our attention and paying attention to details
- **interpretation**—attaching meaning and identification to the recognized stimuli and tolerating a little ambiguity
- **expectation**—avoiding creation of desired outcome through predisposed visions (1980, pp. 131–141)

The Learning Corporation of America developed a training video, "Brain Power" (1986), based on the Albrecht book. Actor John

Houseman describes the perceptual process and explains its impact on effective communication. In the video, he explains that the secret to brainpower is "thinking," as the title implies. Brainpower refers to the ability to use clear and accurate perceptions. In order to improve our perceptual accuracy and precision, we need to remain open-minded, to avoid making assumptions about stimuli we receive, and to seek to maintain a clear, nonjudgmental vision.

The problem is that we become very protective of our perceptions. We keep them in neat little boxes like so many saved thimbles; we take them out to use them but make sure they are put back in the same box afterward. In order to combat differences in perception, we develop what most researchers call defense mechanisms or "filters." We commonly use these mechanisms in our communication processes in order to make sense of the billions of stimuli we receive daily. While some of these "filters" are helpful and necessary to maintain sanity, others are very harmful and disruptive to the communication process (we would literally die if we paid attention to every single stimuli or message we received each day). Avoidance of these "filters" or shields can increase our perceptual accuracy.

Try This Experience

Picture yourself in a children's toy store or a shopping mall a week before the holidays. Close your eyes for 1–2 minutes imagining all the stimuli bombarding you—music, children screaming, parents shouting, lots of moving colored objects, multiple shapes and sizes, flashing lights, and so on. Try to take everything in—do not miss any stimuli—then, open your eyes. Describe your feelings on paper, going through the three steps of the perception process: **recognition, interpretation, and expectation.**

Perceptual Defense Mechanisms and Filters

Leon Festinger (1957) states that humans have a strong desire to keep things basically the same. Although we think that we encourage change and variety, that encouragement is primarily for changes of low risk and immediate gratification. The three basic assumptions about our perceptions that override this surface-level desire for change are:

- that people need consistency among their beliefs, attitudes, and values
- that the awareness of inconsistencies in our frame of reference will produce tensions
- that we will usually do something to reduce the tensions (Brown, 1965; Heider, 1946; Osgood and Tannenbaum, 1955)

These assumptions form what the theorists mentioned above call the **principle of consistency**. We like to keep things stable, orderly, and visually definite. When something disturbs this order, we create an automatic defense mechanism. Have you ever looked at an abstract painting? Our eyes usually try to create order out of the abstraction, even if none exists. We also tend to choose friends who have values that match our values so we can keep our perceptions consistent.

Four common **defense mechanisms** serve as subconscious monitors to maintain consistency in our perceptions—and frequently to change or distort the intended meaning of the message sent. Defense mechanisms act as perceptual "filters" for the stimuli and feedback we are bombarded with daily. These four defense mechanisms disallow accurate perception (Festinger, 1957; McCroskey, Richmond, and Stewart, 1986, p. 220-224). The four mechanisms are:

- **selective exposure**—allowing ourselves to be exposed only to those messages which reinforce our current frames of reference
- **selective attention**—listening only to those messages which reinforce our current frames of reference
- **selective perception**—perceiving and deciphering messages only through our current frames of reference to the point of changing the intent
- **selective retention**—remembering only those parts of the message that reinforce our current frames of reference

What Do You Think?

Mary's Dutch mother was always nice to everyone and had such a pleasant demeanor. Still, Mary was afraid to tell her mother that she was seriously dating a man from India, but she decided to tell her anyway and tried to explain how happy she was in this new relationship. Her mother's comment was that it was very nice that she had a new friend and she was glad she was happy. Then Mary's mother asked, "What's her name and where is she visiting from?" Mary just shook her head and went to her room.

What type of selective defense mechanisms were used here and by whom?

Increasing Perceptual Accuracy

As we have discussed, there are many factors that distort the way we interpret the messages we receive. When we attach meaning to behavior—verbal or nonverbal—that process is referred to as **attribution**. We attribute meaning to both our own actions and to the actions of others, but we often use different interpretations for the two different attributions. There are several perceptual errors that can lead to inaccurate attributions. Ronald B. Adler and Neil Towne identify four such perceptual errors (1993, pp. 103–106):

- we often judge ourselves more charitably than we judge others; a self-serving bias protects our self-image
- we are influenced by what is most obvious
- we cling to first impressions
- we tend to assume others are similar to us

Perceptual Checking

One proposed solution to this perceptual pitfall of attribution is what Adler and Towne (1993, pp. 106–108) call **perceptual checking**, which involves the following three steps:

- a description of the behavior you noticed
- at least two possible interpretations of the behavior
- a request for clarification about how to interpret the behavior

Perceptual checks are designed to assist us in increasing the accuracy of our perceptions about the communication behaviors of others. Instead of assuming that our first interpretation is correct, taking time to do a perceptual check will increase the likelihood that we will understand others more accurately.

What Do You Think?

Jack was interviewing two qualified candidates for the same position. Because this was a factory position, neither candidate wore a business suit—one wore blue jeans and the other wore khakis. Jack hired the candidate wearing khakis. Two weeks later, he had to fire the new employee because he was irresponsible, so Jack called the other candidate to see if he was interested. Unfortunately, Jack was too late; the other candidate had already been hired somewhere else.

Were Jack's perceptions influenced by any nonverbal behaviors that he may have misinterpreted? If so, what were the nonverbal behaviors? What step in perceptual checking did Jack fail to follow?

Semantic Differential

An understanding of the implications of semantic differentiation will assist us in communicating more effectively by providing the knowledge necessary to create more accurate messages. The **semantic differential** scale is used to measure latitudes of meaning that words can have (Osgood, Suci, and Tannenbaum, 1967). Based on individual frames of reference, the semantic differential scale visually displays the differences in meaning that one word can have. While some words have different meanings in different contexts, other meanings are described with different words by different people in the same context. The word "pop" means "father" in the East but refers to carbonated beverages in the Midwest. The slang word "fag" is a derogatory reference to a homosexual in the United States, but in England "fag" refers to a cigarette. When three people are asked to describe an accident they just witnessed, each description will inevitably be surprisingly different. While the first two examples (different meanings for words) are usually easy to figure out once we engage in feedback, the third example (different perceptions for the same event) is the one that creates the most confusion. Why did all three people not "see" or perceive the same thing? Why did they not interpret what they saw in the same manner? Mainly, the differences in their frames of reference create a proportionally larger gap in the semantic differential scale and reduce the overall message clarity and accuracy.

This Really Happened!

Kim and Terry were in Florida on spring break from a northeast university when they decided to order some pizza for dinner. This is the conversation that occurred:

Terry: Hi. We want to order a couple 'a pies to be delivered to the Daytona Beach Inn.

Clerk: We don't sell pies; this is a pizza parlour.

Terry: Yeah, that's what I said. We wanna order two large pies to go.

Clerk: Buddy—I just told ya, we don't sell pies. We only sell pizzas.

Terry: Well just forget it then, you creep!

What was the misunderstanding here? Describe the problem related to the semantic differential.

Punctuation of Communication Events

DeVito refers to a phenomenon called the **punctuation of communication events** (1995, p. 32) which is another way of analyzing the accuracy of our perceptions. While the communication process is continuous, DeVito describes the way individuals see those events as punctuations. He uses the example of a husband-wife argument at a party: Did the husband cause the wife to start drinking because he was flirting, or did the wife cause the husband to flirt because she was drinking? The interpretation of this communication transaction lies in the mind of the perceiver; each person "punctuates" the event differently. These differences in perception concerning which stimuli caused which action result in an egocentric view of the transaction and place the participants in a dichotomous dilemma.

What Do You Think?

Kim and Kelly attended a party together. Kelly was talking to some friends on the other side of the room when Kim "lost it." Kim started screaming at Kelly that acting like that was not acceptable. Kelly got embarrassed and walked away from Kim, and started talking again to some other friends. This just seemed to make Kim madder yet.

Tell the story from Kim's point of view. Tell the story from Kelly's point of view. Who is right?

Summary

Understanding the impact of the perceptual process on human interaction and the barriers that can reduce our perceptual accuracy can assist in our efforts to understand and to be understood through increased perceptual accuracy. There are specific strategies which can be practiced in order to increase our perceptual accuracy which will result in more effective interpersonal communication.

References

Adler, Ronald B. and Neil Towne. *Looking Out, Looking In*, 7th ed. New York: Holt, Rinehart and Winston, 1993.

Albrecht, Karl. *Brain Power: Learn to Improve Your Thinking Skills.* Englewood Cliffs, NJ: Prentice-Hall, 1980.

Brown, R. *Social Psychology.* New York: The Free Press, 1965.

DeVito, Joseph A. *The Interpersonal Communication Book*, 7th ed. New York: HarperCollins, 1995.

Festinger, Leon. *A Theory of Cognitive Dissonance.* New York: Row, Peterson, 1957.

Heider, Fritz. "Attitudes and Cognitive Organization." *Journal of Psychology*, 21, (1946):107–112.

Learning Corporation of America. *Brain Power*. Videocassette, 1986, 11 min.

McCroskey, James C., Virginia P. Richmond, and Robert A. Stewart. *One on One: The Foundations of Interpersonal Communication.* Englewood Cliffs, NJ: Prentice-Hall, 1986.

Osgood, Charles E., George J. Suci, and Percy H. Tannenbaum. *The Measurement of Meaning.* Urbana: University of Illinois Press, 1967.

Osgood, Charles E. and Percy H. Tannenbaum. "The Principle of Congruity in the Prediction of Attitude Change," *Psychological Review*, 62, (1955):42–55.

Case 9

TargetTerms

- selective defense mechanisms
- perception process
- punctuation of communication events
- semantic differential

PreviewNotes

This case illustrates how strongly the selective defense mechanisms can affect our perceptions. Normally we perceive information from our own frame of reference without consideration for how others might perceive that same information.

CaseParticipants

Eric Sutton, Ph.D.—college professor at a well-known university; attempts to make the learning experience meaningful for his students; known to be very "tough" but fair, when it comes to grading

Daniel Torrington—senior student in Dr. Sutton's seminar; although interested in this course, currently he is plagued by the burned-out feeling of "senioritis"

"I didn't think it counted that much . . ."

Professor Sutton began one of the last classes of the semester by passing out last week's graded essays. The tension mounted as Professor Sutton explained that plagiarism had been detected and that he would speak personally to those involved during this week's office hours. The individuals involved would have a note on their papers indicating a request for an immediate office appointment.

Dan Torrington cringed as he received his paper. During office hours later that day, Daniel timidly knocks on the door of his professor's office, as Sutton says:

Sutton: Come in.

Daniel: May I have a word with you, sir? It's about the remarks you made in class this morning. Is there some kind of problem?

Sutton: Some kind of problem?

Daniel: Well it's about the critique I wrote for the lecture series you required us to hear last week. I'm sorry, but I am a little confused. (*He shows his professor the paper to help clarify the situation.*) There's your note, but there is no grade on this. It seems that you didn't read what I wrote (*playing dumb*).

Sutton: That's not exactly correct, although I will admit to not reading the paper with great enthusiasm. Would you care to understand the reasoning behind all this?

Daniel: I guess (*reluctantly and with trepidation*).

Sutton: You know, Mr. Torrington, I, too, went to hear the University Annual Memorial Lecture last week, and I saw you leave the lecture hall just after the ushers passed out the *Lecture Series Program.*

Daniel: I'm not quite sure what my visit to the men's room has to do with this note on my paper.

Sutton: I guess you have missed the point. Truthfully, I was concerned with the fact that you never returned to the auditorium. I was even interested enough to check if you were feeling well, but I knew that I didn't have to worry when I caught a glimpse of you in the Student Center game room when I left.

Daniel: What do you mean? I still don't understand where you are going with this.

Sutton: Ultimately, to the Dean of Academic Affairs.

Daniel: What???

Sutton: I will explain where I stand on this issue. When I read the critical analysis you wrote about speakers that you never heard, I realized that your paper may . . .

Daniel: (*interrupts*) Can you prove that I never came back?

Sutton: If you can remain civil, I will finish the explanation. When I initially perused your paper, I found that your introduction was very interesting and to the point—even had a great "attention-getter." Unfortunately for you, the same "attention-getter" was published in the *Lecture Series Program.* Talk about coincidences!

Daniel: Well, I read the material for an additional source of information before drafting the paper, and I guess some of the wording may have rubbed off a little in my writing.

Sutton: Is that so? Wait a minute—there happens to be a copy of the brochure in the folder on my desk. (*The two scan the paper together.*) Dan, this entire incident is extremely frustrating. Plagiarism is a serious problem in our course as well as in our academic community.

Daniel: It sounds as if I'm guilty without even being asked about my side of this situation.

Sutton: I'm listening.

Daniel: To be honest, I just didn't think that the Lecture Series was any big deal in the course work requirements. I mean, how much can a critique of this type count anyway? You even said that it could be written in longhand and submitted on the evaluation form, instead of it being typed like all of our other formal writing assignments. I mean it wasn't a major assignment or anything.

Sutton: Dan, you're a senior, I think you know better than that.

Daniel: You understand. I know you do. Please . . . I know you know what I mean.

Sutton: So, are you saying that you chose not to do an assignment because you thought it was insignificant?

Daniel: You know, I never thought that it would come to this. Truthfully, I really didn't understand the assignment at all. I am taking eighteen credits this semester to graduate and it feels as if everything is tumbling down on me.

Sutton: What does that have to do with anything that has been discussed so far?

Daniel: I really didn't think that it would even count in our grade.

Sutton: The syllabus states that this is a requirement for course completion.

Daniel: How much is the paper worth anyway in terms of the percentage in our final grade?

Sutton: Dan—that is not the issue here.

Daniel: Can I hand in another analysis?

Sutton: You seem to be missing the seriousness of this situation—and what constitutes "counting," Dan. It's time to account—not so much to me—but to yourself.

Daniel: I still don't see how any of this relates to my final mark. My evaluations have all been pretty good throughout the semester. Are you going to lower my grade?

Sutton: We're talking about more than grade point averages here. Your integrity is what I'm concerned about. (*He starts to get up.*) I'm already late for my next class, so you will have to excuse me. I'm sure we'll be talking again—soon!

CaseConcerns

1. How would you handle the situation in this case, if you were the professor of the course? Would you have perceived it the same or differently?

2. Are there some problems that cannot be resolved due to perceptual misunderstandings? Is this a phenomenon that occurs frequently in our lives? Recreate the particular circumstances of a situation that caused a great deal of discomfort in your own life.

3. By referring directly to the case, specifically discuss the many instances where meanings and messages were misconstrued.

Were the messages intentionally or accidentally lost through selective perception in the individual responses?

4. What role does sarcasm play in the dissemination of the messages in the conversation between Professor Sutton and Daniel? How does sarcasm affect the communication process?

5. Which defense mechanisms are inherently working in this case? For Daniel? For Professor Sutton? Relate the ones you discover to particular instances in the dialogue.

6. Describe how each person "punctuated" this communicative event.

7. Explain where communication began to disintegrate by using Karl Albrecht's principles of perception (recognition, interpretation, expectation).

8. Describe how the use of various defense mechanisms can impair our communication effectiveness. Use examples from this case and from your life.

ReflectiveResponses

1. Describe how your frame of reference operates in class situations? Can you think of a situation where you were perceiving an instructor's message in one way and he or she intended the message to be interpreted in another way? What do you think could have been changed to have made the communication exchange more productive for both the student and for the teacher.

2. Explain why we have a tendency to think that our way of thinking is the right way. What do you suppose influences this type of thinking?

3. As a college student, what are some of the obstacles to your own perceptual processes of communication? How can you personally increase the accuracy of your perceptions in the communication that takes place in any number of your classes this year?

4. What constitutes "what counts" in your final grade? How might your understanding of the implications of semantic differentiation assist you in more effectively creating accurate messages in your classroom communication?

Case 10

TargetTerms

- F.O.R. (frame of reference)
- perceptual framework
- perceptual process
- selective defense mechanisms
- semantic differential

PreviewNotes

When two people have very different frames of reference, low levels of understanding and comprehension result. This case explores the problems of mismatched perceptions.

CaseParticipants

Jodi Kline—21-year-old, graduating, college senior; currently feeling the normal pangs of anxiety which accompany facing the "real world"

Cindy Green—21-year-old, graduating, college senior; nervous about graduating from college; her life is further complicated by not being able to make up her mind about her major commitments

"Would that I could read your mind . . ."

Jodi and Cindy have been college roommates for the past four years of their college life. The two girls are as different as they are alike. Jodi is beautiful, carefree, and wildly independent, while Cindy is attractive, spirited, yet very insecure. Yet through many "ups and downs" the two were known to be inseparable. This conversation takes place at the beginning of a rather hectic June, while they are packing to leave the dorm.

Jodi: Do you think that staying home all summer will make it any easier for you to come to grips with your life?

Cindy: My life—what about yours? Worry about yourself, why don't you!

Jodi: What is the matter with you? You're biting my head off with everything that I say.

Cindy: Me? Listen to yourself!

Jodi: It's a special time in our lives, Cindy. Instead of focusing on the positives, you're putting all of your energies into feeling sorry for yourself.

Cindy: What do you mean? You never told me that you felt that way before. I always stupidly took it for granted that you really cared about what I do after graduation.

Jodi: That's just the point.

Cindy: What point?

Jodi: Would you just let me finish a sentence?

Cindy: Well, you certainly have a very weird way of showing how much you supposedly care. I would think that if you had any thoughts about what I might be feeling, you'd be a little more sensitive.

Jodi: I have my own problems, and you seem to have no real time to listen to any of them. You seem to be so wrapped up in your own self that you have nothing left to give to anyone else's concerns.

Cindy: Sor-ry! It's not as if I haven't tried to make some impact . . .

Jodi: Time out! Do you think that my life is so out of whack that I need you in order to make a "go" of it?

Cindy: Well, if the shoe fits—

Jodi: Just a second now—I've never asked you for a thing. I'm the one who makes her own decisions, independent of what everyone else is doing. I always do what I want and you'll never find me asking for advice.

Cindy: And so what if you do ask for some extra "TLC" in your life? Excuse me for a minute, but what about the nights that I sat up with you until three o'clock in the morning working out your hysterias!

Jodi: That's not what I would call an "impact"!

Cindy: Don't take everything so literally. Someone should only be here to listen to what you are saying. No one would believe that you are for real.

Jodi: You're not playing with a full deck of cards tonight. Are you upset about moving out of here?

Cindy: That has nothing whatsoever to do with what we're talking about.

Jodi: It has everything to do with what we're talking about. You're really not making any sense at all—and whatever you are feeling—you're taking it out on me.

Cindy: All of a sudden you're becoming so analytical. That's not what I'm upset about. Don't I have the right to tell you how I feel once in awhile?

Jodi: So far, you are not telling me anything.

Cindy: You just said so yourself. It depends on what you call "anything."

Jodi: Oh, that's not what I meant and you know it.

Cindy: Not really. I'm not sure how to take what you say anymore. You're getting so "flaky" that I can't even say for sure whether or not you are serious at times.

Jodi: You've got to be kidding about this.

Cindy: See, there you go again! This is a perfect example of how you really don't care what others might say . . . only if it relates to you.

Jodi: Hey, this is hitting below the belt. Does it make you feel better to get this out of your system?

Cindy: Is that all you think I'm doing? Getting stuff out of my system? I just don't understand how you can say that!

CaseConcerns

1. What are the defense mechanisms working in this case?
2. Identify the weak links in the perceptual process from Jodi's point of view; from Cindy's point of view.
3. What is preventing the two girls from understanding each other?

ReflectiveResponses

1. Describe a situation in your life in which "total confusion" resulted from different frames of reference.
2. Describe a situation when uncertainty made you send unclear messages—which you did not realize until later.
3. Why is it possible to misunderstand a significant other in your life when you think you know "everything" about the person? What can be done in certain relationships to deal more effectively with perceptual misunderstanding?

Case 11

TargetTerms

- frame of reference
- perceptual checking
- selective defense mechanisms
- semantic differential
- punctuation of communication events

PreviewNotes

Sometimes, no matter what we say, our message is not clearly understood. This case illustrates the dual responsibility of sender and receiver in creating effective communication. It also points out several problems that can occur. What transpires in the following case study might appear a "bit far-fetched" and perhaps unlikely. However, consider analyzing the following misconstrued messages as a collection of perceptive misunderstandings.

CaseParticipants

Max Kovell—businessman who is accustomed to a great deal of travel; friendly; enjoys the luxury of first class hotel accommodations and services when on the road
Tim Landis—newly-hired front desk clerk at a major hotel chain

"It's just not my day . . ."

Max has been traveling around the country for three weeks making presentations for his new product line. He's tired and this scene finds him ready for a gourmet meal and a good night's sleep in a well-appointed hotel suite. After he hands his car keys to the valet parking attendant, he hurries to "check-in" . . .

Max: Will someone please help me?
Tim: Is there something the matter?

Max: No. Should there be?

Tim: Then, why are you asking for help?

Max: In approximately one second there will be something the matter if I cannot check in.

Tim: Well, why didn't you say so?

Max: Why on earth would I be here with a valet bag over my shoulder if I wasn't intending to stay?

Tim: Maybe, I thought that you were checking out, sir.

Max: Listen—I've just about had it today. I am in no mood for any small talk tonight.

Tim: Just trying to make this midnight hour a little more bearable. Looks like you need a little levity.

Max: Well, you're not succeeding! Let's just check my reservation and let me go to my room, for heaven's sake!

Tim: Name?

Max: Max Kovell. 460 Harris Street, Long Beach.

Tim: Hold on a sec . . . (*waits for a message on the computer screen*) O.K. . . . Nope. Nothing here to indicate a reservation, Mr. Kovell.

Max: What do you mean? I always make reservations through my office and this has never happened before.

Tim: Well, there's always a first. Now let's see where the problem may be. Checking these records there is no Max Kovell from Long Beach, California.

Max: Not Long Beach, California! Long Beach, New York!

Tim: Oh, sorry! (*sees that Max is ready to explode*) I'll be happy to check again. Oops—I guess your reservation was incorrectly processed.

Max: Whose fault is that? I know my address. If your staff makes mistakes, it's not my problem!

Tim: Now, now—O.K., here we go—there seems to be a Mr. Kovell—but, his name has only one ''l''—from New York, but it seems that the reservation was cancelled only this afternoon.

Max: Can't wait to hear this excuse!

Tim: Uh huh . . . (*nodding again and again*). Now I understand. It was a 6 P.M. guaranteed check-in and here it is midnight! You never did check-in, so it was cancelled.

Max: Of course I never checked-in! What do you think I'm doing standing here now?

Tim: But check-in time is at 6 P.M. Sorry, but if our guests do not check in by 6 P.M. without calling, of course, the reservation is automatically cancelled.

Max: How is it that no one ever told me that before?

Tim: (*he just smiles*)

Max: I never heard of anything like this before.

Tim: According to the read-out on the screen, a message was left on your telephone answering machine two weeks ago to confirm your reservation and check-in time.

Max: But, I left my home for this business trip three weeks ago. How was I ever to get that message? What kind of operation are you running here? I'm a preferred customer of this hotel, and I'm going to report this to the manager.

Tim: But the regulations of the hotel reservation system are all indicated clearly on every printed piece of material here in the hotel. We do cover ourselves on this issue.

Max: So where does that get me when I made my reservation one thousand miles from here?

Tim: Rules are rules!

Max: Sometimes, they are meant to be broken.

Tim: Not on the busiest holiday weekend, Mr. Kovell. You look like you could use a drink—can I get you an iced tea while you wait?

Max: Good idea.

MOMENTS LATER

A waiter enters with a tall glass and lots of ice. Max accepts the drink and as he takes a long sip, he begins to gasp and cough.

Max: This tea is so strong it could kill a person!

Waiter: That's the drink you asked for.

Max: This is hard liquor.

Waiter: That's what you ordered—an iced tea.

Max: I wanted a simple iced tea . . . You know, tea bags and ice and water.

Waiter: Ah-ha! Not where we come from! You ordered as if you were back East. Here we're used to something else. Our iced teas are spiked with more than lemons!

CaseConcerns

1. Has there been an incident from your own experience that has been misinterpreted by another party? Try to retrace the steps leading up to the misunderstanding and explain how the particular situation could have been avoided.

2. Why are we quick to jump to conclusions in everyday conversations? Are there any solutions that would help solve this problem?

3. To what extent is Max responsible for the misconstrued reservation information? To what extent is Tim responsible?

4. By role-playing the incident described, how might you handle Max's misunderstanding of the hotel's check-in policy.

5. How was the bull's-eye theory (page 5) demonstrated in this case? Describe an incident where you were guilty of using this faulty concept of communication.

6. At which point in the perceptual process did this incident begin to display poor perceptual ability? How would you suggest "fixing" the negative results of this case?

ReflectiveResponses

1. How can we as speakers and listeners learn to avoid communication breakdowns? Are there any precautionary measures that may be taken to ensure that a message is not misunderstood? Explain your answer.
2. There is probably a little of "Max" and "Tim" in each of us. Identify your perceptual pitfalls that may affect the way you communicate with others.

Case 12

TargetTerms

- F.O.R. (frame of reference)
- perception process
- principle of consistency
- selective perception
- punctuation of communication events

PreviewNotes

When we send unclear messages, we often receive unclear feedback. This case illustrates the problems created when certain important details are omitted from the message.

CaseParticipants

Sharon Sandler—naturally pretty; late 30ish aerobics instructor who is very well respected by the participants in her classes

Larry Michaels—early 40s; owner of the health club where Sharon teaches; has maintained the distinction of being the "brains behind the operation" of the place where people can become fit in both a cardio-vascular and pampered fashion

"How come you never told me?"

Sharon and Larry have worked together for nearly eleven years in the health and fitness industry. It is now five years since Larry took over the ownership of a failing health club and turned it into a major profit making business with Sharon's help. Larry made certain to retain Sharon as both a consultant and as an instructor because of her charisma and talents. For about six months, Sharon has been putting off a discussion with Larry about becoming a full partner for fear of a confrontation which may alter their affection for one another. Finally, Sharon decides she must speak to Larry. On this Saturday night at the 10:30 P.M. closing, Larry approaches Sharon and says:

Larry: How'd it go today?

Sharon: As usual, except tonight Mark Adams has a new love interest in a woman twice his age and Susie's daughter's finally getting married! Actually, in all seriousness, the classes are really getting very large and I'm getting laryngitis yelling "movements" across this room with less than wonderful acoustics. We're bursting at the seams here.

Larry: A credit to you, Sharon. It's obvious, but it never hurts to tell you again how much you mean to the operation of this place. You ought to know that just this morning I firmed up a deal with an architect for additional space. Think about some recommendations as to your personal needs.

Sharon: Well, there is one . . .

Larry: Yes . . .

Sharon: It goes beyond space, Larry. I'm not all that certain about what my role is at this point. I've gradually and willingly become an integral partner in this business, but what do I have to show for it?

Larry: You're just tired.

Sharon: Larry, don't insult my intelligence—

Larry: Hey, settle down. I didn't really mean anything by that. You're tired. I know you always get a little "cranky" and "crabby" on Saturday nights. You need to smile a little more. Come on, let's go and get a quick bite downtown.

Sharon: A quick bite won't make it "all better." There's more to this.

Larry: I'm obviously missing something here.

Sharon: (*Directly to his face*) How long have we known each other?

Larry: Eleven years.

Sharon: And?

Larry: Wait just a minute. You're not going to say what I think you're going to say?

Sharon: What's that?

Larry: That our relationship has undergone certain changes—

Sharon: Well, yes . . .

Larry: And that you're really starting to question your role with me?

Sharon: Well, isn't it just about time to talk about this?

Larry: I was hoping that it wouldn't come to this. I never meant to put you in this position. You really need to believe that.

Sharon: The fact is that you did. And I've been agonizing over this for the past few months.

Larry: I am so sorry. I don't even know what to say. I feel like such an absolute jerk!

Sharon: For the record, though, it is partially my fault. I really should have told you what I was feeling. I mean, how can I expect you to know what was going on in my brain?

Larry: Please believe that I never intended to hurt you.

Sharon: So, now that you seem willing to discuss this, let's have that late supper. I thought you'd hear me out, so I brought some papers to think about, just in case.

Larry: Papers for what?

Sharon: For my proposal.

Larry: Your what?

Sharon: My proposal for what we've just been discussing.

Larry: But, I just said that I didn't realize you felt this way and didn't mean to hurt you and you said that you understood, and that you knew that I thought so highly of you and all that—and after all is said and done, you offer me a "proposal"!

Sharon: Not meaning to be so businesslike, Larry, it's the only way that we can have some valuable legal foundations to what we both agree on. (*She sees his facial expression turn "blank."*) So, you've reconsidered already. I should have known better.

Larry: Sharon, I only want you to be happy. We've known each other for what seems to be forever. We have lived, breathed and worked under the same roof for over ten years. We made a real live dream come true, but throughout our whole time together there were no strings attached. I always thought that this was the way you wanted it to be. I never really considered another option.

Sharon: But, as I'm getting older and feeling the pressures of "making-it" on my own, I need to know that all my hard work and dedication to you will pay off.

Larry: So that's what all this boils down to. Is that what we're calling it now—a "payoff system"?

Sharon: Hardly! I've been your "gal Friday" for so long that this next step of forming a partnership comes quite naturally.

Larry: Sharon, the way that I feel about you and love you is really not the way that I think you want me to feel for you. You are like my alter ego and the truth is that I cannot think of a day without you here. But, to suggest that I can be a trusting and loyal partner is crazy. I'm just not the type to tie myself down to anything permanent. You, of all people, know how I love my freedom.

Sharon: And who is going to stop you from all this independent wandering? Not me! I'm only trying to develop and strengthen a relationship so that you can place some of the burden on me. This way you gain as much as me. I have an interest and you get your freedom without any guilt.

Larry: You are treating this like a real business arrangement.

Sharon: That's what it is!

Larry: Well, sorry for the disappointment, but I just can't comply with any of this.

Sharon: So much for a heart-to-heart talk. I thought this would happen, so I've already decided to be a lady and give you two weeks notice.

Larry: What's this—blackmail?

Sharon: Did I hear that male chauvinistic side of you that never surfaces? What did you think I was proposing, Larry? (*She looks at him and stops talking. She starts to collect her thoughts—and then, gradually, she bursts into a slow, knowing, methodical smile.*) I can't believe—no, I can believe. Do you actually think that I'm proposing—

Larry: (*He cuts her off.*) Then, you weren't asking me to . . .

Sharon: Oh, Larry, Larry, Larry! The proposal is a merging of two talents . . . and nothing more—certainly not what you think! I've been rehearsing this scene for months, only to get it all tangled in the wash. In an attempt to be so sensitive to your feelings, I guess I kind of beat around the bush a lot. Here's the bottom line—what would you think about having a business partner?

Larry: Somehow, this is a great relief to the other alternative.

Sharon: Thanks! (*smiling*) That really adds to my self-esteem! You know, I'm really starving. Let's eat now and we'll talk later—I'll even treat!

CaseConcerns

1. Many times in our lives, messages are inaccurately perceived by the receiver. By relating directly to the case, trace the gaps in communication between Sharon and Larry. How, in fact, did Sharon's objective become so distorted?

2. Would this case be applicable to another type of employee/ employer relationship? Give an example.

3. What happens when business and personal relationships are mixed? How do Karl Albrecht's principles of perception affect both business and personal situations? Are there similarities or differences?

4. Describe how individual frames of reference affect the communication process. When misunderstandings occur, where does the fault lie?

5. How does Larry perceive Sharon? How does Sharon perceive Larry? How do these perceptions affect this or any other relationship?

6. Identify the defense mechanisms at work in this case.

ReflectiveResponses

1. Sometimes we give and we receive messages which are misunderstood in our lives. Can you think of a situation in your life that led to misconstrued messages which were based on inaccurate perceptions? How did the message become clearer to both sender and receiver? If the message was not clarified, what led to the communication breakdown?

2. Why do we frequently jump to conclusions in our communication with others? How can we prevent making assumptions in our communication with others?

4
Chapter

Listening and Feedback

TargetTerms

- listening as understanding
- crazymaking
- hearing
- listening process
- covert response
- feedback
- egospeak
- types of listening
- defensive climates
- supportive climates
- disconfirming responses
- confirming responses

CoreConcepts

1 the need for listening as related to being understood as a person
2 the importance of listening as a skill
3 the difference between hearing and listening
4 the various types of listening
5 interferences to the listening process
6 strategies for effective listening through better feedback

"Didn't I tell you that?"

Overview

Listening is a communication process which we are all expected to be able to know how to do but for which we are never (or rarely) trained. Yes, we are told to "listen carefully" or to "stop, look, and listen," but we are never told HOW to listen. Logically, this process is half of the communication process, for we must listen to others' messages before we can respond with appropriate feedback. Illogically, we are usually trained in the latter process (public speaking, book reports, presentations) but not in the former (how to be a good listener). Poor listening skills are the basis for many of the communication difficulties we experience. If we send a message and the receiver is not listening, the message can be misunderstood, misinterpreted, or even ignored. Listening is a vital component in the communication process and a necessary element for effective interactions.

In this chapter, we will survey the process of listening and the strategies for effective listening. We will explore listening as understanding, the importance of listening, the differences between hearing and listening, the various types of listening, interferences in the listening process, and effective feedback strategies.

Listening as Understanding

As emphasized in chapter 1, "the most basic of all human needs is to understand and to be understood" (Nichols, 1980, p. 4). As a result of attempting to fulfill this need, we spend the majority of our lives trying to make others understand who we are, what we mean, and why we do what we do. The process of "trying to be understood" can be one of the most frustrating and discouraging tasks we attempt, but if we find at least one other person who really understands us, that can be the secret to happiness and personal fulfillment.

All too frequently, human relationships and our personal development can be severely impaired when we do not have a special person to act as our "sounding board" or to listen without comment. Some people pay professional "listeners," because no one else seems to understand. The desire to be listened to is very strong and is related to the need for consensual validation (see chapter 1). We want to know that we matter, that we have an impact on others. George Bach and Ronald Duetsch (1979) refer to this **right to impact**[1] as a vitally important listening need; when left unfulfilled, the result can be what they call **crazymaking**.[2] (A complete description of crazymaking theories are covered in chapter 5.) Not acknowledging the other person in a relationship can form the basis for serious and perplexing problems; being ignored or made to feel that our opinion does not count creates a separateness that can build permanent walls between us and our partners. Unfortunately, our unsuccessful attempts at good listening seem to be reflected in currently reported statistics which indicate a 50 percent divorce rate. Many times we end up confused, angry—and still misunderstood.

What Do You Think?

Think about the person in your life who is the best listener you know. Now, take a moment to describe this person using any adjectives which might characterize him or her. Then, think about the worst listener in your life and describe this person using descriptive adjectives.

What were you able to determine from your findings?

The Importance of Listening

The foundation for better understanding lies in the skill of listening effectively. However, we are rarely told or taught how to accomplish this task. Rather, we are presented with verbal demands such as, "listen carefully" or "listening is important," but we are rarely taught the process. Although almost half of our waking time (45%) is spent in the listening process (Rankin, 1926), relatively few schools actually teach this vital communicative behavior (Nichols and Lewis, 1954, p. 4). However, things are looking up for the recognition of the importance of listening skills. In the 1978 Primary and Secondary Education Act, the U.S. government added listening and speaking skills to reading, writing, and arithmetic as measures of literacy and recognized them as needed components in basic communication competencies (Wolvin and Coakley, 1992, p. 20). This important government act initiated many positive results, not the least of which is the inclusion of learning outcomes for listening in the College Entrance Examination Board's report entitled *Academic Preparation for College: What Students Need to Know and Be Able to Do* (Boileau, 1983, p. 4).

Most listening researchers maintain that listening is a learned skill which must be taught. Being able to listen effectively is not something we can turn on or off like a switch; rather, it is a learned skill that requires knowledge, practice, and behavior modification.

Effective listening skills have been proven to reduce errors and costs (Steil, 1980, p. 65), increase comprehension (Nichols, 1980, p. 56), and improve production efficiency (Hunt and Cusela, 1983, p. 399). A northeastern college attempted to test these hypotheses empirically; the results are promising. Pre- and post-tests administered indicate that listening comprehension scores significantly improve with only five hours of direct listening training (Seidler and Tamesian, 1983). In another single-class experiment administered by the authors, students were told to "really listen" to a story about which one question would be asked. Almost 75 percent of the students did not know the answer at the end of the story. However, after only a few hours of listening training and awareness exercises, the scores reversed themselves revealing only 25 percent failure. Thus, listening is a learnable skill that requires practice and is a distinct behavior not connected to abilities in reasoning, verbal comprehension, attention, auditory resistance, and memory (Spearritt, 1962, p. 3).

Hearing vs. Listening

There is a difference between hearing and listening. We can **hear** something being said or a noise being made but fail to pay any real attention to it. This happens sometimes when we are asked to do something we would prefer not doing—such as a household chore or a classroom assignment. We hear the message but we do not process it, and consequently the message is lost. The **listening process** involves a series of six activities that must be successfully performed in order for effective listening to occur. This requires involvement, both physically and mentally—listening is NOT a passive process. Listening requires ACTIVE participation on the part of the receiver.

Six intricate activities must be successfully performed by the receiver in order for **the listening process** to occur (Wolff et al., 1993; pp. 8–18):

- **hearing**
- **selecting**
- **assimilating**
- **organizing**
- **retaining**
- **covert responses**

Successful performance of these activities will result in listening (rather than just hearing); the degree to which the listening is effective depends on the degree to which the activities are performed accurately and thoroughly. The steps in the process are reciprocal in that they depend on each other for effectiveness. Weak links in the performance of any of the steps will result in a lower level of listening efficiency. For example, if we **hear** the message without interference, **select** the message stimuli as one to which we will attend, **assimilate** this selected message thoroughly, **organize** it in our mind so that it is decipherable, but then fail to **retain** the meaning of the message, the listening process will fail because of the weak link (retaining).

The final step in the process (covert response) deserves some special attention at this point. To clarify, the **covert response** refers to the process of preparing within how we will overtly respond to the speaker. So, the covert response is the preparation of a message (feedback) to send back to the original sender of the message. This process can have a positive or negative result. The process is initially positive because without it there would be no feedback or response to the sender. We need to prepare how we will respond to a message. However, when the process of covert response preparation occurs too soon or is triggered by defense mechanisms working to filter out the intended message, the process can become negative. Edmund Addeo and Robert Burger (1973) refer to this negative process as **egospeak**— when we begin to plan what we are going to say before the other person even has a chance to stop talking. So, instead of listening and letting the six step process occur in a reasonable time frame, we jump ahead and begin our covert response preparation too early, usually because we are trying to figure out how to impress the other person with our response. This is a common fallacy that leads directly to poor listening skills. Instead of listening, we are preparing. Preparing is an essential element—but only after the entire message has passed through the first five steps in the listening process.

Types of Listening

The process of listening can be further delineated by breaking it into four distinctive types of listening, each serving a different purpose (Wolff, Marsnik, Tacey, and Nichols, 1993). **Discriminating listening** is probably the most common type for college students; they routinely listen to lectures and must obtain information and ideas to store for use at a later time. We do **evaluative listening** as we weigh evidence or reason presented in an argument. Gratifying our senses and tastes while striving for maximum pleasure describes the process of **appreciative listening**. Listening to someone's problems with an open ear and an open heart describes our behavior during **empathic listening**. While the first three seem to be more for our own gain, the fourth type aims toward helping others. Although the types may overlap at times, a dominant one will usually emerge depending upon the context. Adapting to the type of listening needed for the situation is the sign of an effective listener.

What Do You Think?

Kelly always turns on the radio upon entering the car to drive to school. After three classes, Kelly meets with three other friends for a study group where they discuss the concepts presented in the lectures that day. On the way home, Kelly cannot wait to turn on the radio again and relax on the drive home.

What types of listening did Kelly do throughout the day? What type of listening did Kelly not do?

Listening Interference

There are many factors that can interfere with effective listening. Some of these things we do ourselves, and some of these things others do to us. Most of us, when asked, could list a number of "pet peeves" or things that interfere with our effective listening skills or bother us about "other peoples' listening behaviors." When people do not listen to us, we get extremely upset; the message we receive from their poor listening behaviors is that they do not care about us or our message. This can be one of the most irritating behaviors with which we have to contend. It reduces our self-esteem, it influences our feedback, and it pushes our anxiety and insecurity buttons. When we are talking, we expect that the other person will listen to us. When that does not occur, anxiety, frustration, anger, fear, and insecurity set in. Not being listened to is one of the most detrimental communication behaviors we experience.

What Do You Think?

Take a few minutes right now to list the ten most irritating poor listening behaviors that others impose on us. Then, after reading over the list, circle which ones YOU do to others. While we can get very good at identifying others' poor communication behaviors and pointing a judgmental finger at factors that influence the communication process, we seldom become objective enough to identify our own poor behaviors. Psychologists claim that the things that bother us most about others are the things that we do or do not like about ourselves. A closer look at this need for objectivity might be helpful in a thorough self-analysis of effective communication behaviors.

Effective Feedback Strategies

One of the ways in which we can become more effective communicators is to analyze our **feedback**, (the covert responses we prepare for overt expression). Two major theories give us some advice for that strategy: communication climates and confirming/disconfirming responses.

Communication Climate

Jack Gibb (1961) describes what he calls a **defensive communication climate** with six distinct communication behaviors that promote a defensive attitude; he then provides us with the appropriate solution by describing the six positive counterparts that promote a **supportive communication climate** (pp. 141–148). These six pairs of defensive and supportive responses are receiver-based interpretations which describe what Gibb calls communication climate. Gibb states, ''the degree to which these reactions occur depends upon the personal level of defensiveness'' of the receiver (p. 141):

- **Evaluation and description** refer to the degree to which a person feels judged.
- **Control and problem orientation** refer to the degree to which a person feels controlled or manipulated in conversation.
- **Strategy and spontaneity** refer to the degree to which a person detects a hidden motive or feels like a pawn in a game rather than like an individual.
- **Neutrality and empathy** refer to the degree to which a person feels apathy or caring from the sender.
- **Superiority and equality** refer to the degree to which a person feels inadequate or equal to the sender.
- **Certainty and provisionalism** refer to the degree to which a person feels the effects of dogmatism.

Arousing defensiveness disrupts the communication process whereas promoting supportive communication climates allows clearer and more open message reception.

What Do You Think?

Terry was easy to be around. Kim always felt listened to and thought Terry's interactions were comfortable and relaxed. Terry had a way of making Kim feel supported and accepted even when they disagreed. Kim liked Terry because their relationship was not competitive.

What type of communication climate did Terry establish in the relationship with Kim? Identify the communication behaviors Terry used to achieve this effect.

Confirming and Disconfirming Responses

Evelyn Sieburg and Carl Larson (1971) operationalized the terms confirmation and disconfirmation and provide us with the second major theory which offers another approach to effective feedback. **Confirming behaviors** are those messages which make the other person feel good about him/herself, messages that tell the other person that you (the sender) value him/her. **Disconfirming behaviors** are the opposite; these are messages that tell the other person that you (the sender) do not like anything about him/her.

The seven **disconfirming responses** are:

- **Impervious**—ignoring the speaker; denying the sender any feedback; failure to acknowledge the person or the message
- **Interrupting**—breaking into the conversation before the other person is finished; cutting off the speaker; beginning to speak while the sender is still speaking
- **Irrelevant**—responses unrelated to the original message; introducing a new topic without warning; disregarding what the speaker just said by switching focus
- **Tangential**—acknowledging the original message but immediately taking the conversation in a different direction; ''Yes, but I . . .
- **Impersonal**—not acknowledging that the other person is present; speaking in generalized terms (''one'' or clichés); conducting a monologue while in the presence of others
- **Incoherent**—responses that are not understandable, rambling, and difficult to follow; using interjections such as ''you know'' and ''I mean''; not making sense
- **Incongruous**—nonvocal and verbal disagreement in the message; when what you say is not reinforced by your behavior; incongruity between verbal intent and nonvocal/nonverbal behavior

The five **confirming responses** are:

- **Direct acknowledgment**—acknowledging the other person's communication message; reacting directly and verbally
- **Agreement about (not on) content**—supporting or reinforcing information expressed by the other; making it clear to the sender that you understand the message
- **Supportive**—responses expressing an understanding of the sender's message; reassuring and attempting to make the sender feel better; supporting the message and/or the sender
- **Clarifying**—responses trying to clarify the message of the sender; eliciting more information; to repeat (in an inquiring way) what was understood; asking questions about intended meaning
- **Expression of positive feeling**—expressing personal positive feelings about the sender's message; demonstrating support and agreement on content

What Do You Think?

Identifying the behaviors described above (positive/defensive climates or confirming/disconfirming) can be helpful in analyzing who we are and how we communicate with others through feedback. Many times we are either unaware of these behaviors or not objective about describing them for ourselves. As a self-awareness exercise, keep a journal for one day, write down your feedback responses to at least one relationship encounter EACH hour, and identify the specific types of behavior. Finish by writing a brief summary of what you learned about the types of feedback responses you use and then set some goals for yourself.

Summary

The processes of listening and responding are the foundations for human interaction. Basically, the process goes something like this: I talk, you talk, I talk, you talk—with "I listen, you listen" segments inserted before the covert response is translated into talk. The "egospeak" concept refers to formulating a response before listening to the entire segment. Thus, we have missed at least part of the sender's message and negated the process of effective listening. In the witty and cynical words of noted author Fran Lebowitz, "The opposite of talking isn't listening. The opposite of talking is waiting" (1981, p. 7). If we are only waiting for our turn instead of listening, we are not participating in an interaction; it may be more polite than interrupting, but it is *not* listening. Better listening skills and careful attention to the timing of covert feedback and overt feedback responses will help us improve these processes. Listening is a crucial element in effective human communication and one of the most important determinants of relationship satisfaction.

Notes

[1] The term "right to impact" refers to the right we have in a relationship to know if we have an effect on the other person. The theorists state that each party deserves to be recognized and acknowledged by the other party (Bach and Deutsch, 1979, pp. 89–106).

[2] "Crazymaking" has been coined by various theorists (Satir, 1972; Bach and Deutsch, 1979). Although most definitions are fairly similar, in this context, this term refers to indirect communication patterns that drive the other person crazy (Bach and Deutsch, 1979, p. 214).

References

Addeo, Edmund G. and Robert E. Burger. *Egospeak*. Radnor, PA: Chilton Book Company, 1973.

Bach, George R. and Ronald M. Deutsch. *Stop! You're Driving Me Crazy*. New York: Berkley Books, 1979.

Boileau, Don, ed. "Education Research Notes Development." *Spectra*, 19 August (1983): 8.

Gibb, Jack R. "Defensive Communication." *Journal of Communication*, 11, no. 3, (1961): 141–148.

Hunt, Gary T. and Louis P. Cusela. "A Field Study of Listening Needs in Organizations." *Communication Education*, 32 (1983): 399.

Lebowitz, Fran. *Social Studies*. New York: Random House, 1981.

Nichols, Ralph G. "Listening Is a 10-Part Skill." *Nation's Business*, 45, July (1957): 56.

_____. "The Struggle to Be Human." Address at the First Annual International Listening Association Convention, Atlanta, February 1980.

Nichols, Ralph G. and Thomas R. Lewis. *Listening and Speaking: A Guide to Effective Oral Communication*. Dubuque, IA: Wm. C. Brown, 1954.

Rankin, Paul T. "The Measurement of the Ability to Understand Spoken Language." Diss. University of Michigan, 1926. *DA*, 12, (1952): 847–848.

Satir Virginia. *PeopleMaking*. Palo Alto, CA: Science and Behavior Books, 1972.

Seidler, Ann and Linda Tamesian. "An Experimental Study of the Effectiveness of Five Hours of Direct Instruction in Listening on the Listening Comprehension Skills of College Students." *Florida Speech Communication Journal*, 11, no. 1, (1983).

Sieburg, Evelyn and Carl E. Larson. "Dimensions of Interpersonal Response." Paper delivered at the International Communication Association, Phoenix, April 1971.

Spearritt, Donald. *Listening Comprehension: A Factorial Analysis*. Melbourne, Australia: G.W. and Sons, 1962.

Steil, Lyman K. "Secrets of Being a Better Listener." *U.S. News and World Report*. 26 May (1980): 65.

Wolff, Florence I., Nadine C. Marsnik, William S. Tacey, and Ralph G. Nichols. *Perceptive Listening*, 2nd ed. New York: Holt, Rinehart and Winston, 1993.

Wolvin, Andrew D. and Carolyn Gwynn Coakley. *Listening*, 4th ed. Dubuque, IA: Wm. C. Brown, 1992.

Case 13

TargetTerms

- confirming/disconfirming responses
- listening as understanding
- hearing versus listening

PreviewNotes

The need to be understood is illustrated in this case. Types of feedback are also highlighted as we discover the difference between hearing and listening.

CaseParticipants

Alena Petit—46-year-old mother of three children; foreign born and educated; exotically attractive; somewhat reserved and hesitant in her manners

Bill Petit—49-year-old business executive; conservative in style; firm in his beliefs; very much the patriarch of the family unit

"Please hear what I'm not saying!"

The Petits met while Bill was stationed oversees in his early twenties. He and Alena married almost immediately and began their lives in the United States after his term of service abroad. The following discussion is a result of Alena's voluntary participation in a marital communication research project where the couples agreed to talk into a recorder for approximately fifteen minutes about various aspects of married life. Bill was eager to participate in the study. When asked about how their budget was handled in their marriage, Bill begins:

    Bill: It is handled by me—
Alena: By both of us!

Bill: Yeah, but I spend the budget money that is set aside for mortgage and important items, and you spend the money that is set aside for the household items, like food shopping, clothing, and the like.

Alena: There are times when you should consider how I would like to spend some money.

Bill: I do that.

Alena: When?

Bill: (*He is quick to jump in . . .*) Are there any movies that you would like to see that I haven't taken you to?

Alena: That's not what I'm saying.

Bill: You never really listen to what I'm trying to tell you. For once, stop thinking about what you're trying to tell me and start thinking about what I'm saying to you when I'm saying it! (*The tape is cut off.*)

Alena: (*after a few moments*) You think you made your point? Just because I still have to think in my language before speaking doesn't mean I'm any less smart than you are.

Bill: And whose fault is that?

Alena: No one in my life here has ever chosen to speak my language. So, I—

Bill: (*There is an obvious interruption.*) The next question wants us to tell about what we think are the roles of the man and of the woman in the marriage.

Alena: The role of the woman is to stay home with the children and take care of the husband, until . . .

Bill: Until such time as she needs to go out and go to work and help with the finances.

Alena: Why couldn't I say that? You keep saying everything for me.

Bill: Who knows when you were going to finally spit it out.

Alena: Give me a chance. And how do you know so much that this is what I was going to say. You are doing it again. You are not listening to me.

Bill: Let's talk about the next question . . . on discipline and how we discipline our children. I guess the first child was disciplined more than the second and third. The reason I guess that, is that the second and third got away with more because maybe we were older and didn't have the patience and time we had with the first one.

Alena: Yeah, but don't forget the time . . . (*The tape is shut off again . . .*)

Bill: Our problem solving is handled by discussion . . .

Alena: Since when is it that we can talk about a problem without you getting upset and not wanting to talk at all? This is supposed to be truthful.

Bill: Yes, it is handled by this type of serious discussion.

Alena: You're making me feel like an idiot again. Whoever is listening to this tape is going to think poorly of me. How come you are not wishing to hear what I have to say?

Bill: Talk . . .

Alena: But, I think we should try to, uh, talk about the problems more often, and try to solve them. Sometimes we try to talk about them but leave them unsolved.

Bill: Sometimes there's no cut and dried answer to them. You just have to leave them.

Alena: No, that is not right. You want to just leave them—still, forgetting about what I have to say.

Bill: Here we go again . . .

Alena: But there are always alternatives to what we're sharing with each other.

Bill: Well, that's what I just said—that we have to sit down and start—

Alena: But we don't do it . . . we don't do it.

Bill: Now you're not hearing me out.

Alena: But what I said is the truth—we don't do it.

Bill: Listen, there is some lack of communication. (*long pause*)

Alena: So as far as you are concerned—explain—how do you feel and I'll tell you how I feel.

Bill: I don't think there's any great lack of communication. You have something to say and you say it—and so do I.

Alena: Yes, but what is the use of saying something when you don't listen. And . . .

Bill: But—

Alena: You hear me, but you don't listen.

Bill: Sometimes you're not asking me something.

Alena: It seems that you don't pay that much attention.

Bill: There is usually no response necessary.

Alena: But there is when I'm telling you something. Of course, I expect a— how do you say—response. But I don't get any response.

Bill: That's because I don't think there's any response necessary. You tell me what you think and that's fine.

Alena: No, that's not it . . .

Bill: I don't have to specifically disagree with what you have—

Alena: Yeah, but that's not fine. That's the problem. You don't agree, you don't disagree—you just don't say anything. And then things stay that way.

Bill: No—that's not the case.

Alena: You see that's what I mean when I say that we don't communicate.

Bill: So how can you improve that?

Alena: I guess that one way to improve—no wait, you said how can "you" improve! We have to start really listening to each other . . . like if you tell me something that bothers me, I should really do something about it. If I don't agree I should make you understand—explain to you—and tell you that I don't agree for this and this reason—and make sure that you are satisfied with my answer and I would like to get that from you.

Bill: Well . . .

Alena: (*she continues*) When it comes to the children—or to money—to any other problem, I would like to solve the problem if there is a problem.

Bill: If I don't see that there is a problem—

Alena: But, if it's a problem for me, it seems—

Bill: But you don't treat the problem as a problem.

Alena: Sometimes there's a problem, for me it seems—and not to you. So, you just turn your back on me and that's the end of it. (*The tape is cut off for an uncertain amount of time and then Alena continues.*)

Alena: You see, I ask you once and you close your mind, because you don't believe in it. And I believe in it. Only an impartial person can step in to make you realize . . .

Bill: (*interrupting*) What are you talking about?

Alena: This is one problem that we have.

Bill: What? (*long pause*) I'm asking you—what is the problem?

CaseConcerns

1. There are several references to the "tape being shut off" in this case. Specifically refer to the case and decide who you feel turned off the tape. How do you think this made the other person feel? How did you arrive at your answers in each particular instance? What kind of listening behavior does this describe?

2. Identify specific confirming and disconfirming responses. How did these responses affect the listening process?

3. After describing Alena's self-concept, explain how her self-concept affects the way she communicates. How does it affect the way she listens? Answer the same questions for Bill.

4. Do you perceive Bill's listening behavior as confirming or disconfirming? Explain your answer.

5. Does Alena feel understood by Bill? Why or why not?

6. How does the concept of "egospeak" apply to this case?

7. What type of listening is occurring in this case? Explain. Is it the most appropriate type for the situation?

ReflectiveResponses

1. Do you accuse people of not listening? What are some of the reasons that you feel this way? Do you ever behave in the same manner?

2. As we work and socialize in the diverse, multicultural society in which we live, do you consider how you might adapt your listening habits to accommodate others who may not speak your language. Think about a situation when you found it difficult to comprehend a person who spoke a different language. How did you deal with the situation?

Case 14

- right to impact
- the listening process
- hearing versus listening
- types of listening
- confirming/disconfirming responses

PreviewNotes

This case illustrates the need for impact on significant others in our lives. During a couple's taped response to questions on a written marital communication survey, we discover how the listening process can malfunction at various stages.

CaseParticipants

Lisa Young—married; age 38; mother of two elementary school-aged sons; upbeat and lively in terms of her outlook on life; her sense of adventure added to the couple's interest in participating in a marital communication research project

Joel Young—Lisa's 42-year-old husband; extremely successful in his occupation involving sales; seemed to be hesitant about taking some moments from his busy schedule to tape the marital communication research project

"Yeah, right . . ."

According to the couple, the following taped discussion was recorded over a cup of late night "decaf" coffee. Joel has had a long day at work and Lisa has also spent the day completing myriad projects. While toying with a seemingly unfamiliar tape recorder, Lisa reads the first question from a marital communication survey and says:

Lisa: Wait a minute—does this work? Joel, I'm calling you. The play button goes down and then we begin. Will you look at me, please, and put down the newspaper when I talk to you? (*She starts to turn the tape recorder on and talks to herself.*) O.K. We're taping now. O.K.? (*She looks at him and he does not answer.*) Question number one—How is our budget handled? When we need money, we use it. Correct?

Joel: Right. (*referring to the tape recorder*) Where do I speak so it will be recorded?

Lisa: I just told you.

Joel: I didn't hear what you said.

Lisa: So what else is new?

Joel: Well, how do you expect me to do this thing if I can't find the microphone. (*She must have pointed somewhere as the tape is now louder in volume.*) Now, what was the question?

Lisa: Joel!

Joel: O.K. I'll really do it. What should I say?

Lisa: Say whatever you want with regard to the fact that we spend money when we need it. Do you agree or disagree?

Joel: Right.

Lisa: Joel!

Joel: You're absolutely right, Lisa. (*His voice becomes very serious.*) We don't have anything called a budget. When we need money, we look in our checkbook.

Lisa: I only take a certain amount of money each week—to run the house—

Joel: Right.

Lisa: And I usually end up giving you money. Because you never have enough money.

Joel: Does that mean that we are on a budget?

Lisa: Yeah, basically.

Joel: I don't consider that a budget. I define a budget as putting said monies away each week and staying within those limits.

Lisa: But, I run the house on a weekly budget—

Joel: (*He interrupts.*) Yeah—right.

Lisa: And if I have money left over, I put it in my "stash," and if you need money or the kids—

Joel: (*interrupting*) Right.

Lisa: But that's kind of a budget.

Joel: Next.

Lisa: How are we going to talk for fifteen minutes?

Joel: We're not. We never ever talked that long in our lives. Even now, I'm having a tough time—I feel as if I'm falling asleep.

Lisa: All right—let's go! Discuss the guidelines under which you would raise children or are currently raising them. How is the discipline structured?

Joel: Well . . . we really don't need to discipline.

Lisa: As far as who's concerned?

Joel: You always tell me that I don't discipline the kids.

Lisa: Since when did you ever listen to what I said to you about the children?

Joel: MmmmHmmm.

Lisa: You don't.

Joel: Don't what?

Lisa: Discipline the kids.

Joel: Right.

Lisa: You do not discipline them—at all!

Joel: I disagree with that.

Lisa: You do?

Joel: I don't discipline them to the extent that you do, but—

Lisa: (*she jumps right in*) —But, you discipline them for the wrong things—like tracking mud in the house, instead of for cracking each other's heads open.

Joel: Didn't I discipline them the other day for not listening? I told them we couldn't "go" for not listening to me.

Lisa: Go where?

Joel: Where was it that I said we couldn't go?

Lisa: When was it? (*He just looks at her.*) So, did you end up going?

Joel: Sure, we did. (*He laughs.*)

Lisa: (*She laughs.*) So what kind of discipline is that?

Joel: That's not a great discipline, I guess. Well, as for disciplining the kids—I guess that you do it better than I do.

Lisa: And that's why they hate me and love you!

Joel: C'mon, Lisa. I'm just fooling around. I know, let's get to the next question. (*He reads the question from the survey.*) "Discuss the lines of communication used in your marriage and how they might be improved." Well, you call me from the bedroom to the family room and I call you from the family room up to the bedroom.

Lisa: I don't think that's really what they meant.

Joel: What do they mean?

Lisa: The channels of communication—how do we discuss things?

Joel: Discuss things. Oh—not through what mechanism do we discuss things?

Lisa: Got it. I don't think "they" care whether or not we use the telephone or what. The lines of communication, that's what it means.

Joel: O.K. Well, we talk.

Lisa: That's our lines of communication?

Joel: What do you want me to say?

Lisa: Say what you want.

Joel: But, if I say the wrong thing, you won't listen to what I'm saying.

Lisa: But, how do I know if it's wrong if you won't say it?

Joel: I have the best idea to solve the problem all together. Let's turn off the tape as we'll never make the fifteen minute time request anyhow and if you want to talk, we'll talk. (*The sounds of a rumpling newspaper and the clicking "on" of a TV is heard in the background.*) If you want me to listen, I'll listen. Just tell me what you want!

CaseConcerns

1. Distractions are a major deterrent to positive listening behaviors. In this case, what are the specific distractions that affect listening behaviors?

2. References have been made to talking "at" as well as talking "to" another person in this chapter. Identify instances in the case when hearing rather than listening was occurring. Identify instances when listening rather than hearing was occurring.

3. Role play this case demonstrating alternative listening behaviors. Reverse the male and female roles. Does the reversal of roles make any difference in the hearing versus listening process?

4. Characterize Joel's listening behaviors with Sieburg and Larson's confirmation and disconfirmation terms. Do the same for Lisa.

ReflectiveResponses

1. What happens when we "second guess" or make assumptions about a message we are receiving? How can this listening behavior be corrected?

2. Much attention has been paid to the area of being understood in the process of human communication. Do you feel that it is solely the sender's responsibility to create a clear, meaningful exchange? How much depends on the listener's sense of what is important to "hear" or "absorb"? Is there or should there be a certain etiquette attached to listening behaviors in general?

3. Have you ever had to tape your responses to a survey? Or, have you ever had the opportunity to listen to responses from a taped survey or interview? Describe your experience.

Case 15

TargetTerms

- egospeak
- the listening process
- types of listening
- communication climates
- confirming/disconfirming responses

PreviewNotes

Answering before the speaker is finished results in constant interruption. When that premature response is focused on personal needs, it is called egospeak which prevents effective listening and feedback.

CaseParticipants

Jerry Landsman—33-year-old account executive, hard-working; has been with the same firm for ten years; handsome and nicely attired

Alan Jacobs—33-year-old managing account executive; known to be a "workaholic"; serious-minded; nice looking and stylish

"I don't care what you say . . ."

Jerry and Alan have worked in the same public relations firm for the last ten years. Alan Jacobs has managed to "land" seven new major accounts which did not go unnoticed by the corporate board of directors; he was promoted to a newly created, top-level position of Senior Vice-President in charge of account coordination. In addition to obtaining and retaining new accounts, Alan now holds complete jurisdiction over Jerry's activities within the company. At the onset of this conversation, Jerry finds himself infuriated by a memo that was just sent by Alan to all account executives regarding a new procedure. Storming into Alan's office, Jerry says:

Jerry: It's about this memo, Alan. What the hell is going on here?

Alan: Excuse me! Let's hold it here just one second and try this again.

Jerry: This is not a particularly great time for trying out your new "Effective Training Techniques for Increased Productivity for the More Seasoned Employees!" I'm out of here tomorrow for the Ames account—my plane leaves at 6 A.M. And I'm not in the mood to be one of your executive training guinea pigs by writing up a major report at the busiest time of the year.

Alan: What's the big deal about asking you to write a follow-up to your accounts? You can even do it on the plane.

Jerry: Because I never did that before. And, you know that you never had to do that either.

Alan: That doesn't make it any more correct. In fact, that is precisely why I'm instituting this new follow-up policy.

Jerry: And what will this report—that will take me about a month to prepare—ultimately prove? You know the numbers—so do I.

Alan: That we're all doing our job, Jerry. And—it helps us keep track of who's doing what, not to mention the importance of follow through.

Jerry: It's more like busy work—and you know it! My job is coordinating and helping to execute an advertising campaign.

Alan: And what you do translates to new business. Final tallies, product consumption and client appeal is what matters.

Jerry: Do you really want me to listen to this? What is incredible is that you forgot to add how very effective you will look through my efforts.

Alan: Unfair! My commitment is the same as yours—to fulfill a promise of providing excellent service to all of our clientele.

Jerry: I have that same commitment—and you know it. Why are you making me feel as if I am some kind of a weak link in this big chain here?

Alan: Don't take this so personally, Jerry—everyone is requested to do the same thing. All I need is the report by the first of the month. (*pause*) Any other problems that I can help you with?

Jerry: There—there you go again with the word "help." I've pretty much been on my own around here making meaningful contributions to this firm without having to spin my wheels by reading and responding to memos or asking for help.

Alan: Hey—look. Let's consider the positive aspects of what you're so negative about, Jerry. The memo I sent saved you time by not having to attend meeting after meeting about this assignment. By assessing the future needs of each of your clients, your business will, I predict, take on a whole new image.

Jerry: Why don't you just say what you really want to say—that my old image is also in question.

Alan: Stop being so defensive and listen to me. The time you are spending complaining about this request could be utilized more effectively.

Jerry: (*slowly and deliberately*) I've been listening to you for the last eighteen months, going on about the same old thing—"Process, then evaluate and evaluate again." What about "response"? Well, here's my response. (*Jerry makes a derogatory gesture as he exits.*)

CaseConcerns

1. Analyze the communication that takes place in this case and determine whether or not the communication climates in this case change as the dialogue progresses.
2. The defensive and supportive communication climates described by Jack Gibb include six distinct communication behaviors. By referring to the confirming and disconfirming responses listed in the chapter, determine which responses are disconfirming. Include why the response is disconfirming by using the seven disconfirming responses in your answer. Do the same with the confirming responses.
3. What advice would you give to both Jerry and Alan that would help them utilize less disconfirming responses.
4. Identify the barriers to effective listening evident in this case.
5. How does egospeak interfere with the listening process in this case?
6. Identify the types of listening behaviors in this case. Why are they appropriate or inappropriate?

ReflectiveResponses

1. What is the difference between listening and hearing. Think about a situation in your personal or professional life where you heard more than you listened? As you think about the situation now, why do you think you responded as you did?
2. As you begin to relate and think about your own communication behavior, do you feel that you are a confirming or a disconfirming listener? On what do you base your answer?
3. Who is the most confirming listener in your life? The most disconfirming? Describe your own behavior when you are in the presence of each of these persons. As you learn more about interpersonal communication competency, how can you now apply your knowledge to effectively deal with the relationships in your life?

Case 16

TargetTerms

- empathic listening
- defensive climates
- disconfirming responses

PreviewNotes

When friends ask for advice, the decision whether or not to give it is difficult. This case illustrates an attempt at empathic listening, with unsuccessful results.

CaseParticipants

Bonnie Palmer—23-year-old, single, professional woman; spends endless hours on the phone with Barbie Hodges, her best friend

Barbie Hodges—24-year-old, single, professional woman; spends endless hours on the phone with Bonnie Palmer, her best friend

"What should I do?"

Bonnie usually can't wait to call Barbie to check-in and talk about the weekend. This time, Bonnie is desperate to confide in her friend but also a little wary about revealing her irresponsible behavior.

Bonnie: Hello, Barbie?
Barbie: Oh, hi, Bon. What's doing?
Bonnie: Oh, lots, I guess.
Barbie: Well—how was your weekend?
Bonnie: O.K.
Barbie: Just O.K.? (*with a touch of nurturing*) So, what's wrong?
Bonnie: How did you know?
Barbie: I know you like a book.

Bonnie: I guess I do need some advice.
Barbie: Oh, really. About what?
Bonnie: Well, I don't know how to say this—
Barbie: Just say it—
Bonnie: I know, I know, but I feel funny about telling you this.
Barbie: Well, I know I can help. What else are friends for? (*She gets no response.*) Well, are you going to tell me or are we going to play guessing games all night?
Bonnie: (*taking a deep, audible breath*) O.K. If I don't tell you now, I'll burst— and besides, I'll probably never be ready to tell anyone about this . . . Well, you know that guy I went out with last weekend? You know, Louis—well, I just spoke to Sue who knows him from way back and I found out that he's an IV drug user and I'm positively—absolutely hysterical.
Barbie: Well, did you sleep with him?
Bonnie: Well, yes. Why else would I be so nuts over this? I'm just so scared that maybe he was HIV positive.
Barbie: Didn't you have safe sex?
Bonnie: The timing wasn't right for that—one thing led to another and before I knew it—it was over.
Barbie: How can you be so stupid? Where have you been all these years— don't you turn on the TV or read the newspaper? How could you?
Bonnie: If you'll let me finish what I was saying—I didn't even realize what was happening.
Barbie: Couldn't you have exhibited some control?
Bonnie: O.K.—alright already. I know. So, now what do I do? Should I get tested? Should I call him now and ask him if he's been tested? C'mon, tell me what to do—I'm scared.
Barbie: Well, why don't you just call this Louis person and tell him how stupid he is for being an IV drug user and then blast him for having the nerve to put you at risk.
Bonnie: How can I do that?
Barbie: You're worried about that! Why didn't you worry last weekend? I'd even start calling everyone you met at the Club you went to and tell them about this jerk!
Bonnie: Barbie, now wait a minute. Aren't you jumping to all sorts of conclusions here? I mean, maybe he's not even infected—
Barbie: What is wrong with you? You just told me that—
Bonnie: Well, maybe he's not even really an IV drug user.
Barbie: (*with tons of sarcasm*) Oh, great! Nice time to back down—listen, if you don't want my advice, then don't ask for it. (*She slams down the receiver as Bonnie bursts into tears.*)

CaseConcerns

1. Describe how Barbie creates a defensive listening climate.
2. When friends ask for advice, are there any guidelines that could be created? Discuss what you believe would be the best approach.

3. Is Barbie an empathic listener? Defend your answer.

4. How does the topic of a conversation affect the listening behavior of the participants?

5. Does empathic listening allow for "advice giving"? Support your answer.

ReflectiveResponses

1. What do you do when someone you know places you in an awkward position and requests advice that you may not want to give? What are your personal unwritten rules about responding to a friend's need for advice.

2. When listening or responding to other people in your life, are there some subjects that you would classify as "taboo." If so, what would you say to another person to let him or her know that you are uncomfortable with a particular topic?

3. How can we use more effective listening techniques to increase our empathic understanding of issues involving AIDS awareness?

4. Think about a time in your life when someone made you feel as if what you had to say was not important. Why types of disconfirming behavior was evident in his or her response? Think now about a time when someone made you feel as if what you had to say was extremely interesting and meaningful. What types of confirming behavior were evident in his or her response?

5
Chapter

Interpersonal Needs

| Specific Goals for Understanding Chapter Five |

TargetTerms

- needs deprivation
- inclusion
- control
- affection
- hierarchy of needs
- crazymaking
- needs suffocation
- caring-too-much syndrome

CoreConcepts

1. needs and how they affect communication
2. interpersonal needs as motivators of communication behavior
3. when needs can suffocate your partner
4. the necessity for balance

"I really need you."

Overview

The concept of needs as motivators in human interaction is prevalent in communication research (Maslow, 1970; Schutz, 1980). Researchers describe our interpersonal needs as strong forces on which we base important decisions about our actions and our interactions. When not met or inadequately met, interpersonal needs become starving monsters who crave satisfaction with insatiable desire. While this may sound like an exaggeration, needs are powerful motivators of human communication behavior.

In this chapter, we will explore the motivating force of interpersonal needs on the way we communicate. We will investigate our interpersonal needs and their effect on the interaction process, their impact as motivators, their strength to overwhelm through suffocation, and the necessity for balance.

Needs and Communication

We all have certain needs that must be filled in order for us to function as human beings. We need food, water, and sleep to maintain our physical health, and we need to give and receive love to maintain our emotional health. The intrapersonal needs of physical health soon lead to interpersonal needs of emotional and psychological health as we grow. Even from birth we experience both types of needs. We know we cannot exist without meeting our physical needs, but can we survive if we are deprived of our emotional and psychological needs? Not really. It depends on what we mean by survive.

Needs deprivation can cause severe problems both physically and emotionally. Researchers tell us that babies deprived of physical love through touch can develop severe psychological and intellectual deficiencies. Verbal and nonverbal communication are the means by which interpersonal needs are met. When we ignore or deny certain needs in our lives, they manifest themselves in strange and inappropriate ways. For example, if I pretend I do not need anyone and that I can live my life by myself, I may develop an anti-social means of relating to others (probably without realizing it) and end up lonely and isolated. Interacting with others allows our interpersonal needs to be fulfilled; this process is accomplished through the various means of communication that are at our disposal. Without acknowledging or recognizing what we need and communicating those needs to others, we deny ourselves the essential ingredients for satisfaction. Others cannot guess what our needs are—even though we may expect them to "if they really love us!" This process has an effect on the way we send and receive messages.

What Do You Think?

Terry: Hi, hon. I'm home. (*there's no response—pause*) Hon?! Oh, there you are. Hi! How ya doing?

Kelly: (*dejected and depressed—head down in a book*) Oh, hi.

Terry: Hey, what's the matter? You look so down.

Kelly: Oh, nothing. I'm just tired.

Terry: Well, it looks like it's more than just being tired to me.

Kelly: No, really. It's nothing.

Terry: If you say so. You up for a movie?

Kelly: Are you kidding? How can you say that? Haven't you got any feelings?

Terry: Geez, I thought you said it was nothing! How am I supposed to know what's wrong when you say it's nothing and it really is something?!

Kelly: Oh, never mind. You just don't understand my needs—if you did, you'd be able to figure it out. It just shows me how much you don't care.

Were Kelly's needs met? Do you think Kelly knew what those needs were? Did Terry really know what Kelly's needs were but just wasn't willing to fulfill them? Who is at fault here? Anyone? How do you identify and communicate what your needs are to significant others?

Needs as Motivators

The process of need fulfillment or deprivation affects our lives in many different ways by motivating our communication behaviors. We communicate in order to satisfy needs. Because we are basically self-centered human beings who need to take care of ourselves, we frequently focus on what we want and need. "But what about me?" is one of the many phrases we use (or hear from others) when needs are not being fulfilled. Whether the needs are not satisfied because we exhibit the wrong needs, or whether the needs are not satisfied because we do not really know what we need, we are still causing problems for ourselves in interpersonal communication. Needs are strong motivators and can become "monsters" if not "fed" properly.

Knowing what motivates us, what we need, and what makes us satisfied contributes to effective communication.

Inclusion, Control and Affection

Psychologist William Schutz (1980) explains the human needs for **inclusion, control**, and **affection**—social needs that we fulfill through communicating. He states that these three needs motivate our behaviors and that we WILL get these needs met, sometimes at any cost. These needs are measured on a continuum from high need to low need. Schutz's test measures and compares exhibited needs and desired needs.

Schutz (1980) defines **inclusion** as the need to feel a sense of belonging in some personal relationship. This need to feel included or to belong extends into all types of relationships—formal and informal. We satisfy this inclusion need in various ways: through friends in class, through jogging partners, or through co-workers on the job. This sense of belonging can also come from clubs we join, contracts we sign (marriage, jobs), or rituals we perform (religion).

Another type of interpersonal need is the need for **control**—the desire to influence others, to feel some sense of power over your own life. While some types of control are normal and obvious, other types are devious and subliminal. Acting as the captain of the cheerleading squad or president of the student council are regular types of control without devious intent (under normal circumstances). Occasionally, the control comes from people without delegated authority, sometimes subliminally and sometimes overtly. This is the type of control that is difficult to understand and creates barriers in effective communication. The couple who is arguing over eating in or out is not really arguing about food; issues of control and power are the primary needs in this case.

Affection is the third interpersonal need according to Schutz (1980). Broadly interpreted, the affection need refers to the need for love, respect, confirmation, and empathy. We need to know that we exist and that we have some impact on others. The affection need is also closely tied to self-concept which is satisfied by the "mirror" that others provide for us. Without this satisfaction, we become isolated, alienated, and alone.

Schutz's theory (1980) claims that if the desired need is significantly different than the exhibited need, some behavior will be created to obtain the true, desired need. For example, if we exhibit a high need for inclusion with others, but we actually love to be alone, we may become frustrated because people will never leave us alone. We communicate to others that we WANT to be included, but we actually DO NOT WANT to be included. This not only confuses the receiver, but frustrates us—the sender. Similar examples could be created for control (autonomy vs. manipulation) and affection (friendly and social vs. underfriendly and undersocial). The goal is to identify and exhibit (communicate) our actual needs so that others can meet them. The first step is to identify specific needs; the second is to communicate them. If we do not tell anyone what we need, it is unrealistic to imagine that those needs will magically be met.

What Do You Think?

Kim: For a change, let's make dinner together.

Chris: O.K. I'll make the salad and you make the pasta.

Kim: Great. Make sure you wash the lettuce—you know—use the salad spinner. It works great!

Chris: Sure. What do you like in your salad?

Kim: Oh, I don't care. You decide. Oh, don't use tap water to wash the lettuce—use this filtered water, so we won't pollute our organic lettuce.

Chris: Fine. Do we have any tomatoes?

Kim: Let's not put in tomatoes. Let's make it a caesar salad.

Chris: Sounds good.

Kim: Did you add the parmesan cheese—and lots of it—I love it!

Chris: Oh, O.K. How's the pasta coming?

Analyze the dialogue above to discover which needs are surfacing for each character.

The Needs Hierarchy

Abraham Maslow (1970) presents us with another model similar to Schutz's called the **hierarchy of needs**. In it, Maslow describes five levels of needs (see Figure 5.1):

1. **physical and biological**—the human need for food, water, sex, and air

2. **self-preservation and safety**—the human need for security, stability, protection, law, order, freedom from fear, anxiety, and chaos

3. **love and belonging**—the human need for friendship, affectionate relationships, and interpersonal acceptance

4. **self-esteem and pride**—the human need for self-evaluation, self-respect, self-esteem, esteem of others, strength, achievement, competency, reputation, prestige, status, fame, and glory

5. **self-actualization**—doing what one is fitted for doing; self-fulfillment and actualizing to one's highest human potential

Figure 5.1: Maslow's Hierarchy of Needs

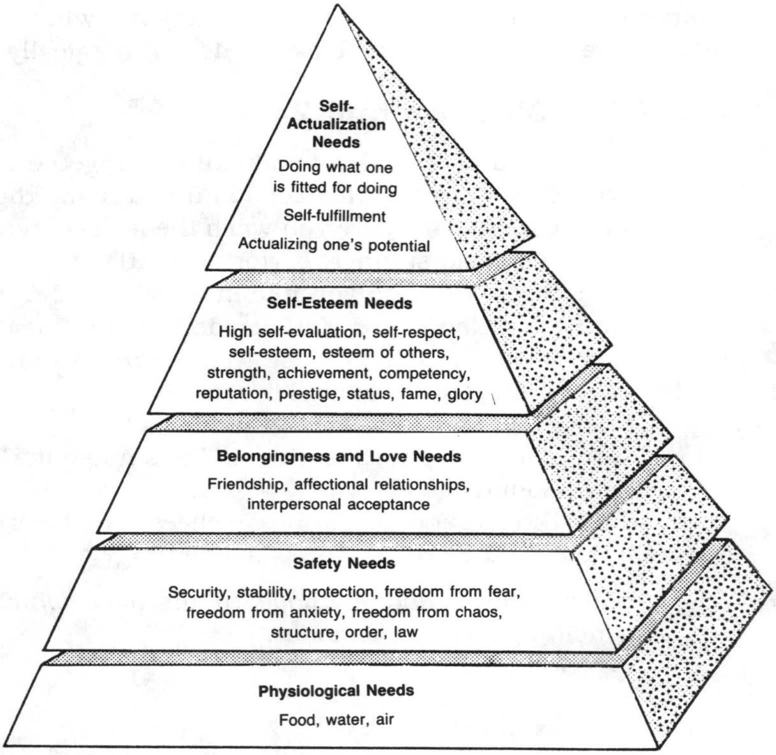

From *Motivation and Personality, Third Edition*, by Abraham H. Maslow. Copyright 1954, 1987 by Harper & Row, Publishers, Inc. Copyright © 1970 by Abraham H. Maslow. Reprinted by permission of the publisher.

We progress through these levels every day, starting at the bottom each morning. Although the levels are somewhat additive, individuals can skip or deny a certain level in order to obtain a need from a higher level. Eventually, the missed level will surface. For example, as college students, you may forget about family and friends while preparing for exams, also missing food and rest. In order to fulfill the need for personal success and achievement, the lower three needs are ignored or denied—but only temporarily. After finals, you go "home" and eat and sleep for days, basking in the comfort of family love and security. Or, individuals can get "stuck" in level four (self-esteem and pride), trying to move up the corporate ladder. Anything will be sacrificed for a promotion: sleep, money, health, even family and intimate relationships. Sometimes realization occurs too late and results in divorce, problems with children, health problems or even death.

What Do You Think?

Try to remember a recent incident that created the feeling of being left out or alone. Vividly recall the experience in your mind and try to recreate the emotions you felt. List two or three of those emotions.

As a result, how did you relate to people when you were feeling this way? What did you say? When the need for love and belonging was not met, how did this affect the way you communicated?

Crazymaking

As mentioned above, if needs are not met, it may be because of the way we communicate those needs or the ways others are communicating with us. Chapter 4 introduced us to George Bach and Ronald Deutsch (1979), who describe what they call the "sabotage of sanity" or the **crazymaking** experience. Through the use of indirect, double-speak language, people send unclear, confusing messages. Quite often when needs are involved, we do not really say what we mean either because we do not know what we need or we are afraid to say what we need for fear of rejection. This "sabotage" is usually done subconsciously, although a deep-seated motive may prompt the confusion. The sender of the crazymaking message is unaware that the message is confusing and may not even realize that it does not say what he/she intended to communicate. The receiver of the crazymaking message feels what they termed the "sabotage of sanity."

Bach and Deutsch (1979) highlight four rights that, if not met, may cause the crazymaking experience:

- **the right to know**—the right to clear and direct information about a significant other
- **the right to feel**—the right to have and express our own feelings and emotions without having a significant other tell us what those feelings and emotions *should or shouldn't* be
- **the right to impact**—the right to have demonstrated to us that we mean something to a significant other
- **the right to space**—the right to have a separate physical space or to have physical or emotional distance from a significant other

Crazymaking results from denial of need fulfillment by the sender. The communication patterns usually center around information that is not the real information. Confrontation with the truth and the "real" reasons are the only solutions that can stop the cycle.

What Do You Think?

Sue is always late when meeting George, her boyfriend, and she always has an excuse which George suspects is not the real reason. After waiting for her for 35 minutes one night at a restaurant, George finally lost his tolerance for her behavior. As

Sue rushed in, she proclaimed problems with the subway and last minute phone calls. George finally had to confront her by asking her why she was consistently late and always had unconvincing excuses. She countered with statements of disbelief and denial, proclaiming her devotion and love for him. George left and said he needed time to think about the problem—alone.

What rights are being violated here? Who is creating the sabotage of sanity? What would you do to solve this dilemma? Why was George feeling the grips of crazymaking?

Needs Suffocation

There are times when we may suffocate our intimate partners by fulfilling needs for them that they do not have. Yes, you read that correctly. Sometimes we may fulfill needs for others that are actually OUR needs, not their needs. In an attempt to meet the needs of another person, we sometimes end up accomplishing our task too well. How so? One cause of **needs suffocation** could be that we are really giving the other person what WE need instead of what they need. We reason, often erroneously, that giving others what we want will help them figure out our needs and how to reciprocate. We fall into this trap because we assume that others have the same needs—at the same time—as we do. Certainly, others have similar needs, but those needs are not always as intense as our needs nor do they occur at the same time. Consequently, our well-intentioned behaviors are met with resistance and confusion on both sides.

Another possible cause of this problem is what we call the **caring-too-much syndrome**. In this case, we may overcompensate for times when we did not feel like satisfying a need of the other person. Or we may be exhibiting a high-level need to control because of a deeply-ingrained insecurity about ourselves or the relationship. Or, as is usually the case, we may be doing what we thought represented caring and loving behaviors. This "over-meeting" of another person's needs happens sometimes when parents do not want to let go of their children or when a person with a low self-concept feels unworthy of the relationship.

What Do You Think?

Don and Winnie were good friends, socially and professionally. Don is a young, single, easy-going, independent, people-pleaser who never wants to hurt anyone's feelings. Winnie is a lonely, retired spinster with lots of energy. Winnie calls Don every day—sometimes up to three or four times. She volunteers to "house-sit" for him when he goes on business trips, and she frequently has movies lined up for them to see. She volunteers to help him with anything at the drop of a hat. Don feels suffocated by Winnie's attention but does not want to hurt her feelings so he does not say anything.

What would you do in this situation? How does Don maintain his personal freedom and privacy without hurting Winnie's feelings? Why is Winnie doing this? Is she caring too much as a friend? Do you have any friends like her? Describe your communication with this person.

The Need for Balancing Needs

In order to develop healthy need levels resulting in a balanced approach to relationships (and effective communication), we need to be aware both of what our needs are and how to exhibit those needs accurately to others—and to read their needs levels as well. As with most elements of life, needs must be balanced in order to function appropriately. When we lie to ourselves by pretending our needs are met, act as if we do not have any, or deny certain basic interpersonal needs, the result can be devastating to us and to our relationships.

What Do You Think?

Kelly: Terry, don't you think you have worked long enough? Come to bed—please—before you collapse.

Terry: Yeah, I'm almost done. Just a little bit longer.

Kelly: I'm worried about you. That's all you do is work, work, work.

Terry: Don't worry about me. I'm fine.

Kelly: What time do you have to be at work tomorrow? Maybe you could go in late.

Terry: Fat chance. I have a 7:30 A.M. breakfast meeting with the big boss.

Kelly: How much longer are you going to keep driving yourself like this? And for what? Sooner or later it's going to take its toll on you, dear.

Terry: I can get by on very little sleep—remember? I don't need more than about 4–5 hours of sleep a night.

Kelly: Oh yea! But what about the person I have to put up with the next day? Not very pleasant—or have you forgotten the last time you did this? It's not fair to me OR you.

Terry: Come on, Kelly. Quit nagging me. Are you really so concerned about me or about how all of this will affect you?!

What need is Terry denying? Why is Kelly so concerned? Is it a selfish concern? What's out of balance here?

Summary

Interpersonal needs motivate our communication behaviors. We realize these needs, either consciously or subconsciously, and seek to get them met in whatever way seems appropriate. When denial, avoidance, and false perceptions cloud our vision, intrapersonal and interpersonal communication problems are manifested through conflict, alienation, and loneliness. There is a need for us to be responsive and sensitive to the interpersonal needs that influence or motivate the communication of others. In addition, as communicators, we must consider using language that allows us to express our individual needs to others. Ultimately, we can develop a better understanding of how interpersonal communication needs differ from relationship to relationship when we adjust our communication to promote relational growth.

References

Bach, George R. and Ronald M. Deutsch. *Stop! You're Driving Me Crazy*. New York: Berkley Books, 1979.

Maslow, Abraham. *Motivation and Personality*. New York: HarperCollins, 1970.

Schutz, William C. *FIRO: A Three Dimensional Theory of Interpersonal Behavior*. New York: Holt, Rinehart and Winston, 1980.

Case 17

TargetTerms

- right to impact
- love and belonging need
- affection need
- right to know

PreviewNotes

Insecurity and uncertainty breeds fear and anxiety in relationships. This case explores the feelings that we get when our needs are not fulfilled.

CaseParticipants

David Sanders—age 21; senior in college; en route to law school; ruggedly handsome; Dean's List student

Kimberly Nichols—age 19; football team cheerleader; college sophomore; psychology major; country-girl look

"Hanging out the white flag"

David Sanders comes from a very comfortable family. He met Kimberly Nichols during her freshman orientation program. They have dated steadily ever since. On this particular evening, David had promised to take Kimberly out for an important dinner date. David is extremely late according to Kimberly's watch. Upon answering the doorbell, she says:

Kimberly: Well, it's about time. Where on earth were you?

David: So now I have to account to you about one more thing! You know that I have a major exam tomorrow, Kim. If I don't do well on this I can kiss my acceptance to law school good-bye.

Kimberly: And where, may I ask, do I fit into this scheme of applications, deadlines, and anxiety attacks?

David: Can't you just try to support me without thinking of yourself for a change? You know that I can't possibly keep up this wild schedule of catering to you, my books, all without a moment's time for "me."

Kimberly: Well, well, well . . . There's a "bottom-liner" if I ever heard one. Tell me, is my assigned role only to sit and wait for you, Mr. Juris Doctor, until you're ready for me? I have needs too, and it would be kind of nice if I could count on knowing that you're there for me for a change.

David: This is just about the most ridiculous conversation we have ever had. All I did was arrive at your place twenty minutes late.

Kimberly: It's not that, and you know it! Your being late is a negative statement toward me. You know how much I always like to be on time.

David: Aren't you getting a bit carried away with your Freudian stuff?

Kimberly: Freudian "stuff"? Oh, I see . . . what I study is not as sophisticated nor as demanding as your studies in litigation.

David: Ah, c'mon—please don't start up with me now. Just tell me what you want!

Kimberly: For an opener, why can't you think before you speak and start considering me for a change. You always negate what I do with my work, especially at the clinic. And how many times do I listen to you tell those sick jokes and dump on what I do.

David: Can't you even take a joke?

Kimberly: No, not when they're at my expense. All you want to do is exercise control over what I do. And, you know what? It's really beginning to bother me.

David: Now, look who is getting carried away! What do you want me to do? Say "I love you" and "I need you" and that "I can't live without you"?

Kimberly: How about if I don't dignify that with an answer. It's quite obvious that you're not even interested in what I'm all about and I don't know if you ever will try to understand or respect me.

David: All this over a twenty minute delay?

Kimberly: Thirty.

David: O.K.! O.K.! I'll hang out the white flag. Look, I'm under the gun. I need to pass this course, and it's the toughest that I have ever taken. I'm nervous for the first time. Is this what you really want from me? To prostate myself before you and let you take over. Well, if that's what you want . . . fine!

Kimberly: (*as she begins to cry*) Let's not do this to each other, David. I guess, with all of my psychology "stuff," that what I'm really trying to tell you is that I'm nervous, too.

David: But don't I always give you everything that you want? Whatever— whenever—I don't care . . .

Kimberly: That's just it. I need you to care. I need to feel important in your life. You're not letting me get involved in your life. (*He does not respond readily*).

David: Listen, I'm beginning to think that I need some space, Kimberly. This conversation is really frustrating me. And to tell you the honest truth, I'm confused. So, do you think you can just lay off for awhile? Just get off my back.

CaseConcerns

1. Identify portions of this conversation separately for Kimberly and for David which can be applied to Abraham Maslow's hierarchy of needs.
2. How would William Schutz analyze the needs of Kimberly? Of David?
3. Is the conflict described in this case realistic in terms of relationships in general? Or is it your belief that this can only apply to certain types of relationships?
4. If you were asked to compose a stream of consciousness of each character's private thoughts in the next hour following the conclusion of the conversation, what would it include?
5. Does hanging out the white flag solve this issue? Other issues? What needs are not being met here for both people? How would you suggest that their needs be met?
6. At various points in the dialogue, Kimberly and David are preoccupied with their own personal needs. What type of effect does this have on the process of communication between them?

ReflectiveResponses

1. Have you ever felt the need for more "space" in a relationship? If so, why? Were you able to deal effectively with the relationship after your decision to back away?
2. How would you feel if a significant other in your life told you that he or she needed some time to reflect about the relationship?
3. Do you feel that you are aware of the needs of the most important people in your life? If so, how did you learn to recognize what those needs were? If not, why do you feel you are unaware of what those needs are?

Case 18

TargetTerms

- inclusion
- exhibited versus desired needs

PreviewNotes

Have you ever had to be all things to all people? Too much inclusion can result in being torn in too many pieces—in too many directions. This case illustrates what happens when exhibited needs for inclusion do not match the desired needs.

CaseParticipants

Suzanne Tisch—overburdened; over-achieving; over-worked

"Needed too much . . ."

Suzanne is the mother of two children, who has made the difficult decision of returning to college to complete a long-overdue degree. Her husband and family initially gave their support in "helping out with everything." Before long, however, everyone at home soon forgot their pledge and needed her more than ever. Suzanne finds it difficult to make room in her private life for time to complete her coursework. While her husband is at a meeting, she puts her two young children to bed and starts work at the computer at 8:45 P.M.

Suzanne: (*thinking to herself*) Finally—peace and quiet. The dishes are done—the kids are asleep, and I can finally sit down and get this paper started so that I can have some peace of mind when I go to class this week. (*She turns on her computer*) All right—think—Suzanne—how do I start this damn thing? The intro must be exactly the way she wants it, so I better start it right. O.K.—calm down and think. What is it that I really want to say? Let's see—O.K.—the concepts are—where—where the hell did I put that notebook? It was just here. (*She sees a drawing of a dinosaur on the front of the class folder.*) Oh, Zachary—why did you do this?

(*She smiles to herself.*) O.K., here it is. Now, I've got it. (*She looks up.*) Now all I need is the strength to do this. (*With tremendous energy and renewed spirit, she almost hypnotically starts to create on the computer—and, even as the telephone rings—she continues to think to herself.*) Why can't I be like everyone else and have an answering machine to screen my calls? (*Picks up the phone*)

Suzanne: Hello.

Peg: Hi.

Suzanne: Who is this?

Peg: Peg. I can't believe that you didn't recognize me.

Suzanne: I'm just real busy.

Peg: I know. That's why I want to take you to lunch tomorrow.

Suzanne: I'd love to, but—

Peg: No buts! You're too busy and I'm not taking "no" for an answer.

Suzanne: I have a big paper due tomorrow and I'm really trying to get about a hundred other things in order.

Peg: Let's not forget about you, Suzanne. You still have to have lunch, you know.

Suzanne: If I get away from this—I'll never get back to it for days.

Peg: This isn't a "no"—is it?

Suzanne: I'm afraid that it is "yes"—that I mean, I can't really go as I just don't do lunch these days.

Peg: Oh, c'mon. Don't be like that. Just for an hour? I'll pick you up.

Suzanne: Well—No—really, it's not that at all. (*hears the beep for call waiting*) Oh, Peg, sorry but I have another call coming in. Can you hold—no—it'll be better if I call you back. Oh—about the lunch—I guess that I could get as much done on the paper before noon— yes, I'll meet you—yes, pick me up. Yes. Yes. (*pause*) No. I won't let you down. Bye . . . (*click*) Hello. Oh, he's not home yet. Sure, I'll be happy to give him the message. (*pause*) Yes, I realize the importance of it. (*pause*) Yes, I'll be glad to add whatever you want to this. (*pause*) Yes, I'll give him the message the second that he comes in. (*pause*) Late. Yes. I expect him in late. (*pause*) Thank you. (*pause*) Yes. (*pause*) Good-bye.

(*She goes back to the computer—irritated that she had to stop what she was doing—when six-year-old Zachary comes into the room with sleepy eyes to tell Suzanne that his "bones tickle" and that he can't sleep. She kisses him, gives him a big hug, and puts him back in bed—hoping desperately that he'll quickly fall back to sleep. She goes back to the computer.*)

Suzanne: (*thinking to herself*) Now, back to the first point that I was trying to discuss. Where was I? Ah—yes—in order to make the con- nection between the ideas—dammit—I can't even think straight. Why did she have to call me when she knows that I have all of this pressure? I never have lunch in my life—and she has to call at 9:00 P.M. to ask me out. What does she want from me? Why can't I even find one lousy moment to do something for me? Now where was I? Point one—to connect the ideas—calm down—it'll come. (*She stops what she is doing and places her hands across her face as if in some type of pain.*) Ugh!—Jen's field trip is tomorrow, and I never got over to the bakery to pick up snacks for the class as requested. Remind me to do that tomorrow. I better write that down or I'll forget. (*It is now 9:30 P.M., and she hears the doorbell ringing. As she looks out of the window, she sees Arnie, her husband.*) Now, why didn't he bring his key? He knows that I'm working up here. (*She goes downstairs to open the door and after he greets her, he goes directly to the refrigerator.*)

Suzanne: Why do you look so ravenous? You said that you were having dinner at the meeting.

Arnie: I just had a quick pizza. Don't worry about me—I'll find something.

Suzanne: Let's not play games—you're hungry and I'll fix you something.

Arnie: Well—don't do anything fancy . . .

(*After making dinner—nothing fancy—she goes back to the computer to continue her "brainstorming" about her work.*)

Suzanne: (*again, thinking to herself*) O.K.! Where was I? Now I've got it— (*as she begins to madly type—quietly—"eating away" at her is the fact that she has to get up very early for the donuts for the class trip—as she continues to think . . .*) Wait—I'll take a break and go now—then—I can write until late tonight without worrying about getting the donuts tomorrow. Arnie—I'm taking a quick ride to "Seven-11" to get the donuts—keep an eye on my computer—will you? (*She goes and returns in a flash and Arnie gives her two phone messages.*)

Arnie: Shari called and says that it is terribly important that you help on the P.T.A. Art Committee—something about you being the only one that has the experience to organize the annual art show? What's that all about?

Suzanne: Oh, just one more thing—

Arnie: Say no.

Suzanne: Who else can do it?

Arnie: So, do it—but, I don't want to hear about how little time you have.

Suzanne: (*looking at the clock*) Oh, it's getting so late—I'm going to finish that paper once and for all.

Arnie: Oh—and you got one other call.

Suzanne: From whom?

Arnie: Your mother.

Suzanne: What, now?

Arnie: She thinks she sprained her ankle—

Suzanne: I know—and can't drive—and she wants me to do her food shopping tomorrow.

Arnie: You got it!

Suzanne: (*ready to burst*) I'm going to finish this paper before the rest of the universe crashes in on me.

(*Back at the computer*) Here we go—it's 10:23 P.M.—okay, the final connection in this analysis—(*phone rings while Arnie is in the shower and she grabs the receiver ready to scream—instead, she answers with a certain pleasant reserve*)

Suzanne: Hello.

Doris: Oh, did I call too late? This is Doris, Doris Langley, P.T.A. President.

Suzanne: Yes?

Doris: We all hear that you are such a fine organizer.

Suzanne: Well, that's not really—

Doris: Oh, but don't underestimate yourself, dear. We want you to head this year's fundraising drive. You're so creative and efficient— why, everyone would just adore working with you. Just say "yes" to heading the Annual Fund Drive. (*Suzanne doesn't answer.*) Are you still there, dear? Please do this for your school and for the children, especially?

Suzanne: I don't know—I have so much going on just now.

Doris: For the sake of the children?

Suzanne: You know, Mrs. Langley, I've got to start doing things for the sake of another person—me! Sorry, but the answer is "no."

Doris: Surely, you'll reconsider.

Suzanne: My reconsidering has just started.

Doris: Good, then, you'll do it?

Suzanne: Sorry, but the best I can do for anyone is saying "no." Did I hear my call waiting beep? Sorry, Doris, but I have another call. I'll see you soon, I'm sure. Bye.
(She hangs up the phone and decides not to take the other call— and goes back to the computer—somewhat content that she has begun to protect her limited free time. Then, slowly, but with a sudden burst of unreleased energy, she turns off the computer, locks herself in the bathroom, and draws a warm bath, adding lots and lots of bubbles.)

CaseConcerns

1. According to Schutz, which of Suzanne's needs are being met and which needs are not being met?
2. According to Maslow, which need is Suzanne attempting to fill in this case? Why?
3. What is Suzanne's exhibited need? What is her desired need?

ReflectiveResponses

1. Can you think of a situation where you exhibited one need (involvement), but actually desired the opposite (privacy). Describe your communication behavior.
2. Identify ways in which you can make others more aware of your needs.
3. Why do people fear telling others what their needs are?

Case 19

- caring-too-much syndrome
- needs suffocation
- control
- affection
- balance of needs

PreviewNotes

Trying to meet someone else's needs is not always easy, especially when we try to guess what those needs may be.

CaseParticipants

Billy—a 22-year-old man starting to work as an accountant
Grandmother Anna—a 75-year-old widowed grandmother
to Billy

"Sorry, I didn't realize . . ."

Billy returns to his hometown after being away at school for four years. He lives in his relatively lonely grandmother's house, but he has his own apartment downstairs. After a long day at work, Billy returns to the apartment.

Anna: (*coming downstairs*) I thought I heard you come in. How come so late tonight?

Billy: I stopped for a quick bite.

Anna: I would have made you dinner, you know. Well, I'm not going to bother you as I guess you have lots of work to do—this being tax season and all.

Billy: Thanks anyway, but I'm going out now.

Anna: In the height of tax season?

Billy: Grandma, please, I'm not in nursery school.

Anna: It's just that you did come in awfully late last night and I know for a fact, Billy, that you went to work real late three times this month.

Billy: What?

Anna: They called you and needed you for something last week and didn't know where you were.

Billy: They called you?

Anna: Well, not exactly. After you left yesterday—I heard the car speed away; you're in such a hurry all the time—I thought I'd give your place a good cleaning. The phone rang and I answered it. Could've been important. The nice lady, a secretary, I think, sounded upset and said that you had an appointment and where were you? I felt so embarrassed and ashamed.

Billy: I can't believe you did that.

Anna: What? Cleaned your place?

Billy: No, answered my phone.

Anna: Oh . . .

Billy: Grandma, can't you just butt out of my life! Just lay off!

Anna: Billy, you would talk to me like this? If your mother ever heard you—

Billy: (*feeling his temper rise out of control*) Can't you just get out of here! I'm not your little Billy boy anymore!

Anna: Well then, I guess, you're a stranger in my house. (*It is apparent that she is holding back tears.*)

Billy: (*goes to her as she backs away*) Grandma, give me a few minutes and I will be upstairs to talk.

Anna: I have nothing to say to you.

Billy: I am sorry, I really am. I don't know what got into me. The last thing that I want to do is to hurt your feelings after you've been so good to me. But, I think that we better talk about what I think is good for me, and not what you think is good for me. Or better, how you and I can live under the same roof while respecting each other for who and what we are.

Anna: Respect—who talks about respect for each other and for who we are? Such college talk, but I like this talk.

Billy: Give me a second, Grandma. I'll be upstairs and I do wanna apologize again. I also think I'm getting hungry. What do you have for me to eat?

CaseConcerns

1. What are Billy's needs in this case? What are Anna's needs? How do the two case participants exhibit their needs to each other?

2. What happens in this case when Billy feels that his needs are not being met? Consider what happens to Anna when she feels that her needs are not being met?

3. Describe how the communication behavior in this case changes toward a productive outcome.

ReflectiveResponses

1. Do you change the way you speak to someone by how old he or she is? Do you have any experience with dealing with a grand-parent, older relative or older family friend where you felt somewhat smothered by affection? Were you able to directly relate how you felt to your relative?

2. Have you ever been involved in a relationship where your needs have not been met? How can you effectively signal your feelings to the other party in your relationship? What are some of the more specific communication skills you can use to more effectively demonstrate what your needs are?

Case 20

Target Terms

- control need
- self-esteem need
- right to impact
- right to know

Preview Notes

The need for control can be demonstrated through withholding the recognized needs of another. What happens when a husband and wife have very different needs in several different areas? This case explores the desire for impact, control, and self-esteem through very mixed messages.

Case Participants

Judith Woods—age 45; petite brunette; tailored, manicured appearance; physically fit and in shape; articulate; well educated

Robert Woods—age 49; tall, thin, dark hair, flecked with grey; formal demeanor; hesitant, but articulate; well educated

"Twenty-three stormy years"

Judith and Robert Woods, married twenty-three years, reside in the outskirts of a large university town in the Northeast. Robert, professor of political science, has recently been promoted to a more prestigious position as Dean of his school. During the early years of the couple's marriage, Judith interrupted her public relations career to raise her three children who are now grown. The following conversation represents a segment of their taped response to a marital communication survey. The first question asks the participants to speak about communication in their marriage. Judith begins:

Judith: . . . communication has been such a problem for me and I've been unhappy about it. You have admitted on occasion that you are difficult to communicate with and that you need to be constantly reminded and opened up and I really don't know that we've done such a good job in that area.

Robert: Well, I think much of it stems from our individual personalities. You have more of a need to discuss things over and over and over again. I don't.

Judith: And you have a need to NOT discuss things at all which is your way of handling a situation for the most part, or a very brief, unsatisfactory, unresolved, conversation is usually sufficient for you . . . and I always feel as though I have to come to some sort of resolve . . . I need you to think of how I feel, you know. I really do think that women especially have that need to discuss things wholly and fully . . . and men don't.

Robert: Well, I think that's basically true, but it's inherently a personality difference.

Judith: Well, I guess it's something that I guess we've, no, I have learned to live with . . . that I've learned to more or less just accept. I accept it the way it is, because it is either "take it or leave it" and I'm not going to leave it, so I just take it. That's my major concern in our relationship—that I can't communicate with you on the level I would like to. I want so much to feel as if you include me in your life. I can't really say that you have ever given me reason to think that I am a part of what you do—or that you are a part of what I do for that matter. Do you understand?

Robert: Well, I feel the same way—to a degree.

Judith: But, you're still speaking on a more intellectual level than an emotional one. I think your complaint has always been that I don't meet your intellectual needs . . . or need to discuss things that interest you, that I have no interest in.

Robert: I don't see a difference. Regardless of whether it might be topics of current events or emotional issues, I might have an interest in discussing certain things and you might not. Neither of us fulfills the other's need to discuss those things. We respect each other, don't we? Isn't that what we're both saying?

Judith: Well, yes—but, I need to know that you care and sometimes I need you to tell me how concerned you really might be—at any given time—or during any specific situation that may arise in our life. To do that, you've got to make time for me. And so I think that . . .

Robert: I think I know what you think. And I'm sure that your dissatisfaction with this all is valid because you choose or prefer to discuss things that you view as emotional in content—and that's because they're more important to you. My interest in discussing everything I need to focus on, I feel, needs to be of interest to me or to my work. What I think is that neither of us is willing to provide that gratification to each other.

Judith: Well, I think that what we've learned to do or learned to accept in our marriage is to satisfy those needs through other people or other relationships. You get more intellectual stimulation from people you work with and see out of work; I communicate on an emotional level that I enjoy with my friends . . . with my women friends.

Robert: I agree.

Judith: I think our relationship is better now after many stormy years . . . twenty-three of them. I think that we've learned to accept who we are in each other. Otherwise, I think that we would have some even greater problems to contend with in our lives. At least for the next twenty-three years, we can have a better handle on what these needs might be.

Robert: Well, I think that part of maturing or learning to deal with each other's needs—or even accepting each other—is not expecting each to provide that complete gratification.

CaseConcerns

1. Write an alternative ending to this case designating each character's exit and final lines.

2. How realistic are the particular interpersonal need problems which were addressed in this case?

3. After reading this case, can you relate to any of your own personal needs not being met? How do you personally deal with not having your needs being met or addressed?

4. Write a short paragraph about the inner dialogue that we didn't hear in this case. Men take Robert's character and women take Judith's character. Then, switch characters.

5. Role play Judith's part strongly emphasizing a high exhibited need for affection and attention. Then, role play Robert's part strongly emphasizing a high need for self-esteem and pride.

ReflectiveResponses

1. How do you suppose a significant other in your life might respond to a question about the communication in your relationship? How would you personally respond? Are you able to make any determinations about respecting each other's interpersonal needs in the relationship?

2. Explain some of your feelings about meeting the needs of someone in your life who may not have similar interests or career goals. Is one able to satisfy another's needs if each person in the relationship is from a different "place"?

6
Chapter

Beliefs, Attitudes, and Values

| Specific Goals for Understanding Chapter Six |

TargetTerms

- beliefs
- attitudes
- values
- drives
- motives
- helix communication model
- principle of consistency
- defense mechanisms

- cognitive dissonance
- entropy
- dogmatism
- black and white perspective
- attraction theory
- trust
- honesty

CoreConcepts

1 an understanding of our beliefs, attitudes, and values (BAVs)
2 developing our BAVs
3 maintaining or changing our BAVs
4 how values can cause conflict in interpersonal communication
5 how values affect relationships
6 the impact of truth and honesty on our communication

"That's the dumbest thing you've ever said!"

Overview

We are all strange creatures when it comes to our beliefs, attitudes, and values (BAVs). We seem to protect them like the family jewels and then defend them to our death. We also feel very uncomfortable when others express differing views from those of our own. This discomfort can surface because we have a fear that we may be wrong and the other person may be right—and we all know the terrible feeling of being wrong. These differences play with our egos, making us question the differences rather than accepting them. We rarely question our attitudes or beliefs; we just assume ours are the right ones. Realizing that our opinions about these issues may differ substantially from the opinions of others is frustrating, but acknowledging these differences is essential. Discovering a difference in beliefs, attitudes, or values can become a battle ground for a communication war when, in actuality, the conflict is unnecessary.

On the one hand, we would like everyone to agree with us and share our BAVs; on the other hand we like to think that we are unique and special, having no other clones made from our mold. This dichotomy produces a paradox for us. We want to be a different, unique, and separate individual, but yet we find ourselves going to extremes not to be too different, unique, or alone (Fromm, 1956). Fromm maintains that becoming aware of ourselves also makes us aware of our separateness and our distinctiveness from other people; this awareness rekindles the desire to create a union with others, to establish human contact, and to seek relatedness with others (pp. 7–31). Simultaneously with being elated in the discovery of our uniqueness, we are also fearful of being too separate, distant, and alone. This paradox intensifies the desire to communicate with others, regardless of the consequences.

BAVs form the basis of our perceptual world. Disclosing our BAVs allows us to share with others who we are. Through interpersonal communication we develop, maintain, and change our BAVs, and that is the focus of this chapter.

In this chapter, we will explore the impact of our value system on the way we communicate. We will discover some definitions of beliefs, attitudes, and values; how we develop our BAVs; some methods of maintaining and changing our BAVs; how our values can cause conflicts; how our values affect our relationships; and the impact of truth and honesty (core values) on our interactions.

Definitions: BAVs

Beliefs

Beliefs are our individual perceptions of what is and what is not, based on our idea of truth or falsity. In contrast, a **fact** is a belief that we all believe or one that we all hold in common. Many times, however, these common beliefs that we think are facts turn out to be false. **Beliefs** are also the little theories or personal truths we carry around in our heads about the correct way to do things. We develop these "theories" through our experiences of what works for us. For example, one type of belief is what psychologist Milton Rokeach (1973) calls a primitive type B belief; this type of belief forms the basis of our belief system. We hold such beliefs regardless of others' agreement or disagreement with us. An example of this type of belief might be the make of car we buy. For instance, my friend had bought foreign cars for several years, and I tried valiantly to convince her to buy an American car. She could not be swayed because for over ten years she had had wonderful success with her brand. As we can see, people have a difficult time changing generalized beliefs based on personal experience and feelings.

Our belief system establishes the foundation for our value structure. In order to exert an influence on someone's value structure, we must first deal with our personal belief system. Without a change in beliefs, any change in attitude or value will be short-lived. Effective change is produced only through a change in belief systems.

Rokeach (1973) provides an outline of a system of beliefs:

- **Type A Belief**—primitive belief with 100% consensus (your name); facts
- **Type B Belief**—also primitive belief but with 0% consensus (prejudices and personal generalized beliefs—"My car is best"); the most difficult belief to change, and the ones which determine our behaviors; we hold these beliefs regardless if anyone agrees
- **Type C Belief**—beliefs derived from authority figures; based on source credibility ("Nine out of ten dentists say that . . .")
- **Type D Belief**—beliefs derived from others and personal experience ("Well, my mother said . . ."); gossip or hearsay
- **Type E Belief**—inconsequential beliefs, ones that really do not matter in the scheme of things; important to us but not to others (pepperoni vs. sausage pizza)

Attitudes

Attitudes are our predispositions toward action based on what we like or do not like. Attitudes can be described by observing how we might act if given a choice. Attitudes are not necessarily linked to values and are easier to change than beliefs or values. However, without a change in beliefs, any change in attitudes will be short-lived. Most attitudes are based on personal preferences and individual likes and dislikes. An example might be our attitude (like or dislike) toward a particular product. Our brand loyalty is based simply on how much we like or dislike the way the product works for us. Advertisers have a difficult job switching us from one product to another.

Values

Values are our individual perceptions of the relative worth of actions, ideas, events, or people. We demonstrate our values when we judge something to be good or bad. Values also demonstrate our preferences for a particular end state. Values are very important to us; our core values are the ones that influence us in making major decisions. Our core values also influence our choice of relationships and establish our conflict agendas. Values are paramount in the creation of our personality, our character, and our communication behaviors.

Rokeach (1973) also provides us with a system of functional (day-to-day) values (such as cleanliness and friendliness) and terminal (long-range, delayed gratification) values (such as a successful life and a world at peace) upon which we base many of our communication behaviors.

The "day-to-day" values influence our daily communication patterns. Some days we may wake up and not feel like talking to anyone—let alone being friendly to anyone. On those days, the value we place on friendliness sinks to the bottom of our hierarchy of values, even though we still hold it in high regard. On other days, our friendliness value will resurface and will be apparent in our communication behaviors again.

The "delayed gratification" values operate in the same way except that their order stays somewhat more stable over longer periods of time; these values provide the more important motivations in our lives. If we decide to seek a college education, we know that for four years we will have to make sacrifices in order to accomplish our goal. Even though we may waiver from time to time, we stick to our focused goal as long as it is a priority. A sense of accomplishment maintains top priority for a long period of time in our system of values.

Thus, even though different values surface almost on a daily basis according to need and priority, our values stay somewhat consistent and stable over time, and we do not change them unless we confront a powerful stimulus.

Developing our BAVs

The process of interaction between our beliefs, attitudes, and values creates a hierarchy of responses. This series of responses describes how our BAVs are developed. On the very lowest level would be our **drives**—the physiological needs generated by our bodies that create the desire for action (hunger). These drives can then be satisfied by our learned behaviors of action or **motives** (eating). These activities or behaviors then begin to create a repertoire of likes and dislikes which can be described as learned predispositions or **attitudes** (our favorite food). **Beliefs** are developed through the ways in which we are socialized, the perceptions learned from others, and our life experiences. Beliefs become our perceptions of what is true or false in life (that favorite food becomes ''good for you''). Finally, **clusters of beliefs** begin to form **values** and those values create our **values system** (eating certain foods is healthy).

Beliefs, attitudes, and values are learned; we obtain them through nurture (socialization) not nature (genetic inheritance), primarily from our parents. Then, as we grow, other people begin to influence the development of these BAVs through various types of relationships. Although the significance and importance of the relationship has some impact, the influence received from others is not always proportional to the value of the relationship. Sometimes a salesclerk (who is NOT a significant other) can strongly influence our communication behavior if we do not get the service we want from him/her. We end up losing control when the relationship really has no significance to us. However, teachers, relatives, peer groups, and the media provide four significant and influential relationship types that do affect our BAVs rather strongly and they are also the primary significant relationship groups.

Frank E.X. Dance's **Helix** (Dance and Larson, 1972) is a **model of communication** that describes how we are influenced by every single person with whom we come into contact. The spiral model can be easily illustrated with a ''slinky'' toy, one for each person we have ever met. Some people's slinkys will become very entwined with our slinky, while others will barely touch our outer spirals. The Helix model, illustrated by the slinky example, describes how complex our continually growing circle of relationships can become. EVERYONE with whom we come into contact has some effect on our BAVs, no matter how major or minor.

Maintaining and/or Changing our BAVs

Understandably, we become very protective of our BAVs. This need for protection of this fundamental system is based on the fact that our

Figure 6.1: Hierarchy of Responses

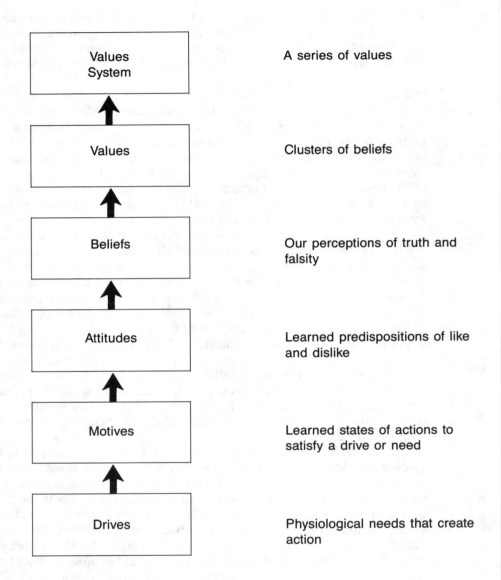

Values System	A series of values
Values	Clusters of beliefs
Beliefs	Our perceptions of truth and falsity
Attitudes	Learned predispositions of like and dislike
Motives	Learned states of actions to satisfy a drive or need
Drives	Physiological needs that create action

Adapted from Winston L. Brembeck and William S. Howell, *Persuasion—A Means of Social Influence,* Englewood Cliffs, NJ: Prentice-Hall, 1976.

BAVs really establish who we are and that we all have a strong need to be right which stems from a need to protect who we are. It is natural to want to protect our identity, and it is also instinctive to fear being wrong. We naturally develop a personal sensitivity to being wrong which is linked to our self-concept. Our fear of change is coupled with the fear of being wrong, and together they produce a very strong defense. Although we talk of the need for change and the desire for something different, we are basically very consistent, unchanging people. Our fundamental need is to have things remain basically the same; otherwise we get scared and rush to the defense of the attacked value or belief. This resistance to change (called the **principle of consistency**) is what protects our BAVs and is the basis for our need to be right, our fear of being wrong, and our need to protect our identity.

We enlist several defense modes in many different ways in order to protect our BAVs. The four selective mechanisms discussed in chapter 3—**selective exposure, selective attention, selective perception**, and **selective retention**—provide the first line of defense. Many times these mechanisms operate unconsciously in order to maintain the necessary balance and consistency we need in our lives and to protect our BAVs. Another process that occurs (usually unconsciously) is the seeking of **consensual validation** (see chapter 1). Consciously or unconsciously, we seek relationships with those people who will reinforce our current BAVs (Mills, Aronson, and Robinson, 1959, pp. 250–253). This means that we normally choose friends who are most similar to us in BAVs. Both of these processes serve to maintain the status quo of our BAVs.

While maintaining our existing BAVs seems difficult enough, changing our current BAVs is not any easier—and perhaps even harder. For example, advertisers know that in order to get us to change any BAV, they need to create cognitive dissonance or entropy in our BAVs. Leon Festinger defines **cognitive dissonance** as a state of discomfort created by two items of knowledge that are psychologically inconsistent (1957). **Entropy** is a chaotic state caused by cognitive dissonance which measures the degree of uncertainty. The existence of dissonance (inconsistency, confusion, or chaos) will motivate people to attempt to reduce the confusion and to re-establish consonance (consistency). When dissonance is present, we also actively avoid situations or information which are likely to increase our feeling of inconsistency or confusion (Festinger, 1957). This is the process that occurs as we attempt to change one of our BAVs. Consequently, changing our foundation of BAVs is uncomfortable and we usually avoid it. That is why we end up making the same mistakes over and over again in our lives—we fail to learn from our mistakes and then we resist any change that would compensate for the mistakes. Rather than go through confusion, discomfort, and the process of decision making necessary for change, most of us would prefer to be confused, consistent, and right. We tend to think it will be easier and more comfortable—even though in actuality it is painful or frustrating; the familiarity is somehow comforting.

What Do You Think?

Tom is very confused and frustrated. He was raised to work hard and be productive, but his body was telling him he had better slow down or he would be in trouble. For some reason, he felt guilty when he relaxed or was not busy. He was longing to take a vacation but he could not make himself believe that he deserved one.

Why is Tom having trouble changing his values. What is he experiencing? What concepts are operating here?

This strong resistance to any kind of change is present except when a very strong stimulus presents itself. The stimulus must be important, influential, and of crisis proportion. Unless such a situation presents itself, we will probably not even realize the need for change. We most likely will not try to change unless we have to—for example, when the stimulus is so strong that it requires us to change. There are times when change is forced on us and there are times when we crave something different. Examples of the above two situations help to visualize these situations. When the death of a loved one occurs, we are forced to look squarely at the situation and make necessary changes. If our job is so unbearable that we can hardly face getting up in the morning, not to mention going to work, we may be forced into doing something about the situation (even if we end up creating the problem that gets us fired or forces us to leave). So a forceful stimulus is necessary in order to act as a catalyst to produce a change in our BAVs.

What Do You Think?

Craig had been divorced twice and was now dating another woman similar to his first two wives. He could not understand why all women were so difficult. What was their problem, anyway? Now his first wife was even putting in a restraining order against him so he could not see his two sons, and his second wife was trying to get more alimony. Craig was so frustrated that he turned to drugs which eventually led to personal bankruptcy. Now at rock bottom, he did not know where to turn.

Why was Craig so resistant to change? What was the stimulus that finally made him see the need for change? Do you have any major blocks like Craig's in your life?

The important thing to remember is that we do have the capacity to change our BAVs, should we find it desirable or necessary. In order to create effective communication patterns, we also need to realize that each person will prioritize his/her personal beliefs, attitudes, and values. Our prioritized lists of BAVs will change as they are influenced by circumstances, events, and significant others. For example, if a core value is friendliness, the way we treat others will probably be reflected in that important value. However, if we are hurt by our best friend, our value of friendship changes and is temporarily reduced in importance. **Our relationships affect our values and our values affect our relationships—it goes both ways.** Change is a necessary component of personal growth and is only possible through interpersonal communication resulting in self-awareness.

Values Conflict

Many of our interpersonal conflicts are caused by a difference in values or differing priorities in values between the two parties concerned. The conflict also can be due to a difference between the exhibited BAVs versus actual BAVs. We may avoid truthful disclosures with others for fear of rejection or other risks that make us vulnerable. Instead of sharing our BAVs, we protect them. No matter what the source, conflict based on **value differences** is frequent and is quite often not identified for what it is. Sometimes we do not realize why we are fighting. While the basis for the argument may be a values difference, we might blame it on something peripheral such as the "burned toast" or "being late." What we are really doing is fighting about being right about our BAVs. It is very difficult for us to realize or admit that someone might have a different value structure or a difference in priorities of those values than we do. As we have discussed, it is hard for us to allow others to be different from us.

What Do You Think?

Sam loves to use money for enjoyment of life, while his wife Sarah was taught to save and conserve everything. Sam's latest purchase was a red Porsche convertible which, for Sarah, was the last straw. Sarah told Sam that if he did not return the car, she was going to leave him. Sam was dumbfounded. It was his money from his personal account, not from their joint account, so why was she so irrational? The following day, Sarah left for her parents' house and Sam was left alone with his car.

What value is surfacing for Sarah? What value is surfacing for Sam? Is there a solution to this values difference?

Interpersonal communication is the only way to resolve and effectively deal with a values conflict. It is only through talking to each other that the participants can come to realize what the real problem is. Most of the time, values conflicts are disguised through arguments about trivial matters while the real conflict is submerged. However, values conflicts do have solutions, even if that solution is to honor each other's differences. Respect and agreeing to disagree are necessary ingredients in values conflict resolution.

We need to foster the importance of openness and tolerance of differences. **Dogmatism** is a dangerous emotion that disallows a clear and focused perception of reality; it is sometimes called tunnel vision, meaning that the victim can only see one path. The danger of dogmatism is that the victim also disallows others their right to differences. This **black and white perspective** (seeing things only as one way or another—opposites) does not respect the differences that others may exhibit and judges others because they are different than us. Consequently, this attitude says to others, "You are wrong," which, in turn, creates a very defensive, disconfirming communication climate. Archie Bunker of "All in the Family" is a good example of a highly dogmatic person whose tunnel vision clouded his relationships with everyone. A nonjudgmental, open-minded attitude—one of respect—is what is needed in order for effective communication to occur.

Relationship Values

While there are many reasons why we choose certain people over others when selecting our friends, it is our values that are the primary influence on our decision-making process. The **attraction theory** states that people like people who share the same values. "Friendship is more frequently based on similarity of ideas (values) than on similarity of personality" (Kline, 1956, p. 106). The classic study by Robert Bales and Arthur Crouch (1969) gives us **four ultimate values** through which we establish relationships:

- **community values**—the importance of adopting the central values of the groups we associate with; treasuring of kin (high inclusion need through groups such as religion, organizations, nationality, or race)
- **other person's unique values**—the importance of appreciating the unique values of the individuals we are related to; treasuring of other people as unique individuals (being selfless, hero worship, imitation)
- **control values**—the importance of making an effort to persuade others or to control others in a situation; treasuring of one's own power in interaction (manipulation, persuasion, coercion)
- **our own unique values**—the importance of asserting one's own individual and unique values; treasuring of one's own individuality (pride, confidence, self-esteem)

The priority we place on these four main value clusters determines our relationships with self and others. Differences in these values will establish differences in communication patterns, or as

Charles Brown and Paul Keller state, "the four ways of behaving with people" (1979, p. 101). A person whose perspectives are primarily focused on control values will communicate manipulative messages to others, desiring control over people and situations. In contrast, a person whose perspectives are primarily focused on community values will communicate high inclusion need values, exhibiting a desire to belong and to be one of the group.

What Do You Think?

Sue loved working at her church. She volunteered 10 hours a week to help in the office with mailing, printing, and filing. She really liked the people who worked there, and she felt proud that she was helping out. It was great to see the results of her efforts on Sundays when the program she designed was used for the service. Some of her other friends keep asking her to join their bowling league, but Sue just does not see the value in that activity. She would rather be at church helping out there.

Which of the four main value clusters was preeminent in Sue's life? How did that value manifest in her life? How did this affect her communication?

Trust and Honesty: Core Values

Trust and honesty could be considered two core or universal values. Although all people do not place the same emphasis or priority on trust and honesty, these two core values could be considered primary motivators in communication behavior. Both seem essential for maintaining an effective, long-lasting relationship, and both of these values appear to claim a high priority for most people.

Trust is a necessary ingredient which can only be provided through appropriate self-disclosure. Sharing personal, intimate information with someone, which is then reciprocated, builds trust in a relationship. When reciprocity does not occur, trust fades. But building trust is difficult because of the risks involved. The ultimate issue becomes, "trusting makes me vulnerable and while I request and require trust from others, it may be difficult for me to give."

Honesty is a fascinating value based on the whole truth, which usually portends to claim top priority, but frequently ends up somewhat lower in the final analysis. Most of us claim to be totally honest in relationships, while, in reality, we are just dishonest to different degrees. We also do not want, nor do we care, to deal with the whole truth; the truth is not always comfortable or pleasant. While we say we crave the truth and even go in search of it, we do not deal well with it in reality and ultimately just want to be appeased in some type of sensitive manner. This old story tells the tale:

I could hardly believe my eyes when I saw the name of the shop: **THE TRUTH SHOP**. The salesperson was very polite. What type of truth did I wish to purchase: partial or whole? The whole truth, of course. No deceptions for me, no defenses, no rationalizations. I wanted my truth plain and unadulterated. She waved me on to another side of the store.

The salesperson there pointed to the price tag. "The price is very high sir," he said. "What is it?" I asked, determined to get the whole truth, no matter what it cost. "Your security, sir," he answered.

I came away with a heavy heart. I still need the safety of my unquestioned beliefs (de Mello, 1985).

So even though we may claim to always want the truth—the whole truth and nothing but the truth—is that what we really want in relationships?

What Do You Think?

Kim: I don't know whether or not to tell Terry that I slept with Chris. Do you think Terry will freak out?

Kelly: Well, I don't know. All I know is that I would certainly be upset if you *didn't* tell me.

Kim: So, you think it's better to tell the truth, even when it could hurt somebody—like me, for example!

Kelly: It may hurt, but in the long run, I think you'll be glad you did.

Kim: But what if Terry tells me it's over—that the relationship is finished? Terry is very important to me and I really don't want to lose . . .

Kelly: (*interrupting*) To me, it looks like you lose either way. I just think it's important to be honest—period. You know the saying, "the truth will set you free."

Kim: There's another part to that saying which is "but first it will make you go through hell." So, what Terry doesn't know won't hurt either one of us.

Kelly: Don't be too sure. I always say honesty is the best policy—no matter what the consequences.

Kim: But you can't be 100 percent honest in a relationship. Nobody would ever stay together. It's too intense.

Kelly: Well, it's your call. Good luck.

Do you think Kim should tell Terry about the affair? Why or why not? What is Kelly's point of view on the subject? Who do you agree with—Kim or Kelly? Is it possible to be 100 percent honest in relationships? Do you want 100 percent honesty? What would that look like? Describe a relationship that was 100 percent honest.

Summary

Beliefs, attitudes, and values have a strong effect on the way we communicate and on how we proceed in the development of relationships. We develop our BAVs through the influence of others and we only change them when we absolutely must. Many conflicts are caused by value differences while other causes may seem to be the culprit on the surface. The fact that everyone has different value priorities scares us and forces us into a resistant pattern of dogmatism to defend what we believe and who we are. Only through openness, respect, and tolerance for other values can we become effective communicators.

References

Bales, Robert F. and Arthur S. Crouch. "The Value Profile: A Factor Analytic Study of Values Statements." *Sociological Inquiry*, 39, no. 1, (1969).

Brown, Charles T. and Paul W. Keller. *Monologue to Dialogue: An Exploration of Interpersonal Communication*. Englewood Cliffs, NJ: Prentice-Hall, 1979.

Dance, Frank E.X. and Carl E. Larson. *Speech Communication: Concepts and Behavior*. New York: Holt, Rinehart and Winston, 1972.

de Mello, Anthony. *Song of the Bird*. San Francisco: Harper San Francisco, 1985.

Festinger, Leon. *A Theory of Cognitive Dissonance*. Stanford: Stanford University Press, 1957.

Fromm, Erich. *The Art of Loving*. New York: HarperCollins, 1956.

Kline, Josephine. *The Study of Groups*. New York: Routledge, Chapman, and Hall, 1956.

Mills, J., E. Aronson, and H. Robinson. "Selectivity in Exposure to Information." *Journal of Abnormal and Social Psychology*, 59 (1959): 250–253.

Rokeach, Milton. *The Nature of Values*. New York: Free Press, 1973.

Case 21

TargetTerms

- selective perception
- cognitive dissonance
- BAVs
- the four ultimate values

PreviewNotes

The beliefs, attitudes, and values that were instilled in us while growing up often come back to haunt us. We can change, but do we?

CaseParticipants

Mark Burke—college graduate who is working in a part-time position on the outskirts of a college town; daring and carefree; tall, sensitive and very much wants to feel needed; dates Audrey Ames steadily and seriously

Audrey Ames—college student in her senior year; innocent and very bright; takes what she does and how she feels very much to heart; dates Mark Burke steadily

"But what will my parents think?"

Mark and Audrey have discussed the possibility of moving in with each other. After finding what appeared to be the perfect new place, Mark finds that Audrey is having second thoughts. He looks at her almost angrily.

Mark: Will you stop agonizing over this. What's the big deal? You spend half of your weekends here anyhow.

Audrey: My parents will have a fit.

Mark: So, they don't have to know.

Audrey: And how am I going to afford carrying the overhead of two apartments?

Mark: Trust me, I'll think of something.

Audrey: Somehow, when I hear that "trust me" line, I get even more worried.

Mark: Any more excuses?

Audrey: They're not excuses, Mark. I just feel real funny about making this commitment.

Mark: Part of the reason that we're doing this is to avoid commitment. No strings—remember?

Audrey: Maybe it's just that I'm so used to a certain kind of bond in a relationship. It's not as if we haven't talked this out enough, but I'm getting cold feet.

Mark: Well, I'm certainly in no position to get married.

Audrey: We're not talking about marriage.

Mark: You didn't have to say anything. I smell it—

Audrey: How?

Mark: It's in your voice.

Audrey: No, it's just that I'm starting to worry about what everyone's going to think.

Mark: We're not living in the turn of the century. Attitudes have changed, you know.

Audrey: I know, but I think that my parents will really be disappointed in me.

Mark: Whose life are you going to live—yours or theirs?

Audrey: Don't throw that garbage at me! At least they care about what I do. Besides, I don't think my parents did such a bad job. You usually like me to be independent—right?

Mark: Sure, that's because you are your own person. What I like is the way you can be so different from everyone else—being able to turn the switch "on and off"—rejecting or accepting what you think is right. That's part of the reason I want to be with you more. It's what I wish I could do.

Audrey: I guess I need some time to figure this out.

Mark: You think that another few days or another week is going to make any difference?

Audrey: I feel so rushed now. School's starting and so is my job. I'm not sure that I'm giving this decision the kind of time it deserves.

Mark: Want me to talk to your parents?

Audrey: Absolutely not, they'd go off the deep end if you talked to them about this.

Mark: What's the matter? I'm not good enough for them?

Audrey: Cut it out. Why are you bringing them into this anyhow?

Mark: You're the one that said your parents would get nuts about this— not me!

Audrey: Try and see it my way. I spent years in religious school with constant warnings about "saving myself" for the man I marry. Although I don't really believe that, I also can't bring myself to announce to the world, "screw it all—I'm going to live with Mark."

Mark: There's one thing here that's important.

Audrey: What's that?

Mark: Do you want to see more of me?

Audrey: You're making it sound like a threat.

Mark: Now you're putting words in my mouth.

Audrey: The more you say Mark, the more I realize that we're not as similar as we think we are. If you can't understand how I feel about this, then I guess you really have no understanding of what I'm about. What I believe is part of what I am. Take it or leave it, I guess.

Mark: Audrey, all that garbage about being brought up with those ridiculous values is not what living is all about! What about all of the late nights we spent talking about not just being another newly married couple—fighting our way through rent payments and having kids to appease our parents?

Audrey: That was not the point of what we said at all. At least get it right. What we said was that we didn't want to make a commitment without being sure that we were being fair to each other. And, truthfully now, I see this living arrangement as another type of commitment. So, we're still going nowhere.

Mark: You are so off base that it's unbelievable!

Audrey: Why? 'Cause I don't think the same way that you do?

Mark: Don't you think it's pretty strange that you don't think about all this "value" nonsense when we start turning off the lights?

Audrey: What are you trying to say? That all I care about is sex?

Mark: You said it—not me!

Audrey: You are being so unfair. Just because I don't agree with you, I'm a hypocrite?

Mark: All I'm saying is your standards seem to shift depending on the time of day.

Audrey: And you really believe that what I'm saying is all an act? That I haven't been brought up with any morals? That because I spend nights at your place—well, that I haven't thought over and over again whether I was doing the right thing?

Mark: Maybe it's time to stop spending so much time thinking—and start living.

Audrey: It would help if you would try to understand how much I want to do just that. But, I just can't. It's not as if I can throw twenty-one years of learning out the window.

Mark: What's so terrific about what you've learned? You never practiced it before.

Audrey: Will you just stop picking on every word I say! I'm damned if I do— and damned if I don't. I just don't know what's right anymore. (*Mark tries to put his arm around her, she pushes him away.*) I'm not in the mood. (*She starts to the bedroom.*) I'm tired. I'm going to sleep—alone.

CaseConcerns

1. Do you think Mark is protective of his BAVs? Explain your answer.

2. If we become protective of our BAVs, what harm does this cause to effective communication?

3. Identify two or three behaviors that demonstrate a protective attitude toward an individual's BAVs.

4. Identify a time in your life when you felt a high level of cognitive dissonance. What did you do about it? What would you do differently now that you have read this chapter?

5. How is selective perception used and by whom?

ReflectiveResponses

1. Do you believe that making a decision to "live with a significant other" depends on one's BAVs? How so?

2. How might communication change in relationships when two people are living together as opposed to dating?

Case 22

- cognitive dissonance
- BAVs
- the four ultimate values
- values differences

PreviewNotes

Roommates with very different values have lots of conflicts. What's fair when sharing the same space when values differ?

CaseParticipants

Lori Adams—18 years old; bubbly and enthusiastic first-year college student; raised in a suburban town; sometimes immature; sensitive about feeling insecure in her new co-ed dorm; very much in need of a warm, inviting friend

Lynn Hagen—18 years old; has seemingly been exposed to college life prior to this first year; mature and independent; simply wants to be left alone to "do her thing" for the next four years

"So, that's the way you feel . . ."

Lori and Lynn have learned through their college orientation program that they are going to be roommates for the first year. As part of the program, Lori and Lynn were able to obtain each other's addresses and phone numbers. Although the girls have corresponded over the summer, they still do not know very much about each other. Lori had to be on campus three days earlier than Lynn, and thus has already moved in the dorm at the time of this conversation. It is now eleven o'clock at night, and Lori decides to go to sleep—somewhat worried about Lynn, who was scheduled to arrive at noon that day. A short time later the room door opens and Lynn enters.

Lynn: Surprise! It's me! Lynn!

Lori: You scared the daylights out of me! (*regaining her composure*) Is everything O.K.? I thought you'd be here much earlier.

Lynn: My plane was late so my connection was all messed up, and then my luggage went somewhere else. If that wasn't enough, the flight attendant put me on stand-by. I screamed and yelled a lot—but, finally, I'm here in one piece!

Lori: (*getting up from her bed*) You know, I had a completely different image of what you'd look like.

Lynn: Me, too.

Lori: Good or bad?

Lynn: Well—just different.

Lori: You can be honest. I mean I feel as if I know you already after all of the letters we wrote. How'd you expect me to be—

Lynn: Just different.

Lori: I get the feeling that you're disappointed.

Lynn: No—no. I'm "me" and you're "you."

Lori: Well, I didn't mean to make a big deal about it. Anyhow, to change the subject—did you bring the bedspreads?

Lynn: Just for the record, I left behind a friend who used to check up on everything I did. I couldn't go to the bathroom without her asking me when I was coming out. Please tell me you're not one of those.

Lori: All I asked was whether you brought the spreads.

Lynn: No, but, don't worry. They're being sent up by the end of the month.

Lori: End of the month? Had I known I was going to wait that long, I would have had my parents bring them.

Lynn: Your parents?

Lori: My parents.

Lynn: Why would they want to bring them up?

Lori: They brought me up here. We have a big car, and one more thing wouldn't have mattered.

Lynn: Who asked what kind of car you had? I couldn't care less what anyone drives—big or small.

Lori: Why are you jumping down my throat?

Lynn: You've got to understand me, that's all. I'm real private. I am not real thrilled about being asked lots of questions, and I couldn't care less if the bed is covered today or next week or three months from now.

Lori: But don't you think that the spreads will make these four walls a little homier?

Lynn: Who cares?

Lori: Me, for one.

Lynn: Well, then get yourself a spread, if it's such a big thing with you.

Lori: But we both chipped in for the decorations. I'd hate to have the money thrown down the drain.

Lynn: I'm tired—I'm cranky—and this whole conversation is making me absolutely nauseous. Good-night!

CaseConcerns

1. What were some of Lori's BAVs? What were some of Lynn's BAVs?
2. Describe the values conflict in this case.
3. Describe the relationship values in this case.
4. Do you believe that the BAVs which both girls exhibited in this case can change? If so, how? If not, why?

ReflectiveResponses

1. When other people exhibit values different than ours, we can get defensive or protective. Why does this happen?
2. How does dogmatism affect the way we communicate? Which case participant do you think exhibited a dogmatic attitude toward her BAVs? Can you explain why?
3. Seeing things as either black or white locks us into a rigid thinking pattern. Identify three ways that might help blend the black and white perspective to a grey perspective.
4. Meeting someone for the first time may be scary. How much of your BAVs should you/can you/would you disclose on the first meeting? Is there a danger of disclosing too much? Too little? What happened in this case regarding the disclosure of BAVs?
5. Describe a time when your BAVs were threatened and you felt that you needed to protect them. What did you do? Why?

Case 23

TargetTerms

- dogmatism
- selective exposure
- selective perception
- tunnel vision
- black and white perspective

PreviewNotes

Sometimes our belief structure gets in the way of our perceptions and reality becomes an illusion. It is hard to believe that everyone doesn't value the same things we do—and sometimes we do things to make other people conform to our values.

CaseParticipants

Gale Higgins—college junior; member of a well-known sorority on campus that houses what appears to be a "select" groups of girls; idealistic; remains consciously aware of her responsibility in her privileged lifestyle

Anita Wyndorf—college senior; also a member of the above mentioned sorority; well bred and extremely conscious of her family background and the responsibility that she thinks it holds

"Well, let's not go against the grain . . ."

Anita and Gale, sorority sisters, live in Grecian Column, a house which was built one hundred years ago. While lounging in the reception area of the house, the two girls begin what starts as an innocent conversation about Susan Parker—who is very anxious to be accepted into the prestigious sorority.

Anita: I have tons of reservations about admitting Susan. It'll open up a giant can of worms.

Gale: But she's got all of the basic qualifications. I mean, she's a cheerleader, writer for the university paper, and on the Dean's List and she's cute.

Anita: But, really, you know what I'm talking about.

Gale: You know how much Susan wants to be a part of our sorority.

Anita: That's all very well and fine. Lots of girls on campus want to get in. But there's other stuff to consider.

Gale: Like what?

Anita: You know what I mean.

Gale: No, I don't.

Anita: I remember your big fuss when Dolores wanted to get in. How quickly we forget.

Gale: But that was different.

Anita: Why?

Gale: Well, she wasn't a campus leader like Susan.

Anita: Sure—sure. We should never have invited her to our teas in the first place. Can't you just go along with the idea that she wouldn't feel comfortable?

Gale: Meaning that her family doesn't have enough money?

Anita: That's not it at all! There are plenty of girls who are like her in *that* respect.

Gale: So, it doesn't matter to you that her mom and dad are part of the housekeeping staff at this school?

Anita: (*hesitantly*) Well . . . ! Her parents might start interfering in our private sorority business. They always seem to be in sight, you know. It can lead to all kinds of other things—their involvement, that is. You know, it's best to stick with your own kind.

Gale: You're beginning to sound like a skinhead!

Anita: Gale, you're making it sound so awful. Look at it this way, if Susan gets in, then she'll have a cousin who will be entering school next fall—or the year after. Then, she'll want her "in" and our whole—

Gale: Our whole what? Your "holier than thou" attitude is beginning to take over this entire sorority.

Anita: And all of a sudden you want to play fairy godmother to everyone and anyone who wants to join.

Gale: Susan Parker would be one of the best pledges this sorority has had in recent years, and you know it!

Anita: Boy, are you missing this point! Yes, she's nice, but nice isn't enough. We have an image to uphold. I mean it's not like we always have to be for all that equal opportunity stuff—

Gale: Equal opportunity stuff? How can you even say anything like that? You're making it sound as if she's some statistic in some weird quota thing we have.

Anita: Don't get so hung up on this. I just like to associate with people who share my goals and ideals.

CaseConcerns

1. What are some of the reasons for clinging to our BAVs as illustrated in this case?
2. What selective mechanisms are Gale and Anita using in this case? Give an example for each person.
3. How does the concept of tunnel vision affect the communication process in this case?
4. Which of the case participants is most dogmatic? Give an example for each.
5. What do you feel will be the outcome of this verbal exchange?

ReflectiveResponses

1. What can happen to our relationships when our BAVs begin to control how we respond? How do we release this control?
2. Can you identify any of your own dogmatic behaviors? If so, how do they interfere with your communication effectiveness?
3. Can someone's BAVs be changed by another person?

Case 24

- trust
- honesty
- BAVs

PreviewNotes

When a confidence is shared, even in—or especially in—a family unit, breaking that trust bond creates problems. Who is right here? Should the parents be able to impose values for their children that they themselves don't follow? Check out this double standard in terms of values.

CaseParticipants

Nancy Hauser—38-year-old mother of Wendy, an only child; enjoys being both confidant and "buddy" to her daughter

Wendy Hauser—17-year-old daughter of Nancy; enjoys the benefits of being the sole interest of her mother; charming and happy

Richard Hauser—43-year-old husband of Nancy; takes pride in knowing that he can personally take care of his two favorite girls, Nancy and Wendy; believed by Wendy to be somewhat old-fashioned and behind the times

"Don't tell anyone . . ."

Nancy, being fairly young and somewhat trendy, has maintained a rather unusual relationship with her daughter. It has become increasingly difficult for Nancy to exert any authority over her daughter's "comings and goings" because of this closeness. Richard, on the other end of the spectrum, is most concerned with insisting that Wendy follow a designated set of proper rules and regulations in her active life as an older teen. Unlike his wife, he is all too firm about having his only daughter cling to certain values. It is a Friday afternoon when Nancy and Wendy have back-to-back opthamologist appointments. They are waiting for the nurse in the doctor's office to call them.

Wendy: Mom, let's play a game.

Nancy: Sounds O.K.—how do you play?

Wendy: Well, we did it at school. Remember the encounter groups from the 60s?

Nancy: Mmmmhmmm.

Wendy: There was a whole thing about being totally honest, and all these people had "encounter sessions"—like "you tell me something and then I'll tell you." But we must keep whatever is said to ourselves.

Nancy: Yes.

Wendy: Well, let's do it.

Nancy: Sounds all right. You start.

Wendy: Now, you promise that we keep this all secret? (*Nancy nods.*) All right. Here goes. (*She hesitates for a moment.*) You sure that you are not going to break my confidence?

Nancy: You know me better than that.

Wendy: Mom, remember the night that you gave me permission to sleep at Linda's even though her parents were not home? You got all bent out of shape that she wouldn't sleep at our house—but then you finally gave in.

Nancy: Uh-oh! I'm not sure I want to hear what you are going to tell me now.

Wendy: C'mon, Mom. You promised. Part of the game is that you don't make any comments—nasty or otherwise.

Nancy: Go on—I'll be serious and listen without saying anything.

Wendy: Well . . . Sure you're ready? (*Nancy smiles and urges her on.*) Well . . . Jeff Anderson came to Linda's house at around 10:30 that night and guess what? (*She pauses for a long while.*)

Nancy: What! Tell me already.

Wendy: He decided to stay for the entire night.

Nancy: What did he tell his parents?

Wendy: Mom! What a dumb question! Only you could think to ask that now.

Nancy: Well, what did he tell his mom?

Wendy: That he was sleeping at Doug's, of course. His parents were away, anyhow, too. I guess that his mom never had any reason to check.

Nancy: And, where, young lady, may I ask—did he sleep?

Wendy: Oh, don't worry, Mom, he slept in her brother's room. Her brother, Greg, is away at college, so Jeff had the whole upstairs to himself.

Nancy: Well, I guess I'm relieved about that.

Wendy: Besides, you know that Linda's pretty prudish and so am I, I guess. But, all the same, it was kind of fun to do something a little different.

Nancy: I guess if you could own up to it—that it wasn't so terrible after all. I'm glad you told me. Sometimes when you hold in things like that, it feels better when you bring them out in the open.

Wendy: Remember, Mom—no lectures. Now, I told you something, and now it's your turn to tell me.

Nancy: Oh, God. I really can't think of anything that is such a big secret. I never keep anything from you.

Wendy: Mom . . . there must be something . . . some itty-bitty-teeny-tiny thing that no one but you knows about.

Nancy: Well, there is something.

Wendy: Go on . . .

Nancy: Just last week in the book store . . . Oh, I can't even say it.

Wendy: Remember, you promised.

Nancy: I might as well just tell you, then. There was a very handsome and well-dressed man who came into the shop. He was standing nearby, and I could sort of make out that he was asking someone what my name was.

Wendy: Uh huh . . .

Nancy: Then, he waited near me, while I was looking through a new book. Well, I started toward the cashier to pay, when he stopped me and told me that I was wasting my time in this town—that I belonged in, of all things, the movies!

Wendy: Mom . . . this is great.

Nancy: As long as we're being honest, he asked if I wanted to have lunch. And since I was fairly famished at that point, I said "yes."

Wendy: And then—what?

Nancy: Nothing.

Wendy: Mom!

Nancy: Well, the truth is that we had a very lovely lunch and we talked and talked for about two hours. Then, we both checked our watches and couldn't believe how the time flew by—and we got up to leave.

Wendy: Who paid the bill?

Nancy: He did.

Wendy: What's his name?

Nancy: That's not in the rule book.

Wendy: I told you!

Nancy: Oh, all right. Mark. Mark Spencer. From Great Hills, if that's what you're going to ask next.

Wendy: Wow, mom. That was even better than what I told you. Are you going to see him again?

Nancy: No, of course not. It was just a lovely way of meeting a new friend and it was very innocent—on both of our parts.

Wendy: Sure, Mom!

Nancy: Sweetheart, no more questions. This "game" was your idea, but as part of the rules, we should respect each other's confidentiality and truthfulness. So, no more questions. I think that the nurse is signaling for you to go in now.

LATER THAT SAME DAY AT HOME

Nancy: (*calls to Richard in a very concerned tone*) Richard, do me a favor and stop what you're doing, please, for a few minutes. I'd like to talk to you about a very important problem that we both have.

Richard: Sure.

Nancy: I was at the eye doctor's with Wendy this morning, and I am very upset about what she discussed with me.

Richard: What's this all about?

Nancy: Well, remember when she was hysterical about sleeping at Linda's last week—

CaseConcerns

1. What do you think about the mother's actions at the conclusion of the case? How might this incident affect the mother/daughter relationship? Discuss what you believe will be the effect on their future communication.

2. How does Richard respond after Nancy tells him about Wendy's secret? Is there a right or wrong way? Evaluate your decision.

ReflectiveResponses

1. Is total honesty possible in a relationship? Why? Why not?

2. What types of information, under what circumstances, can and should be kept from "significant others"? Identify categories of information and circumstances that qualify. Is this being dishonest?

3. Describe an incident where a "trust" or "confidence" has been broken in a relationship of yours. How did this affect the way you communicated with the person afterward?

4. Which BAVs are the most difficult to change? Why? Identify yours.

Case 25

TargetTerms

- cognitive dissonance
- honesty
- BAVs

PreviewNotes

When one of our values is challenged, we feel frustrated and confused. We sometimes begin to question our basis for judging right from wrong. Opposing messages can create this cognitive dissonance for which we ultimately seek balance.

CaseParticipants

Terry—19-year-old sophomore; friend of Chris
Chris—19-year-old sophomore carrying 18 credits during the
spring semester; friend of Terry

"But isn't that cheating?"

Terry and Chris are good friends attending a large university.

Terry: Hi, Chris. What's happening? How's it going?

Chris: O.K., except for my term paper. It's driving me crazy—all those required sources! I'll never get done.

Terry: Oh, come on. That was easy. I finished mine in a breeze. There's this term paper service—you call this company and they send you all the current research on whatever topic you request. They even send you a sample term paper which you can use as a "guide." (*Terry winks at Chris.*)

Chris: Can't you get caught for cheating for stuff like that?

Terry: That's not cheating. It's getting all the current research. Isn't that the goal of the paper?

Chris: Yeah, but what about all those rules about "primary sources" and putting it in your own words. Don't you think the Prof will find out?

Terry: Who's gonna know?

Chris: Well, yeah, but I've always been taught . . .

Terry: Yeah, yeah, yeah . . . but the real world demands the use of modern technology in this new information highway. Come on—

Chris: But, why does it still feel like I'm cheating? It makes me feel really uncomfortable for some reason.

Terry: I don't know. I guess that's something you'll have to deal with—but here's the 800 number—just in case. (*Terry passes Chris a business card.*)

Chris: (*hesitantly*) Thanks, I think.

Terry: Good luck. See you later. (*Terry leaves.*) (*Chris returns to the dorm and starts to dial the 800 number, but hesitates . . .*)

CaseConcerns

1. Describe how you think Chris is feeling about this decision. What do you suppose is going through Chris's mind?
2. What is creating the cognitive dissonance for Chris?
3. Do you think Chris makes the phone call? Why or why not?

ReflectiveResponses

1. Think of a situation in your life when you experienced a conflict in values. How did you deal with this situation? Did you at any point find it necessary to communicate with another about how you felt?
2. Have you changed any of your original core values after experiencing cognitive dissonance? To what do you attribute these changes?

7
Chapter

Self-Disclosure

Specific Goals for Understanding Chapter Seven

TargetTerms

- self-disclosure
- blurting
- Johari Window

CoreConcepts

1   the nature of self-disclosure
2   the levels of self-disclosure
3   the resistance to and fear of self-disclosure
4   the necessity of self-disclosure
5   the rewards and benefits of self-disclosure

"There's something I have to tell you."

Overview

Telling someone else who we are and what we believe in can be one of the most traumatic things we do. Revealing our innermost secrets, hopes, fears, insecurities, and dreams to another person is frightening. What if they laugh? What if they think we are stupid for thinking a certain way or believing in a certain idea? John Powell claims that these fears are very powerful and keep us from sharing ourselves with others (1969). In his book, *Why Am I Afraid to Tell You Who I Am?*, he illustrates our fears and anxieties related to this process and reveals the answer to his proposed title question. Powell states that the reason we are afraid to self-disclose is "because if I tell you who I am, you may not like who I am, and that's all I have to give" (1969, p. 60). The fear of rejection is so strong that many times it keeps us from being honest with ourselves and others.

In this chapter, we will investigate the importance of self-disclosure. We will look at the meaning of self-disclosure, the levels of self-disclosure, resistance to self-disclosure, and the rewards of self-disclosure.

What Is Self-Disclosure?

Most theorists agree that in order for information to be considered **self-disclosure**, it must meet three criteria:
- it must contain personal information about the sender
- the sender must communicate this information verbally
- another person must be the intentional target (Cozby 1973)

Ronald Adler, Lawrence Rosenfeld, and Neil Towne (1992) summarize this definition as "the content of self-disclosure is the self, and information about the self is purposefully communicated to another person'' (p. 182). Other factors that distinguish self-disclosure from other types of communication include honesty, depth, availability of information, context, appropriateness, and the receiver's perception (p. 182).

Another important component for characterizing self-disclosure is offered by David Johnson (1981). He describes **self-disclosure** as any information shared with another person that helps the receiver understand the sender's current behavior. For example, I may have never told you that the reason I dislike guns is because my father accidentally shot and killed himself with one, so it is difficult for you to understand my intense fear, anxiety, and hostility when you discuss your love of hunting. Thus, we can see that the characteristics of self-disclosure are primarily related to understanding and insight in relationships. Part of the consideration in self-disclosure is to think about frames of reference—ours and the receiver's. Our goal is to include a check-up on individual frames of reference.

But self-disclosure is not pouring our problems out on another person, nor is it saying anything at anytime to anyone. Let us not confuse self-disclosure with **blurting** which is communication that is inappropriate, untimely, overdone, and usually out of context. Self-disclosure needs to be planned, focused, and intentional (Jourard, 1971).

What Do You Think?

Mary thought Sue was her best friend and called her several times a day to prove it. Mary told Sue everything—isn't that what best friends are for? And Sue was such a good listener. Sue was beginning to monitor her phone calls with her phone message machine.

Was Mary self-disclosing or blurting? Explain the reason for your answer.

Levels of Self-Disclosure

Powell (1969) reports that there are five levels of self-disclosure:
- **cliché conversation**
- **reporting the facts about others**
- **my ideas and judgments**
- **my feelings and emotions**
- **peak communication**

These five levels describe the type and depth of self-disclosure we can select for each interaction we encounter. We select the level, depending upon the significance of the relationship between the parties to the interaction. As a relationship grows, the level selected may eventually reach the peak communication level. Although both partners are not always at the same level of disclosure, generally the process follows the logical path described above. When the levels of disclosure are unmatched, frustration may occur thus hampering the communication process.

Level one is **cliché conversation**. This is the lowest level of response to another human being and takes the form of meaningless interaction, or **phatic communication**. This "small talk that precedes the big talk opens up the channels of communication" (DeVito, 1986, p. 228) and is characterized by "Hi, how are you?" or "Have a nice day." Phatic communication breaks the ice and allows us time to decide if we want to continue the conversation. Powell (1969) claims that actually no communication occurs here at all and that both parties sense the superficiality of the clichés being used. No sharing occurs on this level, but rather, "everyone remains safely in the isolation of his pretense, sham, or sophistication" (Powell, 1969, p. 55). While little significant meaning is exchanged, phatic communication provides a framework in which we feel comfortable to decide whether another level should be entered. In fact, if this phase is ignored and someone leaps to another level, we are usually decidedly uncomfortable and might seek to end further contact. In other words, phatic communication sets the stage for intensified contact or civil leavetaking.

Level two is when we **report the facts about others**. Here, we still isolate ourselves from participating in any serious or important exchange of information with the other person. We maintain our protective shield by not revealing anything about ourselves, but rather by sharing what others have said; this level borders on gossip. By offering nothing of ourselves, we receive nothing back from others on this level and thus no trust is developed yet. As with all communication, what we choose to say about others does reveal something about ourselves to discerning listeners, but at this stage, we do not make direct statements about our beliefs.

Level three is the beginning of some important communication when we begin to share **our ideas and judgments**. Although we are still somewhat guarded at this level, we are beginning to break down the barriers and shields we have erected. It is here, also, that we may become what Leo Buscaglia (1972) calls "the fake banana." We may begin to say the things we think others want to hear and to act the way we think others want us to act. Although some valuable and necessary outcomes result from this level of disclosure, we still cannot develop an intimate, trusting relationship unless we are willing to advance to the next level.

Level four deals with **personal feelings and emotions**. This is a scary level of disclosure because it is here that we really begin to take a chance on whether or not others will accept us for what we really are. "Actually, the things that most clearly differentiate and individuate me from others, that make the communication of my person a unique knowledge, are my feelings and emotions" (Powell,

1969, p. 57). Without participation on this level, Powell claims we cannot grow, nor can our relationships grow. We also cannot develop trust without using this level of communication. The danger on this level is that it requires total honesty; however, many times we would rather defend our dishonesty on the grounds that the truth might hurt others. In doing so, we settle for superficiality and dangerously repressed emotions.

Level five is **peak communication**, the deepest and fullest level of self-disclosure. Powell (1969) makes a case at this level for absolute openness and honesty. He describes this level of communication as rare, necessary, and desirable. It is the attainment of "almost perfect and mutual empathy" (Powell, 1969, p. 62) and it only happens in unique, infrequent moments, but it is still a goal.

What Do You Think?

Terry loved talking with Kim about their relationship. Terry enjoyed those times when they both really seemed to click in their communication. But Terry could not get Kim to participate in this type of communication all the time; Kim seemed to like to talk more about other people and always seemed to be complaining. Terry just hoped that their deep-level communication would expand as the relationship grew.

Terry: I really love talking with you, Kim.
  Kim: Yeah, me too. How was work today?
Terry: Oh, fine. How do you think our relationship is developing? Are you feeling good about us?
  Kim: Sure, I guess. Why? Aren't you? Is there a problem? I'm fine.
Terry: Well, it's just that I like to talk about our relationship. I want to hear you say what you feel.
  Kim: I do say what I feel. But do I have to talk about it all the time?

What level of disclosure was Terry using? What level of disclosure was Kim using?

Another way to view our levels of self-disclosure is to draw a visual picture of our types of self-disclosure by using the **Johari Window** developed by Joseph Luft and Harry Ingham (Luft, 1969). The Johari Window is a model of how we present ourselves to others and gives us an idea of the image we project to others. The window represents the whole self as we relate and self-disclose to others. The panes in the windows change in accordance with the context, the receiver, our feelings, our motivation, and our awareness. We actually have a different window for each person with whom we interact. The four quadrants of the window identify the type and amount of disclosure we use with each person.

The Open Window

This window identifies all the aspects of ourselves that are known to us and to others. This window is usually quite large as it comprises all of the basic information we share freely without fear or restriction. It includes things like our name, sex, eye color, and things we do not mind admitting or sharing about ourselves (job, marital status). Usually the more comfortable we are in a relationship, the larger this window is.

The Blind Window

This window contains all of the things about ourselves that other people perceive but are not known to us. We may see ourselves as a real comedian, but others may not think we are very funny at all. Sometimes we are perceived by others differently than we perceive ourselves. While this can be frustrating, it may be giving us a message that our communication about ourselves does not match our internal image. We may think we are very friendly, but we may be getting messages from others that we are abrasive or defensive. These cues will give us a picture of our blind window.

The Hidden Window

Here is where we get to exercise control over what we reveal to others. This window is composed of all the things we choose not to disclose to others. These could be silly things like not wanting to tell anyone we failed a biology test or more serious and important things that might be family secrets like our mother is an alcoholic. But they could also be things that we are not necessarily ashamed of or think of as wrong. We are all entitled to our secrets—things we keep private to only ourselves or maybe one or two others. Certain things may remain private and personal and never get disclosed. These hidden things are then unknown to others but known to us only.

The Unknown Window

This window is made up of everything unknown to us and to others. This information can be referred to as our hidden potential or "unleashed energies." It involves things even we do not know about ourselves—yet. As we grow and discover things about ourselves, this window gets smaller but it never disappears. We can never know all there is to know about ourselves. This area can be illustrated through examples of other people noticing our talents or potentials. For example, a teacher may talk about our talents as excellent writers when we never thought of ourselves as such. This begins to unlock some unknown resource or potential for development.

The four window panes are interdependent; changing the size of one pane requires that the other panes change as well. The goal is to increase the open pane in search of a healthy and more accurate self-concept, resulting in greater self-acceptance.

What Do You Think?

Draw your Johari Window for three select persons with whom you have current relationships. Re-read the four types of panes carefully so that your window will be as accurate as possible. Compare the three windows for differences. Now draw your "generalized other" (or a generic person) Johari Window of how you see it now and how you would like it to be if you could make any changes. Write a one page reaction to this exercise.

Resistance to Self-Disclosure

While the levels of self-disclosure seem to provide us with choices about how deep we want the interaction to be, there are several factors that influence our choice of level. These influential factors seem to be based primarily on fear which, as a result, creates a **resistance to self-disclosure**:

- **societal bias**—labels, stereotypes
- **fear of punishment**—rejection
- **fear of self-knowledge**—to share information about ourselves is to learn about ourselves

DeVito (1995, p. 145) describes the resistance as dangers of self-disclosure and refers to the following three risks:

- **personal risks**—rejection from loved ones
- **relational risks**—too much even in long-lasting and close relationships can cause problems and result in negative effects
- **professional risks**—jobs and professional reputations can be ruined and destroyed with information gained from the disclosure

These fears (dangers, risks) keep us from participating in self-disclosure at a deep level—usually not above level three (our ideas and judgments). We create an invisible shield that protects our vulnerability from harm. For example, if you had become pregnant when you were fourteen and had an abortion, you probably would not tell very many people for fear of rejection and harsh judgment about your values and ethics as a person. Ex-convicts would prefer not disclosing their past unless necessary; why would they want to live with a label for the rest of their lives? Reduced disclosure allows people to avoid labels, stereotypes, rejection and multiple other fears. We do not disclose information that we fear others may use to harm us.

Adler, Rosenfeld, and Towne (1992) discuss five risks to be aware of when revealing private information. These are the reasons we are afraid to self-disclose and, as you will see, some of them are reasonable fears. In such cases, we may want to consider not disclosing. The five risks of self-disclosure are:

- rejection or disapproval from the receiver
- projection of a negative image to others resulting in loss of respect
- a decrease in satisfaction obtained from a relationship or disappointment in differing wants and needs
- a loss of control in the relationship through vulnerability
- the hurting of the other person with our truth

Each chapter in this text stresses the necessity of self-understanding. The more aware we are of who we are, the better our chances of communicating successfully. Knowing the risks of self-disclosure helps us distinguish between revealing information that will strengthen trust in our relationships and revealing opinions that will wound the other person. Reflective thinking which considers reciprocal feelings and responsibilities should precede any communication. Without it, blurting can result. As we learned earlier, sometimes no communication is the most appropriate choice and will enhance the relationship. The most important point to remember is that a good communicator learns when to take risks to reach deeper levels of communication and when not to self-disclose. The greatest harm comes from avoiding the process or not understanding it.

What Do You Think?

Erik knew he was gay from a very young age, but he never told anyone. Instead he tried to live the expected life of a heterosexual male. He even has a girlfriend. Erik pretends that he is happy, but he is miserable.

What is Erik afraid of? Why will he not risk self-disclosing his homosexuality?

Rewards of Self-Disclosure

There are rewards and advantages to self-disclosure. Based on the theory that relationships are necessary in order to survive, most theorists would agree that self-disclosure is necessary, for it is through self-disclosure that we develop, maintain, and change our self-concept and our relationships. Sullivan (1953) claims that all personal growth, all personal damage and regression, as well as all personal healing, are a result of our relationships with others. Even though this process makes us vulnerable to the people with whom we disclose, it becomes a necessary function of being human (Jourard, 1971). While it is sometimes necessary to "retreat" from the vulnerability that self-disclosure creates, it is also necessary to get back in the mainstream again so we can continue to participate in our growth and development of our self-concept and our relationships.

There are many contemporary lyrics which tell the story of someone who is hurt in a relationship and consequently becomes withdrawn and fearful of people. Through a chance meeting, a new friend is found who encourages the victim to take another chance. We go through this process in our lives sometimes—we allow ourselves to take a chance and become vulnerable with others until we get hurt, and then we retreat to safety until our wounds are healed. Buscaglia (1972) says that we must try again and again and continue to take another chance even though the process maybe painful, for it is our vulnerability that makes us human.

What Do You Think?

In your next class session, bring in a sample of a popular song which contains lyrics dealing with self-disclosure. Select a one minute or less segment from the song and play it for the class. Provide a brief oral explanation of how the lyrics apply to self-disclosure.

Even though self-disclosure may cause pain, we cannot shield ourselves from this pain forever. Pain is necessary for growth and understanding. Buscaglia (1972) continues by stating that if he had a choice between pain and nothing, he would choose pain—at least then he would know that he is alive. While facing the truth is not easy, it is the only way we can become "real." The following excerpt from *The Velveteen Rabbit* colorfully illustrates the process of becoming "real."

> When the Rabbit asked the Skin Horse "What is REAL?," the Skin Horse answered. "It doesn't happen all at once. You become. It takes a long time. That's why it doesn't often happen to people who break easily, or have sharp edges, or who have to be carefully kept. Generally, by the time you are Real, most of your hair has been loved off, and your eyes drop out and you get loose in the joints and very shabby. But these things don't matter at all, because once you are Real you can't be ugly, except to people who don't understand" (*The Velveteen Rabbit*, Margery Williams, 1975).

When our exterior truly reflects our interior, then, and only then, can we become an authentic, "real" person (Powell, 1969, p. 44).

The rewards or benefits of self-disclosure, however, are sometimes difficult to imagine when we are stuck in our pain and isolation. Benefits are not apparent to us when we are closed and withdrawn. However, it is only through self-disclosure that we can experience some of these benefits and rewards. One of the most rewarding experiences we can have is when someone else really understands us. Through intimate self-disclosure, we can create trust and develop a satisfying, close relationship with another person.

DeVito (1995) and others (Jourard, 1971; Buscaglia, 1972; Powell, 1969) identify many **rewards or advantages** gained through participating in what most researchers claim to be the most important form of communication—self-disclosure:

- better relationships
- psychological and mental health
- intimacy and trust in relationships
- personal growth, self-understanding, and commitment
- ability to cope with life
- self-proclamation and acknowledgment
- improvement of communication effectiveness and clarity
- energy release

These rewards are clearly important and can only be obtained through participation in self-disclosure.

What Do You Think?

Kelly: Terry, you seem really upset these past few weeks. What's going on with you?

Terry: It's really hard for me to talk about . . . I'm scared.

Kelly: Why, it's just me—your best friend. You're not scared of me, are you?

Terry: No, no—I know, but this is not easy to say.

Kelly: Maybe you'll feel better if you tell someone—and it doesn't have to be me.

Terry: I really want—no, have—to tell someone—and I guess you are the best choice. I mean, I really know you are. Thanks for sort of encouraging me and drawing it out of me.

Kelly: Well, maybe not now, but whenever you're ready, you just let me know.

Terry: No . . . no—I'm ready . . . now. Just let me take a breath . . . (*looking Kelly right in the eyes*) Last month I tested HIV positive . . . and I'm scared to death. (*talking faster and faster*) I don't know what to do, who to talk to, where to turn. (*begins crying*)

Kelly: (*with arms around Terry*) I don't know what to say except that I am really sorry that you are going through this, and I want you to know that you do not have to go through any of this alone. (*pause*) I will do anything I can to help you—always! (*another pause while Terry is still sobbing*) I will be here for you no matter what—and I *really* mean that!

Terry: (*sniffling*) Thanks. (*softly and slowly*) I feel a little better already. (*pause*) You have no idea what a relief it is to

say it out loud to someone else . . . and to realize that
you won't disappear or evaporate. (*after a long pause*)
Can you help me find out what I need to know—you
know, the best doctors, the latest medicines, alternative
treatments . . . ?

Kelly: Absolutely. I don't know much, but I'm sure we can find
out everything we need to know—together. Let's start
right now . . .

*How was self-disclosure a reward for Terry? What benefits did
Terry's self-disclosure provide? What was Terry afraid of—why
was he afraid to self-disclose that he was HIV positive? What
type of support did Kelly provide? Can you think of a time when
your self-disclosure provided you with a reward? Describe the
situation and the benefits you received.*

Summary

Self-disclosure may present many fears. We protect our self-concept
and true identity in order to avoid pain and isolation. However, it is
precisely the use of self-disclosure that allows us to remove ourselves
from this self-imposed isolation and shield ourselves from pain and
vulnerability. Once we realize the advantages and rewards of self-
disclosure, we begin to realize that by sharing the truth about who
we are and what we are about, we allow others to come into our lives
and help us grow and develop. Once we are authentic and "real" with
our self-disclosure, we are not so easily bruised and susceptible to pain.
The truth about ourselves, revealed to ourselves and others, may make
us go through pain, but it will also set us free.

References

Adler, Ronald B., Lawrence B. Rosenfeld, and Neil Towne. *Interplay: The
Process of Interpersonal Communication*, 5th ed. New York: Holt,
Rinehart and Winston, 1992.

Buscaglia, Leo. *Love*. New York: Fawcett Crest, 1972.

Cozby, Paul C. "Self-Disclosure: A Literature Review." *Psychological Bulletin*,
79 (1973).

DeVito, Joseph A. *The Communication Handbook: A Dictionary*. New York:
HarperCollins, 1986.

———. *The Interpersonal Communication Book*, 7th ed. New York:
HarperCollins, 1995.

Johnson, David W. *Reaching Out: Interpersonal Effectiveness and Self-
Actualization*. Englewood Cliffs, NJ: Prentice-Hall, 1981.

Jourard, Sidney. *The Transparent Self*, rev. ed. New York: Van Nostrand
Reinhold, 1971.

Luft, Joseph. *Of Human Interaction*. Palo Alto, CA: National Press Books, 1969.

Powell, John S.J. *Why Am I Afraid to Tell You Who I Am?* Niles, IL: Argue Communications, 1969.

Sullivan, Harry Stack. *The Interpersonal Theory of Psychiatry*. New York: Norton, 1953.

Williams, Margery. *The Velveteen Rabbit*. New York: Avon Books, 1975.

Case 26

TargetTerms

- benefits of self-disclosure
- risks of self-disclosure
- trust/honesty

PreviewNotes

We usually feel very comfortable sharing confidences with close friends. It is extremely upsetting to find that what we thought was confidential information was revealed to a third party.

CaseParticipants

Gary Michaels—graduate student; presently studying for "comps" in his major field; best friend to Richard Baker; serious and known to be a good listener

Paula Kohl—graduate student who is also studying for "comps" in the same field of study as Gary Michaels; "study buddy" and friend of Gary; girlfriend of Richard; sincere and serious about her relationships

Richard Baker—graduate student who is not studying for "comps," but is presently completing his studies and thesis; best buddy of Gary and boyfriend of Paula; takes life quite seriously

"I thought you'd understand!"

Paula and Gary are close friends who have Richard Baker as an integral part of both of their lives. During one of many study sessions as the clock ticks on and on, Gary decides that it is time for some type of diversion. This time it will be "food."

Gary: Break time!

Paula: What, again?!

Gary: This is driving me nuts. I have enough information in my brain to start another encyclopedia company. Coffee ice cream is what we need!

Paula: Good. I've been wanting to talk to you anyhow. Care if we walk there?

Gary: You hate walking. So this must really be serious.

Paula: I've been keeping this inside for a long time—and I'm not really sure if talking to you about it is right.

Gary: Look, Richard's my best friend—and now you.

Paula: Thanks! Unfortunately, that's part of the problem—your relationship with Richard. You're such a good friend that I need to talk to you, yet you and Richard are so close. It's about him—and me—we don't seem to have it anymore.

Gary: I'm not sure I know what you mean—or that I want to.

Paula: I don't think we're right for each other. Worst of all, I'm not even attracted to him like I used to be. I'm so afraid of hurting him, but that doesn't change how I feel. I have to tell him, but I can't find the right way. It's tearing me apart. I've never been dishonest about anything in my life.

Gary: Why are you telling this to me? What do you expect me to do?

Paula: I thought maybe you could tell me how not to hurt him.

Gary: That's impossible. I'm going to be real honest with you. I'm not all that happy about hearing about your problems with Richard.

Paula: I haven't said a word about problems to you. I need someone to talk to. You always told me that you'd be here if I needed an extra shoulder. Well, I need one now.

Gary: Yeah, but I never imagined this! Why the change of heart?

Paula: I can't even really explain it to myself. I guess I'm not willing to tie myself down to any one person now.

Gary: He never asked you to tie yourself down to him, did he?

Paula: Not really. But I get the impression he wants to keep the relationship exclusive. Gary, you know him as well as anyone. What should I do?

Gary: Do you want to date other people?

Paula: (*She doesn't answer and he repeats the question.*) You hit a nerve. Since I'm being honest with you, the answer, I suppose, is "yes."

Gary: Well, now we are getting to the bottom of this. Who is he?

Paula: No one in particular.

Gary: Paula?

Paula: I feel as if I can really talk to you. It's almost as if you're easier to talk to than Richard. That's why I know you understand. I can't really lie to you—

Gary: When you say "lie" I'm getting a queasy feeling.

Paula: Oh, all right . . . someone did ask me out, and after a few times of saying "no" and meaning "yes," I finally said "O.K." and went out. I felt so out of sorts the whole time. I know that we have no real commitment or anything—Richard and me, I mean. But, I'm not being fair . . . but then again, he never told me not to date others. And who knows, he can be dating others for all I know!

Gary: And you want me to give you all the right advice on what to do now? Is that all? (*sarcastically*)

Paula: I know it is asking a lot, but at least it feels better getting it off my chest. I've been staying up nights thinking about what to do.

Gary: You like this new guy, huh?

Paula: That's the problem! I think I really do.

Gary: The only thing that I can tell you is that I think you really should not break up with Richard before you know what the score is with this other guy. I mean, if I were you I would kinda keep them both stringing—well—not stringing, but I certainly would see both of them whenever I could. Then, maybe, you'll come to some conclusion about this. I would do that if I were you. I mean, plenty of girls still do that kind of thing. Who knows? Someone might be doing it to me now. Drop this whole thing for now. C'mon kid, don't look so glum! Let's have some ice cream and then we'll get back to the torture chamber and study.

Paula: Gary, you're great! I knew you'd understand. I mean it when I say I love you for being the special friend you are.

LATE THAT NIGHT . . . THE PHONE RINGS IN PAULA'S ROOM

Paula: Yes?

Richard: Paula?

Paula: Oh, hi. Why are you calling so late? Is everything all right?

Richard: Oh, sure! Why should anything be wrong? Everything's fine—just fine! You spend the night with Gary—talk about our relationship and boom—I find out that there's no need for us to be honest with each other. Why should that make me feel that anything is wrong?

Paula: I—(*She stops. The pause and then silence becomes deafening.*)

Richard: You still there? We need to talk—now!

CaseConcerns

1. Did Gary misuse the information disclosed to him by Paula? Defend your answer.

2. Was the information disclosed by Paula to Gary inappropriate? Do you think Gary thought it was inappropriate? Do you think Paula thought it was inappropriate?

3. What risks of self-disclosure did Paula fear to keep her from disclosing this same information to Richard?

4. How will the disclosure of this information affect the future of Paula's relationship with Richard? With Gary?

ReflectiveResponses

1. Discuss how personal information may have been misused by another in your life. How did this affect your relationship with another person?

Case 27

TargetTerms

- feelings/emotions versus ideas/judgments
- unmatched levels of self-disclosure
- resistance to self-disclosure
- rewards of self-disclosure
- necessity of self-disclosure

PreviewNotes

Although at times others would prefer that certain things be left "unsaid," it is important and necessary for us to share intimate feelings with those we love to help both ourselves and others understand who we are.

CaseParticipants

Jane Gardner—23-year-old college graduate working in a city office; sociable and sincere; deliberate in her actions; takes everything about what she does and believes very seriously

Lea Gardner—58 years old, happily married and mother of Jane; active in social and community affairs; quiet and reserved; wishes to have her privacy respected by all with whom she comes into contact

"There's something I want to tell you . . ."

Jane and Lea rarely have the opportunity to really "talk" to each other. Now it has become even more difficult since Jane works out of town. Not only distance separates mother and daughter. Their last visit together was relatively disastrous in terms of sharing what was happening in each of their lives. A cloud of misunderstanding seemed to lurk over the two women, and a visit over Thanksgiving ended with some very negative feelings. Despite the negativity, Jane and Lea planned to spend some time together once again at Christmas. Just before New Year's, another conflict appears to be brewing between the two women. It is late that evening as Jane says:

Jane: Mom, please don't go upstairs just yet. I really want to talk to you— before I go back to work tomorrow. We can't put off what we have to say to each other. I hate to keep you up so late, but we won't get a chance to be alone again before I leave.

Lea: Yes, I know, but we both need our rest, dear. (*starting out of the room*) We'll get to say "good-bye" at breakfast, dear. See you in the morning.

Jane: Really—what's more important to you, Mom—an extra hour of sleep— or my peace of mind? (*deafening silence*) Or should I even bother to ask?

Lea: We've been over this about a thousand times. What you do is your business. I certainly don't want you to know the details of my life—so don't ask me to understand the details of yours. See you at breakfast, dear.

Jane: Look, I'm sorry if it sounds like I'm asking you to get too involved, but I'd really like you to talk to me—like a person—no—like your daughter—not like I'm some member of your social club.

Lea: That's not fair! Why do you think I scheduled all of these dinner parties? Everyone wanted to see you. I, myself, was counting the minutes until your plane landed.

Jane: Mom, seeing me is one thing. Listening to me is another. If you ever want to have an honest relationship with me, I need you to stay with me now—and hear me out. It's taken too long to be able to share this with you at all . . . and now that I'm ready, just give me the chance.

Lea: (*resignedly*) Well, all right. (*She starts to sit down.*) But, do think of me, Jane. Consider my peace of mind, please.

Jane: That is not what we're discussing. You are doing it again—twisting and turning what I say to fit what you feel safe knowing. Well, I've got to start thinking about what is going to make *me* feel good. I've been in such a state of confusion and you have done nothing—not even one little overture of trying to figure out what the problem might be. I feel like a paper doll that you take out and show to people.

Lea: You were always such a good little girl. Why are you saying these things now?

Jane: So that I can tell if you are ready to talk or not. I'm hoping that we don't have to wait another four months to be honest with each other— 'cause I'm ready to burst.

Lea: Honest? Did I hear this right? You don't think we've been honest with each other?

Jane: Let's stop doing this to each other. Please. I don't want the "I'm sorrys" or the "I don't understands" that you've been giving me for the last year. All I want is the time to talk to you to tell you who I really am and how I feel. Won't you do this for me?

Lea: Can't we just keep our mother-daughter relationship a little less personal—especially about knowing each other's business?

Jane: Mom, if I can't talk to you, who am I going to turn to?

Lea: Don't get so hysterical about this, Jane. I want you to understand that I'm very willing to hear what you have to say.

Jane: Provided that it meets whatever standards you might be setting?

Lea: Mind if I say that's a bit unfair?

Jane: Well, I've always played according to your rules. I've always tried to do it your way.

Lea: Not always.

Jane: That's because sometimes, I just couldn't play by anyone else's game plan. I couldn't be hypocritical and do things that I felt uncomfortable doing. I felt scared that if I spoke to you about what I was feeling— well, that you'd be hurt. I always tried not to hurt you.

Lea: But not hard enough.

Jane: Can't you just quit throwing out those damn innuendos? Why don't you say what you really want to tell me?

Lea: Why don't *you*?

Jane: (*with a great deal of reservation*) Because I'm not sure you're ready to listen to me.

Lea: Listen, this so-called "guilt trip" is of your own making.

Jane: (*nearly in tears*) How can you be so unfeeling to call this a guilt trip? How can I share anything with you when you treat me as if I am someone else—someone *you* want me to be—not who I really am. (*Feeling badly that her words seemed so callous, she takes her mom's hand.*) The truth of the matter is that I really need you now. I'm feeling so alone, and I don't want you to let me down.

Lea: (*quieting her down*) I've never let you down. Ever! Don't you forget that! I will always be there for you.

Jane: Even when I tell you that I'm gay—that I'm a lesbian?

Lea: (*absolute silence, then*) What time will you be down for breakfast?

CaseConcerns

1. How does Lea communicate her feelings and emotions to Jane? How does Jane communicate her feelings and emotions to Lea?

2. What are the rewards, if any, of self-disclosure in this case?

3. Explain how this case describes unmatched levels of self-disclosure.

4. Why did Jane feel the necessity of disclosing her homosexuality to her mother? Why didn't her mother want to hear it?

ReflectiveResponses

1. Why do children fear disclosing certain information to their parents?

2. Identify reasons to resist self-disclosure in this case. In your life.

3. What do you do when you are disclosing information of a very personal level and the receiver is listening and responding at a very impersonal level?

4. Make a case for the necessity of self-disclosure.

5. Should the feelings of the other person be considered before you choose to self-disclose? Defend your answer.

Case 28

TargetTerms

- levels of self-disclosure
- appropriateness of self-disclosure
- necessity of self-disclosure

PreviewNotes

Frequently, we have the urge to share a confidence with a certain someone. How often, though, do we stop to think about whether the party on the receiving end really wants to have the responsibility of knowing the secret?

CaseParticipants

Ann Sharf—35-year-old mother of young children; spiritually motivated in many respects in her life; dear friend to Joan Byrnes; enjoys being who she is

Joan Byrnes—38-year-old mother of young children; tends to be extremely opinionated and emotionally charged; presently is going through some difficult moments of self-doubt and worth

"I'm seeing someone . . ."

Ann and Joan have been friends since their kids have been in nursery school together. Although they are also neighbors, they have respected each other's privacies in matters of child rearing and lifestyle. However, in each woman's life, there has been a time when each relied on the other for some type of emotional release or confidence sharing. However, lately Joan has been continuously over-stepping that fine line of being too intrusive in Ann's life. Sometimes it is as if she doesn't know when to back off. On one such

occasion when Ann tries nonchalantly to get off the phone, Joan is
very quick to add just one more thing as she says:

Joan: Yes, I suppose there was a reason for my calling. I'm at the end of my rope now, and I can't keep this all bottled up inside anymore. I don't even know where to begin.

Ann: Well, stop skirting the real issue and tell me what's going on. You're just not yourself.

Joan: And for a very good reason. You are going to really hate me when I tell you this.

Ann: How bad can it be?

Joan: You'll be sorry that you asked.

Ann: Well, I didn't ask—you started this—so, don't leave me hanging now. You'd think that you were having an affair or something.

Joan: Why'd you have to say that? I'm still not sure if I should . . .

Ann: You have two choices, Joanie. Either you tell me or you don't. What'll it be?

Joan: (*pause—silence*) I'm seeing someone.

Ann: (*pause—silence*) What do you want me to say?

Joan: Well—I don't know. You're making me feel so—

Ann: I'm not sure if I should be relieved or in a panic.

Joan: Explain . . .

Ann: All these months of your flying from here to there, and from there to wherever—well, I began to think that something was wrong. I thought that you were real sick and going to some far off place for treatment of some kind. What you're telling me is not really such a welcome relief, either. I mean, how did this happen? Or, more importantly, why did it happen?

Joan: I'll assure you that this didn't happen out of the blue. As you know—

Ann: No, I don't know, nor do I wish to know. Let's consider keeping it at that. I'm too close to both of you guys to get involved. I'm around for you, but I'm also there for Craig.

Joan: It's someone I've known for a long time. In fact, I met up with him again at that high school reunion that I was so indecisive about attending. It was all so crazy—we've been seeing each other ever since.

Ann: Look, you've just got to stop this. Now!

Joan: Please, don't be so judgmental. I've been denying that this is happening. This is one time that I need a friend and not a sermon. (*pause*) I think that I'm in love with him.

Ann: You think? You're not thinking at all. If you were, you wouldn't let your emotions rule you—none of this would be happening.

Joan: Great! Just what I needed now—a lesson on how to control my emotions. Tell me, please, who can I talk to about this, if not you?

Ann: I'm asking the same question. Why me?

Joan: Who would you like me to tell this to—Craig?

Ann: Is this guy married?

Joan: Worse than that.

Ann: How much worse can it be?

Joan: To my best girlfriend from high school.

Ann: You've really done it, haven't you? You didn't miss hurting anyone, did you?

Joan: From your (*sarcastically*) encouraging response to my present situation, Ann, I'm sorry that I opened my mouth.

Ann: And now, you're going to tell me that you want me to forget that we ever had this conversation, right?

Joan: I feel so alone, Ann. I am so mixed up and I care so much about everyone's feelings.

Ann: Any thought about the fact that you have two children?

Joan: So does he.

Ann: My, my! With each answer, the whole thing seems to get more sordid.

Joan: Why'd you have to say that?

Ann: Why'd you have to tell me all of this? What am I supposed to do with this information? Think of me for a minute—and the position you put me in. Sorry, Joan, since you told me this, I'm going to tell you how I feel.

Joan: Ann—I am *really* involved—I can't function on a day-to-day basis without him in my life.

Ann: I didn't hear you just say that. Nor do I want to hear you say it. Hey, look—it's not as if I don't care. I do probably understand more than you think that I do . . . but, you're pushing me right into the middle. You know what is right and what is wrong—

Joan: I'm not saying that I don't know the difference. These things do not happen by accident. There is a reason why they happen to some people and not to others. The timing was just right in my life—for this relationship to form.

Ann: And what about when this old girlfriend of yours finds out? She'll kill you.

Joan: I'm taking my chances. I almost wish she knew. Then, the whole thing would be out in the open.

Ann: You are serious, aren't you?

Joan: I've never been more clear about anything. I guess, now, I'm beginning to understand the type of contentment you have in your life.

Ann: I'm not going to become your victim over this. How you have the absolute gall to tell me that you want to experience the contentment of married life—and then in the same breath, tell me that because you didn't, you decided to find it elsewhere—you just can't say those kinds of things and expect to maintain any type of relationship with anyone. There's a time and a place—and this is not the right thing for me to listen to at any time or in any place. You must understand that if you ask me what I think, you are going to have to be prepared to listen to what I have to say.

Joan: I don't remember asking you what you thought. I merely wanted to tell you how I felt. Was that too much to ask?

CaseConcerns

1. Describe the debilitative emotions that Joan might be feeling. How do these emotions keep her from communicating effectively with Ann?

2. How could fear keep Joan from communicating with Ann at an honest level? Describe a time when you have felt intense fear about self-disclosure. How did this affect the way you communicated?

3. Evaluate the appropriateness or inappropriateness of Ann's responses. Who decides the appropriateness of the disclosure and the response? Defend your answer.

ReflectiveResponses

1. What happens when the person with whom you are communicating minimizes your disclosure? Or when the receiver becomes judgmental?

2. Think of a situation in your life when you may have wished you had not disclosed information to another person. What happened? Were you ever the recipient of inappropriate disclosure?

Case 29

TargetTerms

- levels of self-disclosure
- resistance to self-disclosure
- fear of punishment
- lack of honesty and trust

PreviewNotes

How often do we find ourselves torn between sharing an important problem and running the risk of being criticized for doing so? This case points out what can happen when a problem which needs to be shared is not disclosed due to fear. It also demonstrates how we avoid communicating at an intimate level by sometimes using a safer level.

CaseParticipants

Jeanie Boland—mother of Carly, a 15-year-old teenager; she tries to be concerned, but . . .

Ed Boland—uninvolved and unsupportive in his married and fatherly life

Carly Boland—15 years old; Jeanie and Ed's daughter, who has just discovered she's pregnant and is afraid to tell her parents

"I was afraid to tell you!"

The neighborhood gossip, Phyllis Brennan, has just called Jeanie Boland with some very unexpected information. Calling only to confirm the story, Phyllis has no idea that she was the actual person to break the news to Jeanie and Ed Boland about their daughter. Jeanie, in absolute hysterics, calls Carly and makes her sit down.

Jeanie: I'm sick about this. Can't you see what this is doing to your father and me—that we had to hear this from Phyllis Brennan, the biggest mouth in town? I don't even know what to say. Ed, say something!

Ed: First—well, why didn't you come to us when you found out you were in trouble?

Carly: I knew it—I knew you'd scream at me.

Jeanie: (*very loudly*) We are not screaming. We just want you to understand.

Carly: Even saying that I'm in trouble . . . I just knew, Dad, that would happen. I can't even tell you now how I feel. This whole thing is . . .

Jeanie: Carly, this is not any of your so-called "whole things." You are carrying a baby, for God's sake, and you are a baby yourself!

Carly: I knew you'd do this to me.

Jeanie: Think about what you're doing to us.

Carly: It's not as if I didn't want to tell you that I am pregnant. I've been pretty upset about this myself.

Jeanie: How long has it been?

Carly: Not real . . .

Jeanie: Not real, what?

Carly: Not real long.

Jeanie: Do his parents know?

Carly: He has a name, Mom.

Jeanie: Ex-cuse me! Do Tony's parents know? Or, should I now say, do Mr. and Mrs. Rottimer, Tony's parents, know?

Carly: Yes, and they've been very supportive.

Jeanie: Yeah, because you're not their daughter. Ed, say something! Can you believe that the Rottimers are very supportive of our daughter being pregnant?

Carly: That's why I couldn't tell you. I knew you'd rant and rave, just like you're doing now. You know this wasn't done on purpose.

Jeanie: It shouldn't have been done at all.

Carly: Can't you understand that I don't want to feel any more upset than I do now? I've been feeling sick lately. In fact, I feel pretty lousy, now. And I'm real scared—real, real, scared. (*She starts to cry.*)

Jeanie: Well, what do you expect me to do?

Carly: That's exactly why I never tell you anything. You never want to do anything.

Jeanie: How can you say that to me? Put yourself in my shoes—getting a call from Phyllis Brennan about this. I still can't get over that she had to tell me and you didn't.

Carly: How long is this going to go on—this guilt trip that you're hanging on me? I can't believe that I can't even turn to my own mother and father.

Jeanie: That is not true and you know it.

Carly: Well, it sure as hell seems that way.

Jeanie: Don't you dare speak to us that way.

Carly: Think about how you are speaking to me. You don't even care about how I feel—

Jeanie: No, Carly, that's not so.

Carly: Tell me how else I'm supposed to feel. You're treating me—well—like a piece of dirt.

Jeanie: I'm just—well, a little overwhelmed by all of this—I need some time to adjust. I don't mean to make you feel any worse—(*cuddles her*) Carly—I know it's hard for you to understand this now, but I do care and I am sorry. (*holds her daughter closely, gently questioning her*) Have you seen a doctor? (*looks over at her husband*) Ed, why are you leaving this room? She needs us now.

Ed: I can't believe what I'm hearing. Our daughter's pregnant and you're saying, "I'm sorry," and I want to kill Tony.

Carly: There you go again. I knew you'd punish me with all of this guilt garbage. It's not Tony's fault. It's as much mine. I'm ready to take the responsibility, too.

Ed: And what about the responsibility of raising a child?

Carly: I haven't thought about that yet.

Ed: And when the hell do you expect to start thinking about it?

Jeanie: Ed—stop this! I just said that she needs us now.

Carly: How can you keep going on and on—saying and doing this to me? That's why I could never tell you. I knew you'd do this to me—and worse yet to each other. I said I'm sorry. I really am.

Ed: I can't listen to this anymore. I'm going to sleep.

Jeanie: You know, Carly, it is late and I'm awfully upset. Let's just get some rest—and we'll deal with this tomorrow.

CaseConcerns

1. In the disclosure presented to Carly's parents about her pregnancy, who assumes the victim role and why?

2. Identify the levels of disclosure exemplified in this case. How does this affect the communication between parent and child?

3. After witnessing her parents' reaction to what was disclosed, at what level does Carly's trust allow her to continue disclosing her feeling about this subject?

ReflectiveResponses

1. What fears block children (at any age) from disclosing important information to their parents?

2. How can denial of reality be a destructive force in establishing a healthy family communication pattern?

Case 30

- levels of self-disclosure
- rewards of self-disclosure
- resistance to self-disclosure
- appropriateness of self-disclosure

PreviewNotes

Meeting people for the first time may influence the way we communicate and disclose information about ourselves.

CaseParticipants

Sandy—female college student heading home from school on Amtrak for the holidays

Ron—male college student heading home from school on Amtrak for the holidays

"Strangers on the tracks"

Have you ever had the experience of being a passenger on a bus or a plane when you've met a total stranger with whom you share rather personal information? Although Sandy and Ron attend the same school, they have never met—until the two sit next to each other on the train.

Sandy: (*spying notebooks with a college logo*) Looks like you go to my school. What department are you in?

Ron: I'm studying pre-med. How about you?

Sandy: Oh, so you're going to be a doctor. What kind?

Ron: I don't know yet, but I'm real interested in psychology, so psychiatry might be one of my choices.

Sandy: Ya know, I'm a psychology major. There are some great courses in the department, aren't there?

Ron: Sure. (*continues reading the book*)

Sandy: Why are you studying so hard? You already took your exams, didn't you?

Ron: I'm taking a three-week intercession course and I'm gearing up for it. (*continues to try to read*)

Sandy: You mean that you are doing reading in advance?!

Ron: Sort of, I guess.

Sandy: (*sees that the book has a title that deals with date rape*) Well, the book looks interesting enough. Listen, I'll tell you about what happened to me. I'm sure it's better than anything in that book. You wouldn't believe the mess I got into on campus.

Ron: (*half listening and reading at the same time*) Oh?!

Sandy: After one of our sorority parties at our house, a few guys stayed and tried to help us clean up. The problem was that they wanted to be paid for their work—if you know what I mean.

Ron: (*continues to read*) No, I really don't. If you'll just—

Sandy: Oh, c'mon, you must have heard about it—it was all over the newspaper. About five fraternity brothers came by and started pushing us around. Next thing we knew, the police came—the brothers were put on probation and the campus shut down their fraternity house.

Ron: So why are you telling me this?

Sandy: Well, you're reading about date rape. After that incident, I'm the one who could really tell you firsthand about the subject.

Ron: That didn't sound like date rape to me.

Sandy: After what that guy did to me—how would you like to be shoved around like that? (*Ron doesn't respond.*) You guys are all alike! (*She glares at Ron as he just looks at her in silence.*) Awww—what would you know, anyway? (*She gets up and changes her seat.*)

CaseConcerns

1. What examples of phatic communication are there in this case? Cliché communication? Other levels of self-disclosure?

2. Explain what you believe are the rewards and resistance to communication in this case. Of the two case participants, who is more resistant to hearing about what the other has to say? Why?

ReflectiveResponses

1. Why do we frequently self-disclose to strangers or have strangers self-disclose to us?

2. Think of a situation in your life where you felt differently about a person in a relationship after he or she disclosed to you. Why do you suppose you felt (or feel) the way you did (do)?

3. Describe your own thoughts about disclosing to others. Do you have an unwritten rulebook about telling certain things? To what do you attribute your thinking?

8
Chapter

Emotions

Specific Goals for Understanding Chapter Eight

TargetTerms

- debilitative emotions
- facilitative emotions
- intensity
- duration
- jealousy
- fear
- anger
- crazymaking
- irrational beliefs
- indirect communication
- Rational Emotive Therapy (RET)
- empathy

CoreConcepts

1 the components of emotions
2 identifying our emotions
3 judging our emotions
4 the necessity of expressing emotions
5 types of emotions
6 dealing with debilitative emotions: jealousy, anger, fear
7 irrational beliefs as debilitative emotions
8 guidelines for expressing emotions
9 how emotion relates to empathy

"Stop—you're driving me crazy!"

Overview

Even the best planned strategies with the best intentions fail when strong emotions enter the relationship scene. We can learn and practice the various approaches to communication effectiveness, but when deep feelings and emotions are aroused, all those plans and intentions become impotent. Our emotions sometimes control us, and we are accused of "thinking with our hearts instead of our heads." However, the strength of our emotions is underestimated when it comes to the effect they have on our interpersonal relationships and the intensity with which we pursue those relationships. Emotions are very powerful and need to be understood in order to be utilized to our advantage.

In this chapter we will explore the intensity of emotions and their impact upon our relationships. Together, we will unveil the complex structure and power of emotions on the way we communicate. We will find out how emotions are put together; how to identify them; why we judge them; the need for expressing them; the various types of emotions; how to deal with debilitative emotions such as jealousy, anger, fear, and irrational beliefs; guidelines for expressing our emotions, a unique cognitive approach to emotional control known as Rational Emotive Therapy, and how emotion relates to empathy in our communication.

Components of Emotions

Emotions are hard to describe even though we all seem to know instinctively what they are; we might describe *emotions* as feelings or sensations. Social scientists suggest that generally there are four components to our emotions:

- **physiological changes**—changes in the body that occur when strong emotions are felt; for example, fear results in increased heartbeat, rise in blood pressure, increase in blood sugar, slowing of digestion, and dilation of the pupils

- **nonverbal manifestations**—feelings are usually demonstrated nonverbally
- **cognitive interpretations**—our bodies react similarly to various emotions (our temperature rises whether we are angry, afraid, or surprised); the difference in meaning comes from our interpretation of the emotion
- **verbal expression**—necessary and difficult; can result in counterfeit emotions displaying a lack of congruence between the verbal expression and the emotional meaning of a feeling (Adler, Rosenfeld, and Towne, 1923, pp. 206–233)

This list of factors helps us identify more specifically what our emotions are and how they affect us, but there are some other points we must consider as well. Most of us do not realize that emotions are mostly temporary or transient and that they are also controllable. For example, if we feel miserable and lonely following the ending of an intimate relationship, it seems as though we will never feel better or "back to normal" again. Our emotions consume us, and we become prone to sudden outbursts of uncontrollable feelings. This is a typical reaction and can be viewed as a normal and sometimes necessary response. There are times when there are valued reasons to be emotional just as there are times when we are overreacting emotionally. What we need to realize is that, as the saying goes, time will ease the pain and eventually we will feel good again and be able to control our emotions.

We must also realize that we have a choice about the way we feel. We can choose not to feel bad, or we can choose to be mad only for a short time. This is not easy, but it is possible. So, emotions are mostly transient. We can control them, and we can change the way we feel.

What Do You Think?

Kim's mother could usually tell what Kim was feeling just by looking at Kim's face.

Mom: What's the matter, Kim?
 Kim: Nothing, really.
Mom: Come on, you can tell me. You know you can't fool your mother.
 Kim: No really, I'm fine.
Mom: Then don't look at me like that. You've got anger written all over your face!

Which of the four components of emotions was Kim's mother reading in Kim's face?

Identifying Our Emotions

Figuring out how and why we feel a certain way is not always easy. When someone says, "What's the matter?" and our response is, "Oh, nothing," we probably are having difficulty identifying exactly what it is that is bothering us. Most feelings have a stimulus or a catalyst which activates them; however, we do not always know how to identify these connections. For example, we may receive a low grade on a project that required a considerable amount of work on our part. Later that same day we may start to feel irritable and not know why. We may have dismissed the low grade without much thought, thinking that we had dealt with our anger and frustration already. But later, when we become anxious and irritable, we fail to connect the stimulus (the low grade) with the response (the irritable feelings). This situation exemplifies the difficulty we may have in labeling the feeling itself or the cause of the feeling. In going through this connection process, we can become more cognizant of how emotions affect the way we communicate. Try asking yourself frequently, "Why do I feel this way right now?" With practice, you will become better and better at making the connection between the feeling and the cause of the feeling.

What Do You Think?

Take a few moments right now to identify a feeling that you have experienced today. Identify the feeling by labeling it with a specific emotion. Then, search through your experiences of the day and try to identify the stimulus which activated the feeling. Try to make the connection between the emotion and its stimulus.

Judging Our Emotions

Emotions are also neither good nor bad, they just are. However, we usually are raised with guidelines on how to evaluate our emotions; we are told to "snap out of it" or to "stop crying or I will give you something to cry about." These messages create a false labeling of feelings and a denial of their existence. In our society, men are taught that emotions such as sadness and grief should not be expressed through crying, while women are taught that emotions such as anger should not be expressed verbally. This training can lead to self-punishment and incrimination for feelings that are actually natural and normal; the result is frustration, self-hate, and denial.

We need to allow ourselves to experience the whole range of emotions, whatever they may be. Repressed emotions or emotional denial can lead to serious problems—physically, mentally, and verbally. When little boys are taught that "big boys don't cry," they learn to be scared, not to be brave. Men receive continual reinforcement that denying emotions is masculine; consequently they can develop into emotionally unresponsive and emotionally unavailable people who become a tower of repressed stress and anxiety. Paradoxically, young girls are taught to be responsive to the needs of others while denying their own needs and feelings; consequently they can end up nurturing others rather than themselves. So, it becomes dangerous to judge or deny our emotions.

What Do You Think?

Ed is currently married to his third wife, and he admits that he just does not understand women. After three wives, he is confused. He has more than adequately provided for his wives—a beautiful house, expensive clothes, wonderful vacations, and abundant spending money for food and entertainment. What else could they want from him? What does his current wife, Connie, mean when she says he is emotionally unavailable to her? He just does not get it.

Describe what might have happened to Ed as he was growing up and dealing with his emotions. Is this a typical problem? What does Ed not get?

Necessity of Expressing Emotions

The fear and anxiety of expressing how we feel is programmed into us by society through social and parental conditioning. However, the necessity of expression is validated by social research. Unexpressed feelings are not only dangerous to physical and mental health, they are also destructive to the communication process. We cannot communicate effectively without identifying, expressing, and (to some degree) controlling our emotions. In the worst case scenario, serious diseases are being linked to stress and repressed emotions. Cancer, heart disease, colitis, and ulcers are a few of the diseases that researchers are now beginning to associate with stress-related emotions. Such powerful consequences in terms of personal health concerns seem to indicate a high need for the awareness, identification, and expression of our emotions. However, before deciding to express our emotions, we must consider IF expression will enhance or detract from the relationship. Therefore, it becomes essential to deal appropriately with our emotions in order to communicate more effectively. Adler, Rosenfeld, and Towne, 1992 (pp. 213–215) identify three major **benefits of expressing emotions** appropriately:

- **physical and psychological health**
- **increased intimacy**
- **conflict resolution**

Richard Weaver (1993, pp. 231–233) stresses the importance of understanding emotions as a necessary step to recognizing and expressing them; he identifies five **reasons for the need to understand emotions**:

- **emotion is part of the human condition**
- **emotion is an element of empathy**
- **emotion is an aspect of individual uniqueness**
- **emotion is a supplement to reason**
- **emotion is a means for self-understanding, self-control, and security**

What Do You Think?

Vi is out of her mind with fear because she thinks her son Craig is on cocaine. She does not know what to do or which way to turn.

Craig: Hi, mom. Just thought I'd stop by and see what you're having for dinner. I'm starving, and my refrigerator is bare.

Vi: Why didn't you go to the grocery store?

Craig: Where's dad?

Vi: Where do you think—at the damn shop—where you should be—helping him.

Craig: What did you do today?

Vi: What do you care? You're never around to help me. I have to do everything myself, even though my legs are killing me.

Craig: How are you feeling?

Vi: Fine. What have you been doing lately?

Craig: None of your business, damn it. You're always so nosey. You have to know everything, don't you? (*Craig slams the door on his way out.*)

Vi: (*out loud but to herself*) See, that's why I never say anything.

What happened here? What are Craig and his mother avoiding? What benefits of expressing their feelings might they receive if they were really honest about their emotions with each other? What solutions can you offer?

Debilitative vs. Facilitative Emotions

Emotions can be very strong. The degree of strength that an emotion has is proportional to the degree to which it can become debilitative. The degree to which we can control an emotion is the degree to which that emotion is more facilitative. These two terms are correlated to the manner in which we handle our emotions. **Debilitative emotions** are ones which can prevent or hinder effective communication. **Facilitative emotions** are ones which can contribute to effective functioning in conflict. Intensity and duration are the distinguishing factors between these two categories of emotions. **Intensity** is the degree to which an emotion is felt or the strength of the feeling. **Duration** is the length of time an emotion is felt or retained by a person.

Gerald Kranzler (1974) states that the danger of intense feelings is that they can keep us from thinking clearly and often lead to an urge to act on the feeling. Facilitative emotions are usually less intense and thus more manageable. Holding on to (duration) intense feelings or other debilitative emotions can punish us even more; hate or sorrow maintained for a long period of time can be debilitative. The goal is to transfer our emotions to a facilitative mode in order to improve our communication.

What Do You Think?

Kim and Kelly work together, and socially they are friends. Their relationship has become strained lately. Kim decides to confront the issue.

Kim: How's it going?

Kelly: Oh, pretty well. How about you?

Kim: Well, there is something I would like to talk to you about, if you have a minute.

Kelly: Sure, what's on your mind?

Kim: (*looking Kelly directly in the eyes*) Kelly, I am feeling angry about your missing the deadline last week for our report. I feel hurt that you seemed not to be concerned with how your lateness would make me look to our manager. I thought you were more considerate than that, I mean, I thought we were friends and that we could talk about these types of problems before they occurred. Is there something going on for you that's causing this problem?

Kelly: Gee, Kim, I'm sorry. I didn't realize that I caused a problem for you. I guess I was in my own separate world with the funeral and all.

Kim: What funeral? I didn't know someone died.

Kelly: Oh, I guess I was so stressed I just didn't mention it. My grandfather died last week—right in the middle of our deadlines, and I guess I was trying to pretend it didn't matter.

Kim: Gee, Kelly. I'm really sorry to hear about your grandfather. How did he die?

Kelly: Well, I guess it was just old age. He was 96. But it was still a surprise. My mom is pretty upset; he lived with us.

Kim: Death is never easy to face. Is there anything I can do for you?

Kelly: Well, I could use a nice, quiet dinner with a good friend.

Kim: You got it. I'll get my briefcase. And Kelly, thanks for sharing with me. I hope next time something major—or even minor—happens that you will feel comfortable enough to talk with me.

Kelly: Thanks, Kim. I really appreciate your friendship—not to mention, I don't want to do anything to jeopardize our working relationship, either.

Describe how Kim dealt with the anger and hurt as a result of Kelly's actions. Were the emotions Kim felt treated facilitatively or debilitatively? Explain your answer.

Dealing with Debilitative Emotions

The following sections discuss in more detail specific debilitative emotions and methods for converting emotion to facilitate communication. Emotions are an integral—and unavoidable—fact of life. How we channel the power than comes from emotions determines whether our emotions rule us or whether we recognize and understand how to translate that energy to useful purposes.

Jealousy

Jealousy is the green-eyed monster that haunts us during relationships when the feelings of loneliness, suspicion, or insecurity are intense. Jealousy involves a valued item, a perceived threat of loss of this item, and a robber (Kelley, 1980). Kelley defines **jealousy** as "the fear of losing to a third party something to which one feels one has a right and which one finds desirable" (p. 138). DeVito (1986) is more subtle in definition—"a feeling of dissatisfaction and anxiety resulting from the fear that someone or something belonging to one may be lost or taken away by another" (p. 172).

Matching jealousy to the definition for debilitative emotions, we find that this strong emotion is not necessarily debilitative unless it begins to interfere with the successful development of the relationship (Constantine, 1976). When one partner begins to feel alienated or the jealousy begins to interfere with clear and direct communication processes, it is then that jealousy becomes debilitative. On the other hand, some theorists claim that minimal amounts of facilitative jealousy can be helpful to a relationship. Partners can learn about major differences in perception or can discover signals about the need to clarify relational definitions or guidelines through preliminary jealousy (Brown and Keller, 1979).

However, jealousy also can be one of the most destructive forces experienced in a relationship. Its strength and power can consume us in self-righteous feelings of being right and personal feelings of insecurity and alienation. Jealousy is usually communicated indirectly through "double speak" messages which must be interpreted through the relational level of the process. This is another instance of crazymaking—the process of sending unclear, indirect messages either because we ourselves do not understand what we really want or because we are too afraid to say what we really feel. The most effective method of dealing with these double-speak messages is to attack them directly. Crazymaking begets more crazymaking unless it is stopped by one party.

The insecurity which initiates the feelings of jealousy is usually based on not having enough information. Harry Stack Sullivan states that generally we seek to reduce uncertainty in our lives in order to reduce anxiety and obtain satisfaction and security (1953). When a partner in an intimate relationship withholds information—either intentionally or unintentionally—an insecurity develops. Why did he not tell me about the new woman at the office? Why did she not tell me that she has lunch every week at the club? When we do not know the details of a situation, we create them; in doing so, we end up filling in the blanks with our insecurities (which are usually irrational and illogical conclusions). So, if the husband fails to tell the wife about the new woman at the office, the wife begins to imagine reasons why he did not inform her. These "created" reasons are most often inaccurate and most frequently based on the insecurity created by not knowing and the fear created by the possibility of rejection. This is a foundation in the development of jealousy.

Jealousy in relationships, then, seems to be based on insecurity and fear of rejection or loss. As Sullivan (1953) claims, the strongest desire we have is the one for certainty and security. When these needs do not come from the significant others in our lives, the insecurity monster rears up with jealous fangs. The more insecure we feel, the more intense the anxiety can become. These are strong feelings that can really dictate our behaviors if we do not control them and make them more facilitative.

Fear

Fear has to be one of the most debilitating emotions we can experience. It encompasses multiple targets and sources; the source of fear can come from many places and we aim its vengeance at many different targets. Our lives become the imprint of our fears—*we are what we fear*. If we are deathly afraid of water because of a near drowning during childhood, we will miss all the potential enjoyment that the ocean, a pool, water sports, and other water-based activities can provide for us. Our **fears** dictate our actions, limit our income, restrict our freedom, and run our lives. To a large extent, what we fear determines who we are.

Gerald Jampolsky (1979) connects *fear* with the inability to love and develop relationships. His book, *Love is Letting Go of Fear*, explains that we cannot love openly and honestly until we deal with our fears. Perhaps we may never completely rid ourselves of all fear, but certainly there are ways of controlling our fears and making them work for us instead of against us. Jampolsky maintains that our fears are based on our obsessions and that it is our past and future obsessions that we must release in order to be able to love. Samuel Kirschner (1987) says that fear abbreviates itself as *False Evidence Appearing Real*. We often create fear by jumping to false conclusions—you know, one fear leads to another and pretty soon the creak in the house becomes a burglar who is going to kill us. Marianne Williamson (1992), in her best-selling book, *A Return To Love*, suggests the use of the *Workbook* from *A Course in Miracles*, which is a 365-day set of psychological exercises which provides a very specific curriculum for relinquishing a thought system based on fear and accepting instead a thought system based on love. She claims that we were all born with a natural tendency to focus on love, but our world has taught us to focus on fear instead.

All three of these authors (Jampolsky, 1979; Kirschner, 1987; Williamson, 1992) maintain that there are really only two basic emotions: love and fear. If we are not coming from a place of love, then our communication behaviors are some manifestation of our fears. Fear debilitates us by irrationalizing our thinking processes and clouding our logic; it immobilizes us, restricting us from taking necessary and positive actions. Fear ruins our relationships by fostering manipulation, defensiveness and many other debilitative emotions and actions.

Anger

Anger usually results from a need to be right. For example, the next time you are mad, ask yourself the question, "Am I mad because the other person did not do what I wanted them to do?" If the answer is even close to a "yes" or a "maybe," a need to be right may have surfaced through anger. This need to be right can be debilitating in relationships. Louise Hay (1986) claims that you can either be right or you can be happy, but you cannot be both. She maintains that **anger** is based on the need to be right which always results in unhappiness. Giving up the need to be right is the only solution.

Anger can be an effective motivator, just as can jealousy and fear; however, the intensity and duration of any of these emotions frequently causes them to be debilitative. On the positive side, anger can assist us in accomplishing a necessary task. We can get mad at ourselves with a positive result, not involving other people, and the anger we feel can be facilitative. But for anger in a relationship to be facilitative, it takes a great deal of energy to control and direct it in a positive path.

It is not negative that we feel these emotions, because they are basically inevitable; the negative part can be the result of what you DO with these emotions. Remember, we do not have to act on every emotion we feel. So it is what we do with the feeling that makes it facilitative or debilitative.

What Do You Think?

Jill and Todd are always fighting. Even though they have been together for over three years, they just cannot seem to get along with each other.

Jill: You make me so mad!

Todd: (*surprised*) What? I mean what's wrong?

Jill: Oh, you know. It's not like we haven't had this conversation before, and you know it.

Todd: Come on, be reasonable. Give me a break, anyway.

Jill: I'll give you a break, right in your head if you don't stop treating me like this.

Todd: Like what?

Jill: I mean if you don't stop acting like such a spoiled brat and treating me like a possession.

Todd: What did I do? I take you out to nice restaurants, I buy you nice presents, I give . . .

Jill: Yeah, yeah, yeah, and I go out of my way to be nice to you and what do I get—obnoxious behavior. I've just about had it with you.

How are Jill's emotions debilitative in this scene? How can you suggest that she turn them into facilitative emotions?

Crazymaking

In chapter 5, we discussed **crazymaking** and listed four essential elements which, if not met, lead to crazymaking: **the right to clear information; the right to express how we feel without contradiction; the right to know we significantly matter to someone else; and the right to physical and/or emotional distance.** As mentioned earlier, the doublespeak messages of crazymaking must be attacked directly. Good communicators need to be alert to the signs of crazymaking. Violations of the rights summarized above are excellent clues. If partners in an exchange do not recognize crazymaking, emotions takeover and a downward spiral results. The second partner may become so enraged and/or frustrated by crazymaking remarks that he or she also engages in confusing, disconfirming communication.

What Do You Think?

Sue: Honey, I am so excited. I just got accepted at the university to finish my undergrad degree.

Tim: What?! How can you be happy about something that will completely change our lives? What about the kids? What about the house?

Sue: But I'm so happy about going back to school. It's my dream to complete my education. You always encouraged me to finish.

Tim: Well, I think it's stupid, foolish, and selfish—and I just don't see how we can manage this new part of your life. How can you possibly be happy?

What right is Tim violating or denying for Sue? How is Tim sabotaging Sue's feelings? Any suggestions for solutions to this problem?

Irrational Beliefs

Albert Ellis (Ellis and Harper, 1977) claims that we are socialized to believe many irrational beliefs that can act as debilitative emotions in relationships. These **irrational beliefs**, or fallacies, lead to illogical conclusions and result in debilitative emotions (Alder, Rosenfeld, and Towne, 1992, p. 219). Ellis provides us with seven fallacies upon which some of our irrational beliefs are based:

- **fallacy of perfection**—the irrational belief that we can be perfect if we just try hard enough
- **fallacy of approval**—the irrational belief that it is vital to obtain everyone's approval
- **fallacy of shoulds**—the inability to distinguish between what "is" and what "should be"; operating from a perspective that everything should be the way we want it
- **fallacy of overgeneralization**—making statements that are based on inadequate information which are usually phrased as absolutes ("you never listen to me") and are almost always false; low-level accuracy in messages
- **fallacy of causation**—the irrational belief that we can cause others to feel a certain way
- **fallacy of helplessness**—the irrational belief that satisfaction in life is determined by forces beyond control
- **fallacy of catastrophic expectations**—operating on the assumption that if something bad can happen, it will (Adler et al., pp. 219–224)

Many of these fallacies are ideological ideas that we were socialized to believe. For example, many of us were socialized to believe that we are victims and that there is nothing we can do about our inherited problems (fallacy of helplessness). We might buy into phrases such as, "I'm from a broken home so I will never be successful," or "My whole family is fat so I don't have a choice," or "That's just the way I am; there's nothing I can do about it." Or maybe we were raised to be perfect, which rationally we know is an impossible task, one that will frustrate us throughout out lives if we try to obtain it (fallacy of perfection). We might have been socialized to believe that we can control life and that everything "should" be the way we want it to be. As we all know, that philosophy causes a continually frustrating series of disappointments when things frequently do not go the way we want them to (fallacy of shoulds). Belief in these fallacies are irrational if we analyze the logic of their presuppositions. Life just does not work like that. By identifying the irrational beliefs that we may have, we will be able to remove a great deal of anger, fear, frustration, and conflict from our lives. This knowledge can help to improve the communication effectiveness in all of our relationships.

What Do You Think?

Jon was really upset. As the manager of his department, there seemed to be some employees who did not like him. They seemed impervious to his ideas and instructions. They did their work, but Jon wanted them to like him and their job. Was he not doing a good job? Why did some people not seem to like him? Finally he decided that if these unfriendly people did not like him or their job, then he would fire them. Let them find a job they enjoyed.

Which fallacy listed above did Jon buy into? What problems did it cause him?

Guidelines for Expressing Emotions

Emotions can be expressed verbally and nonverbally. Many times repressed emotions "leak" out through our nonverbal behaviors. If we do not allow them to be expressed verbally because we are denying or suppressing them, the emotions will be expressed through various nonverbal channels. Our goal is to make our verbal expression of emotions match our nonverbal expression. Incongruity between the verbal and nonverbal messages creates great confusion in the receiver causing low-level clarity in the intended message. Many times conflicts in relationships are based on these types of incongruent messages.

One of the biggest problems in expressing our emotions is the fear of doing so. We are afraid that the other person will be hurt, will reject us, or will misunderstand what we really feel. While these fears are legitimate fears, we must face our avoidance tendencies. If we do not, resistance to the expression of our feelings (for whatever reason) will probably surface in the form of indirect communication. **Indirect communication** is not saying what we really mean; it is sending messages that do not deal directly with the issue or problem. If I am angry at you for not keeping our agreement about keeping our apartment clean because you did not do your fair share, my message to you can be either direct or indirect:

Direct: "I feel angry because you did not uphold your part of the agreement about cleaning."

Indirect: "What are you doing this afternoon? Do you have any free time?"

OR "Have you seen Jane's apartment lately? It is such a mess. It makes me crazy. I could never live with her."

While direct communication is more effective and certainly more clear, it is also more difficult for most of us. It takes practice and a great deal of effort to keep your "buttons" from being pushed.

John Powell (1974) describes *five rules for disclosing feelings* at what he calls the "gut level" of communication (see chapter 7):

- gut level communication or emotional openness and honesty must never imply a judgment of the other
- emotions are not moral—there are no good or bad emotions, so do not judge yours or others
- feelings and emotions must be integrated with the intellect and the will
- emotions must be "reported"
- with rare exceptions, emotions must be reported at the time that they are being experienced (Powell, pp. 65–77)

David Johnson (1971) claims that not being aware of our feelings, not accepting our feelings, and low-level skill ability in expressing our feelings lead to indirect communication. Rather than sending clear, direct messages about our feelings, our feelings are communicated through the use of labels, commands, questions, accusations, sarcasm, approval, disapproval, "crazymaking," and name calling. Although these tactics are fairly common, they are equally ineffective in the development of productive communication skills.

Gay and Kathlyn Hendricks (1992) maintain that emotions should be expressed respectfully and immediately (or as soon as reasonably possible). In the '60s, this process was commonly called an encounter session. However, their recommended procedure of direct and immediate confrontation of feelings can be threatening to others who are not as "in touch" with their emotions as the sender of the message. Their recommendation for expressing emotions seems to necessitate a mutual agreement on and permission for these confrontations. Each person needs to be prepared or at least alerted to the fact that this "different" approach is being initiated—before it is used. The Hendricks claim that this process, which they call "conscious loving" (the title of their popular book) establishes an atmosphere of honesty, trust, and respect for each other when used in a loving, committed relationship. They caution, however, about using this process without permission, understanding, and prior consent from the other person.

What Do You Think?

Terry: Kelly, I'm really frustrated about our living situation. I need to talk to you about it.

Kelly: Not now, Terry.

Terry: But this is important to me, and I really need to talk to you about it.

Kelly: What could be so important, and why do we have to talk about everything all the time?

Terry: We hardly ever talk about things. You always say you don't want to or you can't imagine what's so important.

Kelly: Well, what is so important that you have to disturb my relaxing Sunday afternoon with your problems?

Terry: Oh, never mind.

What rule for self-disclosing feelings is Terry trying to utilize? Is this problem typical?

A Cognitive Approach to Emotion Control

Although emotions are difficult to identify and even more difficult to express, there are methods that attempt to assist us in doing so. Albert Ellis pioneered a therapeutic approach to emotion control (Ellis and Harper, 1977). **Rational Emotive Therapy** (RET) assumes that people make irrational assumptions that create emotional and behavioral problems. The technique involves substituting logical and rational premises for the irrational ones. For example, a friend tells us that another friend said something negative about us, so we irrationally decide not to speak to the offender ever again. Logically, a discussion with the offender might come first—before we make our decision. The four-step process Ellis suggests is aimed at helping us reduce irrational assumptions and self-defeating thoughts which lead to debilitative emotions:

How to Catch Yourself in the Act through R.E.T.

1 **monitor your emotional reactions**—record and register debilitative emotions, recognize what emotion you are feeling (anger and frustration)

2 **notice the activating event**—following the awareness of your feelings, figure out what event activated this particular response or emotion (the bumper-to-bumper traffic you experience everyday commuting)

3 **record your self-talk**—now record and analyze the thoughts that link the activating event to the feeling ("It makes me so angry when I have to sit in rush hour traffic. I'm so frustrated wasting all this time.")

4 **dispute your irrational beliefs**—using Adler's list of irrational beliefs that lead to debilitative feelings, identify which of these irrational beliefs are causing the feelings (fallacy of should and belief in the possibility of control) (Adler et al., 1992, pp. 224–225)

So, Rational Emotive Therapy asks us to dispute these irrational beliefs and substitute logic and reason. The final outcome is the realization that we are feeling an emotion caused by an irrational belief.

What Do You Think?

Using Ellis' Rational Emotive Therapy (RET), go through his four steps to discover any fallacies or irrational beliefs that you may have. Start with a small or inconsequential problem that you have recently dealt with and graduate to more crucial issues.

How Emotion Relates to Empathy

Without the expression of emotion, there can be no empathy. It is only through the expression of emotions and feelings that we begin to understand what empathy is and can exhibit it to others. If we deny our emotions, we remove our capacity for giving empathy. By definition, **empathy** means accepting another's feelings or demonstrating care for someone to show that you understand how they are feeling. This process requires feeling, emotion, and action. "Since emotion is a prime factor in achieving empathy, a clearer understanding of emotion is likely to add to the potential usefulness of empathy" (Weaver, 1993, p. 232). Emotion is a necessary component in Weaver's **four phases of empathy**:

- **feeling phase**—letting the other's feelings act on us
- **incorporation phase**—adding those feelings into ourselves
- **reverberation phase**—interacting with the feelings experienced by the other person
- **detachment phase**—pulling back and maintaining objectivity, having successfully engaged in the first three phases (p. 232)

The ability to express empathy creates a method of bonding that also provides tolerance for the differences in relationships. Our feelings and emotions make us perceive and act as we do; empathy is the process of understanding and appreciating another's feelings and perceptions which allows a bonding to occur. Without empathy, relationships are shallow and difficult at best. We cannot relate to each other well if we do not first understand each other and second appreciate each other for our individual differences.

Empathy is a key ingredient necessary for effective interpersonal communication (Keefe, 1976). Empathy refers to the ability to show our conversational partner that we understand his or her situation and that we share his or her emotional reactions to the situation (Gladstein, 1986). Empathy is also receiver based. Despite all our efforts to appear empathic, if the receiver does not perceive our communication behaviors as empathic, then the message of empathy we were trying to send was not received.

What Do You Think?

Terry: Damn, I'm so upset. I got a "D" on the test!

  Kim: Gee, I'm sorry, Terry. But don't worry about it; this one test won't affect your semester grade that much.

Terry: That's easy for you to say. You get all As.

  Kim: Well . . .

Terry: I don't need anyone to feel sorry for me—especially you.

Did Kim intend to provide an empathic response to Terry? Do you think Kim sent an empathic response? Did Terry think Kim sent an empathic response? How would you change the responses?

Summary

Emotions exert a strong force over our communication processes, so powerful that they can make us forget all that we have learned about effective interaction. While learning to identify our emotions is difficult enough, finding appropriate and effective ways of expressing them is even harder. However, not only is this process necessary but it is also helpful. Separating the debilitative feelings from the facilitative feelings will help us even more in the process of discovering effective ways of dealing with our emotions. Emotion is the pathway to empathy, for without emotion, empathy cannot exist. Empathy is a fundamental and necessary ingredient in the development of interpersonal competencies. Dealing effectively with emotion allows us to demonstrate appropriate expressions of empathy.

References

Adler, Ronald B., Lawrence B. Rosenfeld, and Neil Towne. *Interplay: The Process of Interpersonal Communication*, 5th ed. New York: Holt, Rinehart and Winston, 1992.

Bach, George R. and Ronald M. Deutsch. *Stop! You're Driving Me Crazy*. New York: Berkley Books, 1979.

Brown, Charles T. and Paul W. Keller. *Monologue to Dialogue: An Exploration of Interpersonal Communication*. Englewood Cliffs, NJ: Prentice-Hall, 1979.

Constantine, Larry L. *Treating Relationships*. Lake Mills, IA: Graphic, 1976.

A Course in Miracles. Tiburon, CA: Foundation for Inner Peace, 1976.

DeVito, Joseph A. *The Communication Handbook: A Dictionary*. New York: HarperCollins, 1986.

Ellis, Albert and Robert A. Harper. *A New Guide to Rational Living*. North Hollywood, CA: Wilshire Books, 1977.

Gladstein, G. A. "Understanding Empathy: Integrating Counseling, Development and Social Psychology Perspectives," *Journal of Counseling Psychology*, 30, (1986): 467–82.

Hay, Louise L. *You Can Heal Your Life*. Santa Monica: Hay House, 1986.

Hendricks, Gay and Kathlyn Hendricks. *Conscious Loving*. New York: Bantam Books, 1992.

Jampolsky, Gerald G. *Love Is Letting Go of Fear*. Berkeley, CA: Celestial Arts, 1979.

Johnson, David. "The Effects of Expressing Warmth and Anger upon the Actor and the Listener," *Journal of Counseling Psychology*, 18 (1971): 571–78.

Keefe, T. "Empathy: The Critical Skill," *Social Work*, 21 (1976): 10–14.

Kelley, Colleen. "Jealousy: A Proactive Approach." In *The 1980 Annual Handbook for Group Facilitators*, J. William Pfeiffer and John E. Jones, eds. La Jolla: University Associates, Inc., 1980.

Kirschner, Samuel. (Speaker). *Coming Home To Yourself*, (cassette recording). New York: Invincible Voices, 1987.

Kranzler, Gerald. *You Can Change How You Feel: A Rational-Emotive Approach*. Eugene, OR: RETC Press, 1974.

Powell, John. *The Secret of Staying in Love*. Niles, IL: Argus Communications, 1974.

Sullivan, Harry S. *The Interpersonal Theory of Psychiatry*. New York: Norton, 1953.

Weaver, Richard L. II. *Understanding Interpersonal Communication*, 6th ed. Glenview, IL: Scott, Foresman, 1993.

Williamson, Marianne. *A Return to Love*. New York: HarperCollins, 1992.

Case 31

TargetTerms

- crazymaking
- right to know
- right to impact
- jealousy

- debilitative emotions
- fallacy of shoulds
- fallacy of helplessness
- fallacy of overgeneralization

PreviewNotes

Uncertainty causes insecurity—if we are not reassured in relationships, we begin to question others' intentions and our self worth. Jealousy can emerge because of our insecurity.

CaseParticipants

Joan Byrnes—38 years old, married, mother of young children; shared the circumstances of her extramarital relationship with her friend, Ann Sharf (Case 28), presently is involved with Brandon Reynolds and is going through some difficult moments of self-doubt and worth

Brandon Reynolds—42 years old, married, practicing physician; father of two grown children; seriously and illicitly involved with Joan Byrnes

"Green with insecurity"

In the past year, Joan and Brandon have been meeting each other secretly following a high school reunion. As careful as they are about not being "found out," Joan has still found it necessary to disclose the relationship to her friend—and lately, is not having an easy time with this secret life. Joan tries to convey this to Brandon when she calls him one morning at the office.

Joan: I'm sorry that I caught you in the middle of something, but I couldn't let this go without talking to you.

Brandon: We've been over this at least a thousand times before—(*rather emphatically*)—try to avoid calling me while I'm seeing patients.

Joan: I can't believe that you're doing this to me.

Brandon: Look, I'll get back to you in an hour or so. (*whispering*) I just can't talk right now.

Joan: I guess I have no choice. I'll wait for your call. Speak to you later.

SEVEN HOURS LATER

Brandon: Hi! Is this a bad time?

Joan: No-no. I'm so glad to finally hear your voice. You had me so worried. You specifically told me that you would call me right back. I've been waiting all day.

Brandon: I said I'd call back.

Joan: Earlier than this.

Brandon: Listen, I'll get to see you tomorrow afternoon. I'm sure whatever it is can wait.

Joan: For a man who is so proud of keeping his word, you certainly are changing your tune these days.

Brandon: What is that supposed to mean?

Joan: Don't you have any idea of what I go through to see you each week?

Brandon: I don't deserve this—over not having the chance to call you while a patient was in respiratory distress? C'mon . . .

Joan: I was literally going crazy waiting for you to call.

Brandon: Well, now you're not going crazy anymore, so let's forget it. Now on to a brighter note, I can't wait to see you tomorrow because I want to take you somewhere very special.

Joan: You can't turn hot and cold on me just like that.

Brandon: What is with you today?

Joan: You are totally oblivious to what is going on in my life. It's as if we don't know each other at all.

Brandon: All right. If it will make you feel any better, talk.

Joan: What makes you think that I can just "talk"?

Brandon: What else did you say you wanted to do when you called? (*thinking that this is almost funny*) Am I crazy or did you say that you wanted to "talk" to me about something very important?

Joan: (*thinking that this is not so funny*) Will you stop patronizing me? I'm not one of your kids.

Brandon: I told you never to bring them into this.

Joan: You know what I meant.

Brandon: Obviously, I didn't.

Joan: How come this is not coming out right at all?

Brandon: We made a promise—remember?

Joan: What promise?

Brandon: Not to let our emotions rule us.

Joan: How would you know about emotions? I'm the one who literally has everything to lose.

Brandon: Are we into "measuring" now?

Joan: Oh, I don't know. I just had lunch with Ann today.

Brandon: Now, I'm getting the picture. She with the happy home—you're feeling good and sorry for yourself.

Joan: Do you realize what you put me through waiting for your call?

Brandon: You've got to start being more objective and think of what I go through during a day.

Joan: Will you try to understand that if anything terrible ever happened to you—which I made myself hysterical thinking about—that I would probably be the last person to know—and I spend so much time with you! I think that stinks!

Brandon: Joan, you are being irrational now.

Joan: Tell that kind of stuff to your patients—not me.

Brandon: Will it make you feel any better knowing that we'll see each other tomorrow for the entire afternoon?

Joan: I'm feeling so helpless.

Brandon: It'll work out. Believe me.

Joan: How can you possibly know what I'm feeling?

Brandon: Don't you think I know?

Joan: I wish I could believe that.

CaseConcerns

1. What crazymaking "rights" does Joan have in this case? Which ones does Brandon have? Explain.
2. Explain how the debilitative emotions of jealousy and fear have affected Joan's communication ability and effectiveness.
3. Albert Ellis identifies seven fallacies upon which our irrational beliefs are based. Identify which fallacies affect Joan and how.

ReflectiveResponses

1. Identify a situation when you were a victim of irrational belief fallacy. What did you do about it? How did you handle it?
2. Identify any crazymaking rights that you are guilty of misusing with significant others. Then identify areas in which you feel you have been violated.
3. Why do you think we feel insecure or jealous in relationships?
4. Jealousy is a powerful emotion. How do you deal with it in your intimate relationships?

Case 32

TargetTerms

- crazymaking
- right to impact
- anger
- debilitative emotions
- fallacy of shoulds

PreviewNotes

People view and use time in very different ways. The anger created when two different perspectives collide is usually based on irrational beliefs. Do we have the right to expect people to live up to their commitments or our expectations? How do we learn to respect each other's differences?

CaseParticipants

Hal Johnston—32-year-old employee of a downtown service station and garage; athletic, very much the outdoor type; hates to waste time and likes to keep his life in order

Josh Macintyre—30-year-old professional sports trainer; spends the better part of his life toning up and keeping fit

"Well, it's about time!"

For the past three years Josh and Hal, long-time buddies, have been steady racquetball partners. Since their work schedules are fairly tight in terms of leisure time, they try to set aside a few hours each week when they can "hit" together. This time also gives them a chance to find out how "life" has been going for each of them. However, this morning of play presents a problem for Hal, as he has been waiting for almost half an hour for Josh to meet him at the town racquetball courts. Since this is not the first time this has happened, Hal is especially aggravated when Josh finally shows— and doesn't seem to be the least bit apologetic about being late.

Hal: What the hell is the story with you?

Josh: What do you mean?

Hal: Oh, jeez—you don't even know why I'm pissed off.

Josh: So, why are ya?

Hal: Do you know what time it is?

Josh: No—what time is it?

Hal: Twenty-five minutes after you were supposed to be here.

Josh: Well, that's your problem. Why didn't you go have a stiff drink or something—seems like you might need one.

Hal: Because someone was looking like he wanted the court and I wasn't willing to give it up.

Josh: So what's the problem?

Hal: Dammit, why are you always so late?

Josh: I was stuck at the dentist.

Hal: (*angrily*) Well, you know what time we meet. You should have taken that into account.

Josh: Listen, I wasn't especially thrilled about being tortured with a drill all morning. That's not my idea of having fun, ya know.

Hal: Why couldn't you have called?

Josh: You see a paging system here? Make a big deal of this, why don't you!

Hal: My time is money, and if you knew you'd be cutting it so close—

Josh: What was I supposed to do? A filling came out, and before I died from eating another thing that touched the damn tooth, I took care of it. Playing racquetball still beats the hell out of getting your tooth drilled!

Hal: (*still angry*) Last week, it was an emergency foreign car job, and next week it'll be a flat tire.

Josh: What's with you today? Boy—did you ever get up on the wrong side of the bed! (*He walks off the court.*)

CaseConcerns

1. Who was "right" in this case?
2. Why is Hal mad? Should he be? Does he have a right to be angry? Why does Josh feel like this is not a big deal? What role do you play most often?

ReflectiveResponses

1. When someone is late for an appointment or a meeting, what crazymaking "right" has he or she violated? Why does this situation make us feel so angry or upset?

2. Describe your "time" behavior and identify realistically its impact on others. Do you violate any crazymaking "rights"?

3. What is the message that people send to others if they are late. What circumstances allow tardiness? Which do not? How does your use of time affect the way you communicate in your relationships? Think of one example.

Case 33

TargetTerms

- debilitative emotions
- anger
- fallacy of perfection
- fallacy of shoulds
- Rational Emotive Therapy

PreviewNotes

When we have a strong need to be right and a belief in perfectionism, we sometimes let our emotions take control. The strength of our emotions then overshadows our logical reasoning resulting in ineffective communication.

CaseParticipants

Susan—renowned decorator who has a tendency to be a
     perfectionist
Ted—Susan's husband
Contractor—person in charge of the renovation project

"My way or else!"

The following case depicts a scene where we meet Susan, a well-known interior designer, who is fastidious about her design work. She demands that her instructions be executed exactly. Thus, she often finds herself frustrated by things she cannot control and the people who are not precise in performing their tasks. Susan has decided to renovate and update her own residence. On one shopping trip to the city for the project, her husband suggests that he accompany her. The following conversation takes place in a showroom.

Susan: So do you like the fabric?

Ted: Not really.

Susan: Hmmmm—you never expressed an interest in my work before. All of a sudden you're an expert!

Ted: You asked me—remember?

Susan: No—you asked to accompany me.

Ted: Whatever! (*He begins to raise his voice.*) You asked me, and I told you that I don't like the color, the texture or the design.

Susan: What do you know? You're a lawyer. And stop yelling. You're making a scene—I see these people daily and they will think we're both nuts.

Ted: Susan, my patience is wearing thin.

Susan: (*She places her arm in his and leads him toward the exit.*) Well, so is mine. C'mon, let's go. I'll order the fabric over the phone. It'll certainly be far less trouble.

THREE MONTHS LATER

With fabrics, wallcoverings, and furnishings chosen, Susan is immersed in her renovation project. Workmen are all around the house, and Susan appears to be in her glory while orchestrating the project. While inspecting the overhead lighting placement, Susan goes crazy. Abruptly calling over the foreman, Susan angrily draws out the blueprints and says:

Susan: (*climbing the ladder with ruler in hand.*) Look! Each light is thirty-two inches from the other—not thirty-four as the plans stipulate.

Contractor: (*smiling at her*) Yes.

Susan: How can you be so stupid? This is wrong—this is all wrong. You didn't follow my plans.

Contractor: Hey, listen, lady—there's a stud in the wall. I took the liberty of spacing the lights differently to finish the electrical work. The sheetrock people are coming in tomorrow—the lighting effect will be the same.

Susan: It's not the same. The overheads were not hung according to plan, and I am furious! That's not what I designed—nor did I tell you to do that. How could you not consult me?

Contractor: I am just doing my job. (*with a touch of sarcasm*) I also know what I'm doing. And besides—the men from the next crew will be on the job in just another hour, and I wanted to take advantage of the timing.

Susan: Take it all down.

Contractor: But the timing on the project will be completely off with this change. It will back up all the other contractors . . .

Susan: I don't care—I want it done right.

Contractor: It'll be another month, lady, since we have another job to do.

Susan: (*angrily, and almost crying*) You made a commitment to me, and I can promise you that I will never refer you for any work again.

Contractor: (*signals to his crew to come down from the ladders*) That's just too bad. (*He looks directly at her.*) Don't worry lady—we're outta here!

Susan watches with horror as the men gather their belongings while walking off the job.

CaseConcerns

1. Identify the debilitative emotions demonstrated by Susan's behavior in this case. Why were they debilitative?
2. Under what irrational belief fallacies did Susan operate? How did they affect her communication behavior? What was the result?
3. Describe how Susan could use Ellis' Rational Emotive Therapy (RET). What might have changed about this case had Susan used this method of dealing with debilitative emotions? Do you think this method is realistic?

ReflectiveResponses

1. How do you deal with the need for perfection? Does it affect the way you communicate with others? Give an example of how it does or does not.
2. What happens to your communication behavior when you cannot get something you want from others? Describe a situation in which this debilitative emotion (perfectionism and control) affected your communication. What did you do about it? What was the result?

9
Chapter

Sex Roles

Specific Goals for Understanding Chapter Nine

TargetTerms

- sex
- gender
- sex role
- gender role
- stereotype

- instrumental orientation
- expressive orientation
- platonic relationship
- sexual harassment
- androgyny

CoreConcepts

1 the definitions of sex roles, gender roles, and stereotypes
2 the research background on sex-role and gender-role stereotypes
3 the relationship consequences of stereotypes: friendships, intimate relationships, and parental relationships
4 the gender differences in human communication
5 dealing with sexual harassment
6 the development of balanced relationships through androgyny

"It's not my job . . ."

Overview

A common argument that ensues during relationships is the one about who is supposed to do what. We are taught to believe that along with our biological sex comes certain duties and responsibilities. These sex-role stereotypes restrict us. If males are trained to think that they are not supposed to clean houses or care for children and women are trained to think that they are supposed to do these things, a pattern of "shoulds" develops that restricts the behaviors of both sexes. These learned behaviors then turn into roles that we play and end up becoming sex-specific when, in fact, they have no connection to biological functioning but rather are psychological and sociological orientations. Susan Basow (1980) argues that sex-role stereotypes are based on few actual sex differences; they also "seriously limit individual functioning and have a negative effect on relationships" (p. 4).

In this chapter, we will explore sex-role stereotypes and their impact upon our relationships. We will discover the definitions of important terms such as sex roles, gender roles, and stereotypes; the background relevant to specific sex-role and gender-role stereotypes; the consequences of stereotypes on our friendships, our intimate relationships, and our parental roles; the gender differences in human communication; and the potential of androgyny to create more balanced, healthy relationships.

Definitions and Background

Definitions

Most people confuse the terms sex and gender, which, when defined, help clarify a fundamental misconception. As communication writers we often find that there are disparities in usage in personal, social, and business applications of sex and gender labels. How often have we seen surveys that ask for our gender in the response instead of correctly asking to identify our sex as male or female. **Sex** is a biological term; people are either male or female according to their sex organs and genes. **Sex roles** are those assigned to people by virtue of their biological sex. **Gender** is a psychological and cultural term; it refers to our subjective feelings of maleness or femaleness and provides each person with a gender identity (Basow, 1980). When society influences this identity, an evaluation of an individual's behaviors as masculine or feminine is produced and the behavior becomes a **gender role**. A **role** is "a cluster of socially or culturally defined expectations that individuals in a given situation are expected to fulfill" (Chafetz, 1978, p. 4). These oversimplified conceptions of our behaviors as males and females can become either **sex-role stereotypes** or **gender-role stereotypes**. Sometimes society creates these stereotypes. If we accept them and believe that they are true, we perpetuate the stereotype. For example, many in our society still maintain that men are the primary breadwinners; fortunately, this stereotype is gradually diminishing in its impact and power on society.

What Do You Think?

David loved art. His goal was to be a sculptor, but his father wanted him to take over the family business and fulfill his role as a provider. David was frustrated because he did not really want to do what his father wanted him to do. As a result, he never communicated his feelings.

Was David a victim of sex-role or gender-role stereotyping? Explain his father's philosophy regarding sex and gender roles.

L. Wrightsman (1977) defines **stereotype** as "a relatively rigid and oversimplified conception of a group of people in which all individuals in the group are labeled with the so-called group characteristics" (p. 672). Saying that all young toddlers whine does not account for the fact that there are happy, pleasant children who never whine. These strongly held overgeneralizations are learned through the socialization process and can be universally perpetuated within a society, causing restrictive behavior and reduced human potential. Labeling people with generalized characteristics disallows individuality and personal growth.

Background

Many researchers have found evidence of these existing sex-role and gender-role stereotypes in our society. Most indicate that about 75 percent of all people believe in and strongly uphold differences in characteristics between males and females based on their sex alone.[1] This means that most people label males and females by stereotypical sex-role traits. The traditional distinctions are that males are aggressive, logical, unemotional, objective, and independent (**instrumental**

orientation); females are traditionally viewed as non-aggressive, illogical, emotional, subjective, and dependent (**expressive orientation**). In addition, both males and females typically rate the male characteristic as more desirable.[2] However, research does not support this "opposite trait philosophy" but rather indicates little or no correlation between the male and female role (Bem, 1974; Spence and Helmreich, 1978). People are just not that simple that they are either all masculine or all feminine; some men are genuinely sensitive to the needs of others and some women can be very competitive and aggressive. Unfortunately, negative connotations are usually implied when these people deviate from the norm (the stereotype that society has established). For example, a majority of people may find it more acceptable for a female to become a ballet dancer than it is for a male. While our society seems to be advancing its perceptions to more open-mindedness, the stereotype still, for the most part, reinforces the norm. Masculinity and femininity simply are not bipolar opposites and are not necessarily connected directly or only with one sex.

What Do You Think?

Debbie had always wanted to organize things and take control as a leader. She was very assertive and worked hard to get what she wanted. As a little girl, she was referred to as "bossy," and as she grew up people started calling her a bitch.

Was Debbie exhibiting instrumental or expressive character-istics? Why were people so cruel to her by calling her those names? What does society do to women who demonstrate masculine characteristics such as leadership, aggressiveness, or determination? If Debbie were a man, would the same communication occur? Why or why not?

The culprit of this unrealistic, sex-linked dichotomy is the original division of labor by sex in our society. What once seemed practical and necessary developed into a rigid structure of sex-specific roles. Now, despite the fact that a division of labor is no longer functional or even practical, the stereotypes remain. However, the argument is that "rigid sex typing is neither necessary nor functional to the individual, to her or his relationships, or to society as a whole" (Basow, 1980, p. 163). The consequences far outweigh the benefits when people are restricted in the development of human potentiation through sex-role stereotyping.

Relationship Consequences of Sex-Role Stereotypes

Not only do sex-role stereotypes restrict individual development, they also strongly affect the relationships we have with others. Logically, if an individual is restricted in behaviors which might enhance self-development, that restriction will also affect the way he or she interacts with others. The negative effects on friendships (same sex and opposite sex), intimate relationships, and parental relationships are pervasive. Both sexes would benefit from an androgynous approach to communication competency (McCroskey, Richmond, and Stewart, 1986, p. 285), which will be discussed later in the chapter.

Friendships

Friendship is an interpersonal relationship between two persons that is mutually productive and characterized by mutual positive regard (DeVito, 1995, p. 428). How we treat those friends is often decided by their sex rather than their gender. Unfortunately, treating people like a stereotype (in this case a sex-role stereotype) usually results in poor relationship communication because the person does not feel as though you understand them. Do you communicate with your same-sex friends in the same way that you communicate with your opposite-sex friends? Probably not, and although this may be appropriate sometimes, other times it is harmful to the relationship. People generally do not like being treated stereotypically.

Friendships are influenced by the sex of the friend. While males tend to have a large number of casual, same-sex friends, females tend to engage in fewer but more intimate same-sex relationships (Basow, 1980). Male relationships tend to be more superficial and developed primarily through the instrumental function; however, they are restricted by four barriers:

- emphasis on competition and being right
- suppression of emotions
- homophobia
- lack of adequate positive role models (Basow, 1980, pp. 211–217; McCroskey et al., 1986, pp. 247–248).

While same-sex female relationships seem to run on a continuum between intimacy and rejection (Bardwick, 1979), females develop friendships for three major reasons:

- recreation/shared activities
- personal support/need for a confidant
- problem solving (McCroskey et al., 1986, pp. 247–248)

Reciprocity is more obvious in same-sex female relationships than in the parallel male type, but females are more likely to give up a female friendship for a relationship with a male. Males develop friendships with other males in order to get what they can from the relationships without tending to reciprocate; this is an extension of the male instrumental orientation in contrast to the female expressive orientation (McCroskey et al., 1986, pp. 247–251).

What Do You Think?

Ray and Jim were best friends and buddies. They did almost everything together. People would ask where the other one was if they were ever seen alone. But pretty soon the questions became insinuations of homosexuality. Doesn't it seem like Ray and Jim are a little "too close" as friends? Don't they seem too intimate for men?

Why are people uncomfortable with intimacy between men? Can men have emotional intimacy without the accusation of physical intimacy? What stereotypes are operating here? If Ray and Jim were lovers, why does society have to be so judgmental about two people who really love each other? If Ray and Jim were not lovers but rather close, intimate same-sex friends, why does society have to be so judgmental about two people of the same sex who love each other?

Opposite-sex friendships are viewed negatively by our society because of stereotypical sex-role behaviors; the norms and expectations of these stereotypes impact upon the development of the relationship. Single men and women seem to have a difficult time establishing a non-sexual or platonic relationship. Societal norms and expectations force sexual overtures and impede the development of a platonic relationship. Males have a difficult time with intimacy, especially without sex. Consequently, these **platonic relationships** receive low-level acceptance and have a low success rate in our culture. While many college students might claim otherwise, the work world seems to follow these societal norms. A woman is viewed negatively if she travels with another man, even if on a business trip.

Intimate Relationships

Life is filled with examples of how roles restrict males and females in intimate relationships. Whether we consider the concept of power, interpersonal needs, self-concept, values, or self-disclosure, the effects of the roles we play and the games we act out because of these roles can play havoc with our relationships. When a relationship becomes important to us, we start to create rules, regulations, and roles which become rigid and restrictive. Add these to the sex-roles we already play, and the impact on the relationship is devastating. Game-playing and manipulation is prevalent in intimate relationships which disallows the development of healthy relationships.

What Do You Think?

Tony and Lisa were living together for three years and having a wonderful relationship. They always talked to each other about different matters. Recently, they decided to get married. Six months later, Tony and Lisa were at each others' throats about money and were having constant arguments over who is supposed to do what in a marriage.

What happened to this relationship? Why do you suppose their interpersonal communication changed after their marriage?

Parental Relationships

Playing the role of a parent in and of itself creates many restrictions. Add to these preliminary role restrictions, the restrictions of sex-role expectations, and we create an even more difficult situation. In many cases, men traditionally have fallen into the role of the breadwinner and women into the roles of motherhood and homemaker. These limitations disallow men and women from performing other valuable roles that could contribute to their effectiveness in parenting. For example, men can help with car pools and women can coach little league. If we subscribe to narrow roles, we limit our contributions to parenting, thus depriving children of the benefits of each parent's strengths.

What Do You Think?

Mary: Stan, can you pick up Suzie at school and take her to the dentist tomorrow at 4:30?

Stan: That means I have to rearrange my afternoon schedule and I really don't want to do that.

Mary: Well, too bad. I don't really want to do a lot of the running around I do for the kids, but I do, and you can help.

Stan: Why can't you do it? It's your job, not mine.

Mary: Because I have an important meeting at the office which I can't miss—and what do you mean, it's my job?

Stan: Just what I said. The wife's job is to take care of the kids.

Mary: Even if she's employed?

What sex-role stereotypes does Stan follow? How does this affect the way he communicates with his wife?

Gender Differences in Communication

While there are no sex-linked differences in the way males and females communicate, there are gender-role differences that distinguish the sexes in the communication process. These learned, gender-role communication patterns are taught to us by society—parents, friends, teachers, peers, and the media. Strangely enough, these gender-role differences have come to be perceived as sex-role differences, when, in fact, they are not linked to our biological sex. The most evident **gender differences in communication** are:

- **the type and amount of information self-disclosed**
- **the language used**
- **the subject matter discussed**
- **nonverbal communication patterns** (eye contact, facial expression, posture, personal space, and touch) (McCroskey et al., 1986, pp. 241–247).

Use and interpretation of these communication behaviors distinguishes the differences between our psychological gender roles in the communication process. The danger comes when we treat others as though their sex requires them to be responsible for a certain role or task.

What Do You Think?

Liz: I've been thinking. I would like to talk about our sex life to see where we can improve it. What do you think?

Joe: What? You must be kidding. Our sex life is great!

Liz: Well, maybe that's what you think, but I have been reading some articles on things we can do to increase the spontaneity and increase the passion in our relationship through sex.

Joe: Good grief. I can't believe we're talking about this. As a matter of fact, I will not talk about this. You don't plan your sex life; it just happens.

Liz: No, I mean I think our sex is great. I just want to talk about it to see if we can improve it in any way. Do you know what I mean?

Joe: No, I don't know what you mean and I don't care. Now, what time is dinner? I'm starving.

Which gender differences in communication are evident in this scene?

Dealing with Sexual Harassment

A prominent issue in the workplace is how to deal with sexual harassment. **Sexual harassment** represents a negative form of interpersonal communication and is defined through a description of the actions taken against a person and the feelings that person has about those actions (Neher and Waite, 1993). The Equal Employment Opportunity Commission (EEOC) is the major federal agency responsible for defining and enforcing regulations regarding sexual harassment in the workplace. While sexual harassment can occur between coworkers, it is of particular concern in the superior-subordinate relationship. When the aggrieved person is a victim of unwelcome sexual suggestions, requests, remarks, or actions by someone who has or is perceived to have power over the victim, that is sexual harassment. As a result of such behaviors, the aggrieved person feels that an environment of intimidation and hostility has been created which interferes with their performance.

At its most blatant, sexual harassment consists of a supervisor's demanding sexual favors from a subordinate in return for some reward or promotion (Neher and Waite, 1993). However, the courts have recently ruled through various cases that the behavior need not be that blatant nor even involve physical contact. "The key is whether or not a so-called hostile or intimidating climate has been created" (p. 143).

Sexual harassment and the results of cases recently tried in court remind us about the need for empathy and respect in interpersonal communication. We must attempt to see the other person's frame of reference. We need to visualize how the other person perceives our communication message. Most organizations and companies have developed very specific policies describing sexual harassment and the penalties for it. We as individuals need to evaluate our interpersonal communication behaviors to discover any abusive language or actions toward others. How we talk to others has a high impact on our relationships.

What Do You Think?

Jack: Lisa, please come in to my office for a minute.

Lisa: Certainly, Mr. Thompson. What is it?

Jack: I really need help on this, and I know you're the one to do the job.

Lisa: Well, you know I always try my best to do a good job for you and the company.

Jack: If you can pull this off, there's gonna be a promotion in it for you. I think it's time.

Lisa: Why thanks, Mr. Thompson. I appreciate your recognition of my efforts.

Jack: Your appreciation is acknowledged. Now, can you solve this Henderson project mess? We're going to lose this client unless they get special service and no doubletalk about the problems they're raising. Can you be upfront and straightforward with them and untangle this disaster?

Lisa: I will certainly try. I know the problems pretty well, and I'm pretty sure I can convince them to stay on with our company.

Jack: Thanks. I feel relieved that you are in charge. (*stands to thank her as she gets up to exit*)

Lisa: I'll get right on it.

Jack: (*puts his arm around her waist*) I just bet you will—as I said, I know you've got what it takes to get that promotion. (*He winks at her and pats her on the butt.*)

What would you do if you were Lisa? Is this an example of sexual harassment? Why or why not.

Androgyny and Balanced Relationships

In order to have healthy, balanced relationships, certain traits must be fostered and the rigid sex-role and gender-role stereotypes must be removed. Bem (1974, 1975, 1976) offers the concept of **androgyny**, the integration of masculine and feminine character traits within a single individual. This ability to endorse characteristics that are typically male or female allows an individual to have a wider range of role behaviors, thus establishing a flexibility in selection of communication patterns. Sex-typed individuals limit themselves in their choices of communication behavior patterns because they endorse only those characteristics that are "approved" for their sex. Sex-typed males endorse sex-role stereotyped male behaviors (instrumental orientation) and sex-typed females endorse sex-role stereotyped female behaviors (expressive orientation). On the other hand, androgynous individuals can be assertive as a leader in the board room and sensitive as a volunteer at the day care center—whether they are male or female. Androgyny implies nothing about one's sexual identity or orientation; it implies the degree of flexibility one has over imposed sex-role stereotypical behaviors (Basow, 1980, p. 10).

McCroskey et al. (1986) present the Bem-Wheeless concept of androgyny as a necessary competency-based skill which is required in order to be considered "communicatively competent" (p. 281). Along with assertiveness (instrumental orientation) and responsiveness (expressive orientation), these researchers maintain that the ability to endorse and display communication behaviors that are both masculine (assertive) and feminine (responsive) establishes the balanced mixture which enhances effective, competent communication behaviors and promotes healthy, balanced relationships.

What Do You Think?

David was a very unusual father, at least according to the traditional norms of fatherhood. He loved watching his children, taking care of them when they were hurt or sick, and nurturing them by spending quality time with them whenever possible. He put his children first—before his job and usually even before himself. David was the manager of his department and had to make difficult decisions every day. He was aggressive in working his way up the corporate ladder in order to achieve success for himself and his family.

Do you think David is demonstrating the characteristics of androgyny? How and why?

Summary

Distinguishing between sex and gender is vital to the understanding of how we unconsciously label ourselves and others with sex-role stereotypes. Our sex in no way determines our characteristics as a human being; it is our acceptance of the socialized sex-role stereotype that defines and restricts our communication effectiveness. Releasing ourselves and others from this trap of rigid behavior patterns frees us from limited development as a person and allows us to utilize a full repertoire of human communication patterns. By not accepting or endorsing the restrictions thrust upon us by society because of our sex, we can more easily develop a wider spectrum of effective communication patterns. Androgyny, then, becomes the desired goal in developing balanced, healthy relationships.

Notes

[1] Two studies discovered that strong agreement exists about the differing characteristics of men and women (Broverman, Vogel, Broverman, Clarkson, and Rosenkrantz, 1972; Rosenkrantz, Vogel, Bee, Broverman, and Broverman, 1968).

[2] More recent studies verify this data (for example, Foushee, Helmreich, and Spence, 1979; Gilbert, Deutsch, and Strahan, 1979; Tunnell, 1979).

References

Bardwick, J. M. *In Transition*. New York: Holt, Rinehart and Winston, 1979.

Basow, Susan A. *Sex-Role Stereotypes: Traditions and Alternatives*. Monterey, CA: Brooks/Cole, 1980.

Bem, Sandra L. "The Measurement of Psychological Androgyny." *Journal of Consulting and Clinical Psychology*, 42 (1974): 155–162.

_____. "Sex-Role Adaptability: One Consequence of Psychological Androgyny." *Journal of Personality and Social Psychology*, 31 (1975): 634–643.

_____. "Probing the Promise of Androgyny." In *Beyond Sex-Role Stereotypes: Readings toward a Psychology of Androgyny*, A. Kaplan and J. Bean, eds. Boston, MA: Little, Brown, 1976.

Broverman, I., S. R. Vogel, D. M. Broverman, F. Clarkson, and P. S. Rosenkrantz. "Sex-Role Stereotypes: A Current Appraisal." *Journal of Social Issues*, 28 (1972): 59–78.

Chafetz, J. S. *Masculine/Feminine or Human?* 2nd ed. Itasca, IL: Peacock, 1978.

DeVito, Joseph A. *The Interpersonal Communication Book*, 7th ed. New York: HarperCollins, 1995.

Foushee, H. C., R. L. Helmreich, and J. T. Spence. "Implicit Theories of Masculinity and Femininity: Dualistic or Bipolar?" *Psychology of Women Quarterly*, 3 (1979): 259–269.

Gilbert, L. A., C. J. Deutsch, and R. F. Strahan. "Feminine and Masculine Dimensions of the Typical, Desirable, and Ideal Woman and Man," *Sex Roles*, 4 (1979): 767–778.

McCroskey, James C., Virginia P. Richmond, and Robert A. Stewart. *One on One: The Foundations of Interpersonal Communication*. Englewood Cliffs, NJ: Prentice-Hall, 1986.

Neher, William W. and David H. Waite. *The Business and Professional Communicator*. Boston: Allyn and Bacon, 1993.

Rosenkrantz, P., S. R. Vogel, H. Bee, I. K. Broverman, and D. M. Broverman. "Sex-Role Stereotypes and Self Concepts in College Students," *Journal of Consulting and Clinical Psychology* 32 (1968): 287–295.

Spence, J. T. and R. L. Helmreich. *Masculinity and Femininity: The Psychological Dimensions, Correlates and Antecedents*. Austin: University of Texas Press, 1978.

Tunnell, G. "Age and Sex Effects on Social Desirability of Sex-Role Characteristics." Paper presented at the American Psychological Association Convention, New York, September, 1979.

Wrightsman, L. *Social Psychology*, 2nd ed. Monterey, CA: Brooks/Cole, 1977.

Case 34

TargetTerms

- sex roles
- gender roles
- stereotypes
- norms

PreviewNotes

He was trained to think one way. She was trained to think another. Can a happy medium be met so that they can ultimately understand each other's point of view? Sometimes it's very hard, especially when it comes to sex roles.

CaseParticipants

Carol O'Donnell—30-year-old mother of a boy and a girl, Jim, Jr. and Susie, ages eighteen months and seven years old respectively; determined and sometimes known to be stubborn; has a special relationship with both of her children

Jim O'Donnell—34-year-old father to Jim, Jr., and Susie; married for nine years to Carol; hard worker and thinks of himself as more of a family man than anything else

"My son will not wear bows!"

Jim and Carol are at the mall on a Saturday afternoon doing errands—some of which involve Christmas preparations. One of the items on the list is to outfit the newest family addition, Jim, Jr., for the family holiday gathering. Jim seems annoyed by the crowds of shoppers and wants to go home. Carol spies something in the window of a store, saying:

Carol: Oh, look, there's a cute French shop where we can buy Jim Jr. an outfit. I love the one in the window. Let's go in.

Jim: Just for a few minutes. I want to get back to the game at home.

Carol: Oh, c'mon. Don't be so grouchy. (*enters the store*) Look how adorable everything is. Oh, honey, just look at this one.

Jim: Which one?

Carol: (*very tenderly*) This cute rainbow-colored overall set with all of the appliques on it.

Jim: What about the big bow on the top? My son is not wearing that.

Carol: It's not a bow. It's a tie, and I love it.

Jim: It has two loops and polka dots on it, and no son of mine will be caught dead in that.

Carol: Jim—he's just a baby. Little boys should look like little boys. I hate when children look so sophisticated—

Jim: That's not the issue. I'm not raising him to be a sissy.

Carol: Stop getting so excited. You sound ridiculous.

Jim: That is not a tie. Anyone can see that it's a bow. Just ask that woman over there.

Woman: Sorry, but I couldn't help hearing—

Carol: That's because my husband doesn't know when to lower his voice. (*turns to the lady*) Well, what do you think?

Woman: It does look like a bow to me.

Carol: (*She turns away.*) Well, I love the outfit, and that's really what matters. With his eyes against that color, he'll look adorable for Christmas.

Jim: He'll look like an idiot in it. Besides that, the family will think I'm the idiot for allowing you to let him wear it.

Carol: So, now, you're "allowing" me to buy Jim Jr.'s clothes. Did I ever need your consent to buy Susie's baby clothes?

Jim: Well, she's a girl.

Carol: Thank you for that enlightening piece of information. So, how come you never took an interest if she had a tie on her dress? Huh?

Jim: It was O.K. if she had a tie.

Carol: But she can have bows, too?

Jim: Ah, Carol—you know what I mean!

Carol: Yeah, what's good for the goose isn't necessarily good for the gander.

Jim: Don't make a big deal of this.

Carol: I never knew that you were so chauvinistic!

Jim: Stop it—I'm not.

Carol: Well, what do you call it? You never bossed me around like this before. So, you are a chauvinist. And I'm buying the outfit.

Jim: If you do, he won't wear it.

Carol: And how often do you stay around to see him dressed? (*paying the clerk for the outfit*) You'll never even know if he wears it anyway.

CaseConcerns

1. In this case with whom do you agree—the husband or the wife? Why?
2. Is the issue over sex or gender in this case?
3. Describe the communication that takes place between the husband and the wife. Are there any examples of sex and gender stereotypical language which you can identify?

ReflectiveResponses

1. Describe the gender-roles you would like your children to follow. On what did you base your decision?
2. Do you think it is possible to raise your children so that they are free of sex-role and gender-role stereotypes? Is androgyny a feasible solution?
3. What stereotypes are difficult to break? What sex-role stereotypes do you hold? What effect do they have on your communication?
4. Identify the origin of sex-role stereotypes.

Case 35

TargetTerms

• sexual harassment

PreviewNotes

Knowing what is meant by sexual harassment is important to organizational communication. How we talk to others in the workplace has a high impact on our relationships in business.

CaseParticipants

Susan—28 years old, newly-married financial analyst who has worked successfully for six years for Acme Electronics

Helen—well-respected, older executive secretary to the Senior Vice-President of Acme Electronics

Howard Davis—son of the President of Acme Electronics

"C'mon—he was only kidding around!"

At the end of a work day at Acme Electronics, a large international corporation, Susan hesitates before knocking on Helen's door.

Helen: *(upon seeing Susan's face)* And what can I do for you today?
Susan: I think we need to close the door.
Helen: Is there something wrong?
Susan: I guess it's getting late and you look like you're busy and besides— well, if anyone sees me talking to you—
Helen: You're going a mile a minute! Sit down, Susan. Whatever I'm doing can wait. Now, what's wrong?
Susan: I didn't know who else to talk to about this, and you're the one who seems to know everyone best.
Helen: *(smiling)* I think what you're really trying to say is that I'm the busybody around here. What seems to be upsetting you? Or has someone said something to you that—
Susan: *(takes a deep breath)* I just can't stand it anymore. If it's not his

jokes, it's his language, or his penetrating stares all day long. I can't even do my work any more.

Helen: Now, I'm getting the picture. But who may "he" be?

Susan: (*very hesitantly*) Howard Davis. My supervisor.

Helen: (*strong silence*) I see.

Susan: All day long, when I'm trying to work, all he says is he wants to see the pictures of my Caribbean honeymoon. Without pictures, he told me, he just uses his imagination to wonder what I look like in a bathing suit. And that's nothing—he's now into talking about the water shortage here and wants to know if I'm wasting water and showering alone these days! And those eyes!

Helen: And what do the others on your team do while he's saying this?

Susan: They listen, add to it and laugh—just like we're at one big party all day long.

Helen: Does he kid around with the other people in the office?

Susan: There, you said it yourself—kidding around. Is that what you call it—kidding around? I call it sexual harassment.

Helen: Susan, he's just trying to see how far he can go. Did you ever tell him that he offended you?

Susan: Of course, I did. I threatened to report him and his answer was, "To whom?" (*uncomfortable pause*) Hey, look, I'm really sorry that I bothered you with this. If seeing how far he can go is your way of saying he's harmless, I don't buy it. (*As she rises from her chair about to leave, she sees Howard Davis entering the room unannounced.*)

Howard: (*to Helen*) Did I ever tell you how gorgeous Susan is, Helen? (*to Susan*) I don't know, since you got married you have a distinct glow—Hmmm, wonder what that's all about! (*Susan continues on her way.*)

Helen: Where are you going? We didn't really get a chance to talk.

Susan: To Human Resources, down the hall—where I should've gone in the first place.

CaseConcerns

1. What are your views about this case being an example of sexual harassment?
2. Why did Susan wait so long to report Howard's behavior?
3. If you were Susan, how would you have handled the situation prior to coming to Helen?
4. Imagine that you are Helen at the end of this scene. What would you do with the information you have just heard?

ReflectiveResponses

1. Specifically, what are some of the laws in your state about issues of sexual harassment?
2. How do you respond to innuendoes based on sex and gender issues in your life? What are your personal guidelines of acceptable behavior between men and women in the workplace?
3. Read about a sexual harassment case which is currently in the news or has been a source of news in the past. Determine how the participants in the case communicated their views about their respective situations.
4. Design a training workshop to inform prospective students, employers and workers on how to deal with sexual harassment in the workplace, school or in social situations. Determine what you would tell others about sexual harassment. Be creative.

Case 36

TargetTerms

- sex and gender roles
- instrumental and expressive orientation

PreviewNotes

Teaching our children to be open-minded and flexible is difficult when it comes to sex and gender roles and values.

CaseParticipants

Jonathan—10-year-old son of Marsha
Marsha—35-year-old mother of Jonathan; open-minded

"Not in my house!"

Marsha feels confident that she is a conscientious parent having made an effort to raise Jonathan with as few "hang-ups" about human sexuality as possible. Jonathan was given an early educa-tion in sex education, and his curiosity was always satisfied with sensible answers to any questions. In a further attempt to foster a healthy attitude toward the human body, Marsha would walk around her bedroom nude after a shower or while changing rather than putting on a robe or closing the door. She had done this from the time that Jonathan was a baby. However, as time went on in Jonathan's primary school years, Marsha noticed more and more resistance to her free behavior in her own home as Jonathan says:

Jonathan: Mom! I hate this running around naked all over the house!
Marsha: Aren't you exaggerating a bit? I'm getting dressed. You act as if I'm performing in a strip joint.
Jonathan: The other mothers never run around naked.
Marsha: Oh, really? Do I make you feel uncomfortable?
Jonathan: Yeah!
Marsha: Why didn't you ever say anything to me before?

Jonathan: I never really thought about it until now.

Marsha: Well, if that's the case, I will promise to keep your feelings in mind when I get dressed. Funny thing is that my intention was only to try to make you more comfortable—and look what I did! Now—march down the hall, I'm trying to get dressed. (*Jonathan smiles and walks to his room.*)

CaseConcerns

1. What are your feelings about Marsha's "before and after" behavior in this case? Do you feel that Jonathan will have any "hang-ups" as a result of the incident described in this situation?
2. Where do you stand in this case? Why?

ReflectiveResponses

1. Why do you think that children are so free and unrestricted in their sex-role and gender-role behaviors? As we grow older, how do we lose this freedom of self-expression?

Case 37

TargetTerms

- sex-role stereotypes
- gender-role stereotypes

PreviewNotes

We communicate in certain ways because of learned sex and gender roles. How we apply these roles to social situations is a central focus of this case.

CaseParticipants

Loretta—45ish in appearance; apparently en route to a resort area as suggested by the sun hat she carries to the departure gate; seemingly friendly

Janine—35ish in appearance; traveling with an attaché case which houses her business papers; departing from the same gate as the other woman to some type of resort area

"And I thought I was so liberal in my thinking . . ."

While hearing the announcement to board the plane, two women passengers begin to gather their belongings. Loretta approaches Janine with an intentional air of nonchalance and says:

Loretta: You, too? We've got the same problem.

Janine: I beg your pardon.

Loretta: Oh, the briefcase, you know.

Janine: Excuse me?

Loretta: Well, here we are on a week's trip to the secluded Caribbean and we're trudging along with these overloaded briefcases for our husbands. I'm glad I'm not the only wife on the plane lugging her husband's stuff. You'd think they'd know how to relax—without all of this added weight—wouldn't you? Guess it's not just my Harry, huh? You've got one like that, too? (*senses no response*) Husband, I mean.

Janine: (*somewhat troubled by the remark, with a touch of intentional cynicism*) Sorry—there's no husband in my life!

Loretta: (*looks quizzically at her*) Sorry, but I . . .

Janine: The fact is that I am not married—

Loretta: So, it's your boyfriend's briefcase—oh, sorrr—rry!

Janine: And, for the record, this happens to be my briefcase. I have no boyfriend. And furthermore, these also happen to be my papers, and what difference should it make if I carry an attaché on board the plane?

Loretta: Well, you being a lady and all, I thought we were in the same boat, you know. I was just making a little conversation while Harry's making some last minute calls. Sorr-rry! (*call to the phone area*) C'mon Harry, the plane's gonna board!

CaseConcerns

1. Do you think that the times are changing making this case a bit unthinkable as we approach a new century?

2. What are some of the sex-role and gender-role stereotypes that are inherent in this case? How do these roles affect communication?

3. Do you believe that Loretta can ever learn to understand Janine's thinking about her gender roles? Can Janine ever learn to understand Loretta's? Use support in your answer.

ReflectiveResponses

1. How do you determine what is comfortable for you in your own sex and gender role taking?

Case 38

TargetTerms

- sex
- gender
- sex and gender roles
- stereotypes

PreviewNotes

Raising children brings up all our BAVs about sex roles. How do our beliefs about sex and gender impact child-rearing?

CaseParticipants

Al Brady—successful stockbroker; father of a 14-year-old son, Bob; former college Hall of Fame football player; forceful in his manner

Sally Brady—housewife; gourmet cook; caring wife to Al and sensitive mother to Bob; actively involved in the Parent Teacher Association; quiet and reserved in her demeanor

"Can't tackle this one . . ."

Al and Sally have been married for fifteen years and have agreed on most issues. However, there have been major disagreements about sports and their son. Al has always dreamed of watching his son make touchdown after touchdown on the high school football field. Knowing how physically able-bodied his son already is, the possibilities of additional training add to Al's excitement. On the other hand, Sally will not even entertain the thought of having her son get near other players who may, as she says, "beat him to a pulp" while he is under all of "those people" in a "tackle." Let's see what happens when Sally tries to enforce her BAVs.

Sally: He's not playing this fall, and that's final.

Al: Sally, we've been over this before. He can hurt himself just as easily playing soccer or tennis.

Sally: But—he won't be tackled on the field with a tennis racquet in his hand.

Al: That's pushing it a bit. Why don't we ask Bob how he feels? That seems to be the most logical way of handling this.

Sally: He's not capable of making this decision, Al. He needs our guidance.

Al: And you've proven my point—that we can help him make a sensible decision about his fall sport. You know as well as I do that he will decide to do what he thinks is right. Above all—he's a good kid.

Sally: What young kid thinks of cracking his head open? All Bob thinks about is pleasing you and the others in the crowd as he fantasizes about the winning touchdown he'll make.

Al: You're not giving him the credit he deserves. The kid's got the skills and talent beyond his years.

Sally: See it from a mother's point of view, please.

Al: I can't support you on your thinking, Sally. To me, this sounds as if one of us loses whichever way we go . . .

Sally: My mind is made up.

CaseConcerns

1. Defend or criticize the mother's perspective. The father's perspective.
2. What is Sally trying to teach her son by taking such a stance? What is Al reinforcing through his position?
3. If you were Bob, what would you do? Describe his reaction to the entire case from his point of view.
4. What does Sally mean when she says, "see it from a mother's point of view"? Is there such a viewpoint?

ReflectiveResponses

1. Have you ever been in a situation where your parents have taken opposite positions? Describe the situation and explain your communication behavior.
2. Describe a time when you were required (or strongly encouraged) to do something which you did not want to do by your parents. How did the incident make you feel? Did it require you to be someone you were not?

10
Chapter

Power

"You're wrong — that's all there is to it!"

Overview

Power is inherent in all relationships. We cannot have a relationship that does not involve power on some level. Although we aspire toward a relationship of equality, most researchers dispel that possibility. Power is not always a negative term, just as the conflict it can cause is not always negative. Developing the ability to respect others can reduce the need for power, while the quest for power can destroy relationships.

In this chapter, we will investigate the nature of power in relationships. We will examine the natural existence of power in all relationships, our need for power, how power develops, our need to be right, the use of language as power, the types of power relationships, the sources of power, and the impact of power on our relationships.

The Natural Existence of Power

Three-year-olds are noted for their temper tantrums which are usually based on an inability to see beyond their immediate wants. This selfish, self-centered time period is an awkward time for parents and an important learning time for us as children. During this period in our development, we should begin to realize that there are other people in the world who also have needs. This process, known as **decentering**, allows us to learn sharing, caring, and giving. We begin to discover how to empathize, to realize that we cannot always have our own way, and that we are not the only person with needs. Without experiencing this decentering process, we continue through our lives with the behaviors of a self-centered three-year-old.

Some people hold on to this need for being right, being in control, and thinking only of personal needs. These needs are actually based on the need for power, and this power need can get very out of control.

C. G. Browne and Thomas Cohen (1958) define **power** as "the capacity to induce another person to act or change in a given direction," (p. 375) and this manipulative approach can be damaging to the communication process. Whether the influence of power in communication is positive or negative, researchers maintain that its existence is pervasive. "Human life is inconceivable without it, yet power is dangerous because it is deeply involved with the way humans communicate" (Brown and Keller, 1979, p. 214). Consequently, many theorists hypothesize that power is the most important factor to consider in any communication context.

The Need for Power

William Schutz (1958) maintains that the need for power is based in our human need for control and the learned behavior of the need to be right. We take on one of three roles: 1) the abdicratic, 2) the autocratic, or 3) the democratic. Loyal followers are **abdicrats**; although they feel hostility and anger, they do not openly voice it. Abdicrats are "go-along-with-the-crowd" people but may engage in hidden or subtle reactions rather than open ones. They do not see themselves as responsible or capable, so they allow others to make decisions for them. Then there are the competitors, the fighters—the ones who exercise power at every opportunity. These **autocrats** have an "I'll-show-them" attitude, usually because of an inferiority complex. Their self-concept is similar to that of the abdicrat; however, their response is opposite. Schutz (1958) calls the **democrat** the most desired response to power. These people see power as an equal exchange—a give-and-take situation in interaction. Democrats also use power appropriately and are not compulsive about its use. However, as communicators we must realize that the appropriateness of these roles somewhat depends on the situation.

Charles Brown and Paul Keller (1979) summarize by stating that the "compulsive need to exercise power, or the persistent effort to resist or escape it, seems to be developed early in life" (p. 214). Our power orientation is a learned behavior, "taught by the way significant others have used power in their relationships with us" (p. 214). Two hypotheses are posited by Brown and Keller about the results of this phenomena:

- When used between people, power distorts perceptions of what each is saying to the other, causing them to omit, misinterpret, and garble
- Power relationships between people restrain them from saying what they would otherwise say, thereby robbing the listener of a chance to appropriately assess the unspoken feelings or ideas of the other (p. 215)

In summary, the use of power in the communication process causes selectivity in our perceptions and restricts our self-disclosure. It is developed as a need when insecurities are not satisfied or when decentering has not occurred thoroughly in childhood. The need for power is then manifested in a need for control and the need to be right.

What Do You Think?

Kelly: Hi, Terry. Do you want to go to the movies tonight?
Terry: Oh, hi Kelly. Sure. I have a lot to do, but what the heck.
Kelly: Well, what would you like to see?
Terry: Oh, I don't care. You decide.
Kelly: OK, I'll check the schedules and pick something exciting.
Terry: Just let me know what time to be ready.
Kelly: OK, see you later.

What kind of control is Terry exhibiting: abdicratic, autocratic, or democratic?

The Need to be Right—The Need to Win

John Stewart (1990) describes communication conflict and power as a war; when two people both need to be right and both need power, then the communication process becomes more similar to a war than a verbal exchange of ideas. Our strongly human, learned need to be right interferes with our need to be accepted and loved—**and** our desire to be happy. Stewart maintains that our fear of not being right scares our ego into thinking that we have to fight to win rather than communicate with respect and love.

Louise Hay (1986), new age philosopher/author, poses the question we encountered in chapter 7, "Would you rather be right, or would you rather be happy?" This perspective from the *Course in Miracles* (1976) states that we cannot be both at the same time. Being stuck in the need to be right obviates or disallows the ability to be happy. Interpersonal conflict theorists maintain that the basis for all conflict is the need for power, status, and rightness. The statement, "the reason I am mad is because you did not do what I wanted you to do" is one whose truth is hard to swallow. If we let others do what they want to do without our judgment, why would we get angry?

What Do You Think?

Write a one-page essay on the topic, "Would you rather be right, or would you rather be happy?" Consider the possibility that you cannot be both. Prepare a brief oral statement that you might be willing to share with the class about this topic.

Language as Power

Because language is the essential tool that people use for making an impact on others (Jacobson, 1972, p. 141), the nature of their power determines the character of their language. Leaders and persons in authority can only obtain power through the messages they send. For example, if Mary is elected president of her sorority because she voiced valuable ideas, her power will be maintained as long as she demonstrates integrity which is congruent with her previous messages. If Mary begins to criticize others, boss them around, exert dictatorial behaviors and messages, then she will not remain in power for very long. If Mary knows how to word her requests carefully and effectively, she will be a more successful leader; if she becomes demanding, she will fall from power.

Our struggle to exert control in relationships is characterized by Paul Watzlawick (1964). He begins by identifying two levels present in every communication act:

- **the content level**—the words chosen to create the intended message
- **the relationship level**—the implied status and metacommunication message about how the sender views the receiver

Watzlawick states that we train others how to treat us by giving them messages about how we view them through the relationship level of interaction, not the content level. This usually involves some level of power and is most often nonverbal. For example, if I scream with authority, "Jim, close the door" I am giving two messages: 1) that I want the door closed, and 2) that I have power over Jim to demand that he do it. On the other hand, if I request with friendliness the same message, I have sent the same content message but quite a different relational message (one of equality and request). These two levels of communication manifest themselves in the two basic types of relationships—**symmetrical** and **complementary.**

What Do You Think?

Don: Kathryn, did you do your homework?
Kate: Yes, I sure did.
Don: Good. Do you want to watch television now?
Kate: Sure, what's on?

Read these lines in three ways. First as a father and young daughter, second as a boyfriend and girlfriend, and third as brother and sister. What is the difference in the content level of the message? What is the difference in the relationship level of the message? What nonverbal implications do you notice on the relationship level?

Types of Power Relationships

A **symmetrical relationship** is one that is based on a subtle struggle to establish or maintain equality and can be characterized as "birds of a feather flock together." Sometimes this struggle results in "one-upmanship"; sarcasm begets more sarcasm and control creates a stronger desire for control. Although one would think that similarities would assist in the development of a relationship, this type of relationship can be unstable and difficult to maintain. Both partners want the same thing and may be too much alike. Watzlawick (1964) maintains that with both partners vying for the same rewards, conflict is certain to ensue. Any attempt to gain an upper hand by one partner is met with equal force by the other. This undefined power produces frustration and anxiety.

A **complementary relationship** is one based on "the acceptance and enjoyment of difference" (Watzlawick, 1964). Generally, most communication is of this type and is sometimes referred to by the phrase "opposites attract." The differences that each partner brings to the relationship complements the other's contributions. Although it would seem that this type of relationship is not as desirable because of our resistance to differences, these small differences are usually what make the relationship work. Because we are actually more alike than we are different, we usually seek what we do not have to complement our traits. If we are with a partner who is too much like us, we will both be vying for the same rewards. While some of this "likeness" is necessary, too much of it creates a power struggle or boredom.

The major difference between these two types of relationships is the way in which the partners define the relationship. In a symmetrical relationship, each partner usually defines the relationship differently (yet exactly the same), thus creating a power struggle ("I'm in charge" "No, I'm in charge"). In contrast, in the complementary relationship, each partner agrees on the definition of the relationship ("I need your help to solve my problem" "OK, I know I can help you"). If we agree that I will be dominant and you will be submissive, we have a complementary relationship. If we both want to be dominant or submissive at the same time, we have a symmetrical relationship and, consequently, conflict.

Timothy Leary (1957) opts for an agreed-upon balance on two opposite dimensions: love/hate and dominance/submission. If partners agree upon sharing this power, the relationship will be balanced; if not, it becomes symmetrical or complementary, neither of which are desirable, says Leary. The agreement is the important factor here. For example, if Bob agrees to let Mary be dominant on household decisions and Mary agrees to let Bob be dominant on investment decisions, then we have a balanced relationship. However, if both Mary and Bob want to make the investment decisions or they cannot agree on who will make them, then they are stuck in an unbalanced position. Watzlawick (1964) refers to this as the **symmetrical-complementary compromise** while D. D. Jackson (1959) calls it **parallel**.

While the name that we call this type of relationship may differ, most theorists agree that in long-term, stable relationships, this pattern of balance is a necessary development. The important thing is that the power is shared. "Interdependence is the essential state of human relationships" (Brown and Keller, 1979, p. 219). The essence is the mutual acceptance and respect of both parties involved. This "solution" to the problem of power in relationships focuses on a sense of union and mutual need which leads to mutual agreement on the division of power (p. 219). It is basically our similarities that bring us together and our differences that keep us together—as long as the differences are not too large, not too overwhelming, and do not cross too many core values.

What Do You Think?

Sue: Why do you always have to be in charge of the money? I would like to be involved with that process, too. I feel left out.

Mike: You're in charge of other things, Sue. You know that we decided to divide our duties this way.

Sue: Yes, I know, but I didn't think it meant not being involved at all.

Mike: Well, you don't tell me about the groceries or the kids' after school appointments. What's the big deal?

Sue: The big deal is I feel . . . oh, never mind.

What is Sue feeling? Why is she feeling that way? How would you describe this relationship? What type is it? What is the power?

Power Sources

Most theorists would agree that all interpersonal relationships have a power structure of some sort. This power can be derived from various sources. John French and Bertram Raven (1959) provide us with five possible **sources of power** in relationships.

- **Reward power** is the ability to deliver something of value which the other person wants. It can be material goods, warmth and supportiveness, or access to others who can provide the reward. (You know someone who has a connection to help me get a job.)

- **Coercive power** is the ability to punish the other person. Punishment includes removal of rewards which the person presently enjoys, such as a position of status and power. It includes requiring the person to perform some disliked task, and it may even include corporal punishment. (Your mother takes the car keys away because you came in late.)

- **Expert power** is the ability to deliver some special service because you have special knowledge or abilities. One person may type better while the other cooks better. (Your teacher can suggest improvements for your resume to make you more marketable.)

- **Legitimate power** is derived from our different roles and positions in the social structure. Sometimes legitimate power is codified in our legal structure, but often it is simply a matter of tradition and the norms which we have been taught. Employers assign tasks to employees. Children obey parents. Whenever people suggest that we ought to obey them because ''that's the way things are,'' they are invoking their perceived legitimate power (not that we need to agree, of course).

- **Referent power** can be exercised over someone when that person idolizes or looks up to us and aspires to be more like us. We are a model, quite often without realizing it. The other person may want to be like us in some way. We have referent power over people when they do what we do. Also, generally, they want us to like them.

What Do You Think?

Kim: I don't care what you say, you can't go.
Kelly: Don't be silly, I have to go. It's part of my job.
Kim: Well, I say you can't go on an out-of-town business trip with Chris.
Kelly: Well, you'll just have to get over it, because I am going.

What type of power does Kim try to use on Kelly? Does the type of relationship make any difference in this case?

The Impact of Power on Relationships

Richard Emerson (1962) argues that power in a relationship is based on the dependency within that relationship. If Steve is dependent on Gary for his job and thus a source of income, Gary has something that Steve wants and needs—money (or the power to provide it). If Steve is also unlikely to change jobs due to availability and geographics, then Gary has additional power over Steve because Steve is unlikely to get his need (money) fulfilled elsewhere. This want or need can also be physical or psychological as well as material. This description of power explains the sources of dependency which give others power over us (Verderber and Verderber, 1992, p. 160).

Joyce Hocker and William Wilmot (1994) claim that we do not possess power but rather it is a product of the relationship. Other people give us power. "All power in interpersonal relationships is a property of the social relationship rather than a quality of the individual" (p. 51). "Power is always interpersonal" (May, 1972, p. 23); it does not reside in people. Hocker and Wilmot (1994) summarize their view of how power operates in interpersonal conflict with six axioms:

- Parties are interdependent
- Parties have resources that another is dependent upon to reach their goals
- The ability to influence the goal attainment of the other is the power you have over him/her
- Each person in a conflict has some degree of power
- Persons in conflicts can make choices that define power either equally or unequally
- Using power productively to achieve both individual and relational goals is a skill that can be learned (p. 52)

Finally, R. V. Sampson (1965) points out that "to the extent that we develop our capacity for power we weaken our capacity for love; and conversely, to the extent that we grow in our ability to love we disqualify ourselves for success in the competition for power" (pp. 59–69). Developing the ability to give and receive love in all its forms, which some theorists define as effective interpersonal communication (Rogers, 1972; Buscaglia, 1972; May, 1972), seems to obviate our need for control and power. Thus, the desire for happiness may win over the need for being right.

What Do You Think?

Kelly: Honey, can you find my black shoes—I can't seem to locate them and I'm in a real hurry?

Terry: OK, just a minute.

Kelly: Did you hear me say I am in a hurry?

Terry: Yes, I did, and I'm calmly trying to find your shoes.

Kelly: I really need your help—and you're telling me you don't want to get excited? I don't get it—do you want to help me or not?

Terry: Alright, alright, already! Just calm down. Here are your shoes—under the bed.

Kelly: Thanks, hon. I didn't mean to yell at you. I just got frantic and wanted you to be frantic, too, and that's not fair. (*They kiss.*)

Terry: Now off you go before you're late . . .

What impact does power have on this relationship? How do Kelly and Terry use power separately and as a couple?

Summary

Decentering allows us to become less egocentric and to release the need for control and to be right. The need to feel important seems to be a natural human need and has been perpetuated by the "me" generation and our individualistic society. These needs can develop into a need for power which is then derived from others and is dependent upon the relationship definition, context, and circumstances. The types of relationships we form are determined by our perceived power needs. Other sources of power come from the roles we play and the dependency we feel on others. A balance of power provides the healthiest relationship allowing for agreed-upon definitions. Power in relationships can have positive or negative effects, depending on its use.

References

Browne, C. G. and Thomas S. Cohen. *The Study of Leadership*. Danville, IL: Interstate Printers and Publishers, 1958.

Brown, Charles T. and Paul W. Keller. *Monologue to Dialogue: An Exploration of Interpersonal Communication*, 2nd ed. Englewood Cliffs, NJ: Prentice-Hall, 1979.

Buscaglia, Leo. *Love*. New York: Fawcett Crest, 1972.

A Course in Miracles. Tiburon, CA: Foundation for Inner Peace, 1976.

Emerson, Richard M. "Power-Dependence Relations." In *Problems in Social Psychology*, Carl W. Backman and Paul F. Secord, eds. New York: McGraw Hill, 1962.

French, John R. P. and Bertram Raven. "The Bases for Social Power." In *Studies in Social Power*, Dorwin Cartwright, ed. Ann Arbor, MI: Institute for Social Research, 1959.

Hay, Louise L. *You Can Heal Your Life*. Santa Monica: Hay House, 1986.

Hocker, Joyce and William W. Wilmot. *Interpersonal Conflict*, 4th ed. Dubuque, IA: Wm. C. Brown, 1994.

Jackson, D. D. "Family Interaction, Family Homeostasis and Some Implications For Conjoint Family Psychotherapy." In *Individual and Familial Dynamics*, J. G. Masserman, ed. New York: Grune & Stratton, 1959.

Jacobson, Wally D. *Power and Interpersonal Relations*. Belmont, CA: Wadsworth, 1972.

Leary, Timothy. *Interpersonal Diagnosis of Personality*. New York: The Ronald Press, 1957.

May, Rollo. *Power and Innocence*. New York: Norton, 1972.

Rogers, Carl R. *On Becoming A Person*. Boston: Houghton Mifflin, 1972.

Sampson, R. V. *The Psychology of Power*. New York: Pantheon Books, 1965.

Schutz, William C. *The Interpersonal Underworld*. Palo Alto, CA: Science and Behavior Books, 1958.

Stewart, John. *Bridges Not Walls: A Book About Interpersonal Communication*, 4th ed. New York: Random House, 1990.

Verderber, Rudolph F. and Kathleen S. Verderber. *Inter-Act: Using Interpersonal Communication Skills*, 7th ed. Belmont, CA: Wadsworth, 1993.

Watzlawick, Paul. *Anthology of Human Communication*. Palo Alto, CA: Science and Behavior Books, 1964.

Case 39

TargetTerms

- the need for power: autocratic control
- symmetrical relationship
- sources of power

PreviewNotes

This case illustrates the conflict that can develop when power interferes in a mother-daughter relationship.

CaseParticipants

Lenore Crowell—mother of two daughters, both of whom are in their thirties; precise in choice of words; dominant; enjoys being right

Caroline Crowell Jennings—mother of two children; very much at ease with herself; athletic and suntanned; free spirited and open minded; enjoys being fair

"What price power!"

Mr. and Mrs. Crowell, both retired senior citizens, live a substantial distance from their married children. Although their visits are not all that frequent, both daughters usually insist on having their parents stay for a long weekend. On one such weekend at younger daughter Caroline's house, Mrs. Crowell, sitting over a cup of tea, tries to vie for her granddaughter's attention. Eight-year-old Tara is, instead, far more interested in her group of friends in the front yard. As Tara leaps from the table to the back door, Lenore Crowell begins to tap her fingers against the teacup, and says:

Lenore: I don't know what it is with your kids these days!
You'd think that Tara would at least kiss her grandmother "hello."

Lenore: You know, dear, I didn't raise you like that at all. She's so—well—

Caroline: So . . .?

Lenore: Well, spoiled is what I mean. I'm very sorry to have to say this—

Caroline: Mom, no one asked you to say anything.

Lenore: Caroline, don't get so curt with me. I'm merely suggesting that you are heading into some stormy waters if you let her grow up like this. The handwriting is on the wall for when she gets older.

Caroline: Mother! She's got her friends here. It's not as if you're going home in ten minutes and she hasn't spent a moment with you. You're going to be here for the entire weekend. Calm down! You're making too much of it—she's only a kid.

Lenore: This is not the first time Tara whizzed past me. She's simply being given the signal that she needn't respect her elders.

Caroline: Given the signal by whom?

Lenore: Well, certainly not me. I always raised you and your sister to be a little more concerned with the feelings of others.

Caroline: Here we go again . . . I hoped the comparisons about the wonderful job that you did of bringing us up would stop. We're twenty years beyond those days.

Lenore: Oh, now I see. I'm old-fashioned—out of date—now things are different.

Caroline: You're twisting my words. Mom, I really love you a lot, but the fact that you and I disagree on minor things is not all that terrible, you know.

Lenore: I never disagreed with my parents. If they said that they were coming to see me, I dropped every plan I had and spent time with them. As far as your kids are concerned, it's a much different story. They don't even know who their grandparents are.

Caroline: Now, let's be serious.

Lenore: And that I am. Whatever happened to the notion of family?

Caroline: Just because you're my mother does not mean that we have to think exactly the same. I happen to believe that Tara will be happier now with her friends than sitting here and listening to us talk.

Lenore: An eight-year-old should know better. You knew very well that Dad and I were coming out to see you this weekend. You know who feels it even more than me?—your father—he's hurt and feels like he's a nonperson in your life and your kids' lives.

Caroline: You can't really mean that.

Lenore: And why not? We have no real part or place in your lives. You seem so involved in your carpools, tennis games, and trips that we're really not crucial to any part of your life style. Anything your Dad and I say is wrong—we're beginning to realize that we have to start looking out for our own needs—alone.

Caroline: What kind of a statement is that?

Lenore: It used to be that parents had some type of control over the comings and goings of their children. You have made it extremely clear that you are not interested in our decisions and our advice, so we're taking three giant steps back.

Caroline: My God, Mom. I always listen to what you have to say. We love you and respect you and we always consider what you have to say.

Lenore: I'm telling you how I feel. And if a mother can't tell a child how she feels—

Caroline: But, you raised me to be my own person.

Lenore: Yes, but I should hope that we threw in a couple of training sessions on respecting other people's authority.

Caroline: How can you liken this to respecting authority?

Lenore: This is your mother talking.

Caroline: And?

Lenore: I have waited for the day that I could come into my daughter's home and be a grandmother—and be absolutely adored by my grandchildren. Now the whole picture is wrong. (*Tara runs in again and asks for something to drink for her friends.*) See what I mean! She doesn't even notice that I am standing two feet away from her—nor does she introduce me to her friends.

Caroline: Mom, I can assure you that she really loves you. She is just not the ''kissy-huggy'' type.

Lenore: And, not even the ''say hello'' type!

Caroline: Mom, stop doing this. Do me a favor and think back for a few minutes and try to remember when you told me that it was O.K. if I quarreled with my sister but that it was never O.K. if someone else said something bad about her. You were right when you said it would make me feel really horrible if anyone else said something that would hurt her feelings. Well, that's sort of the way I feel about you talking about Tara. She's mine and if I'm being possessive, I'm also being really honest with you.

Lenore: This is not meant to hurt you, darling. I'm just trying to show you how to bring the best out in your children, and how to raise them properly. Tara can't go through life ignoring those around her.

Caroline: I'm beginning to feel pushed—

Lenore: Nonsense! I've never, *ever* told you what to do or when to do it.

Caroline: How—after this conversation—can you say that?

Lenore: Say what?

CaseConcerns

1. Describe the power struggle in this case. What type of power relationship do Caroline and her mother have?

2. This case touches on the need to be ''right.'' What are some of the consequences in this case when both mother and daughter want the same end result—through very different methods?

3. Through the study of power structures, French and Raven provide an overview of sources of power. Which of the sources of power are evident in this situation? Which character has which source? Why?

4. At the relationship level of communication, what is Lenore saying to her daughter? How does this differ from the content level message?

5. Louise Hay talks about the need to be right interfering with our desire to be happy. Apply this concept to this case. Apply this concept to you.

6. How would Schutz describe Lenore's need for power? Is she abdicratic, autocratic, or democratic? How about Caroline?

ReflectiveResponses

1. Hou would you describe the balance of power in your family structure?

2. Focus on a relationship you have with a member of your family—a sister, brother, mother or father. Can you think of an incident where you can identify when two different levels of communication transpired in your interaction? What were the circumstances and why do you suppose the content level came into play in your transaction? Why the relationship level?

Case 40

TargetTerms

- decentering
- the need for power: abdicratic control
- symmetrical relationship
- source of power
- relational level messages
- need to be right

PreviewNotes

The struggle for power in a relationship can result in major conflict. This case explores the need to be right and the struggle for equality.

CaseParticipants

Steven Clark—49-year-old businessman; frequently puts in late hours at the office; currently handles the major aspects of running his house; seems content with his triple role as businessman, husband and father

Michelle Clark—Steven's second wife who has never been married previously; sensitive but uncertain about herself and her surroundings; wants very much to feel needed without being obtrusive

"How can you do this to me?"

Steven and Michelle have been involved in a rather tumultuous relationship for the past 17 years. After a short first marriage, Steven was intent on marrying Michelle, an old girlfriend. Michelle leads a fairly contented life as the mother of three children. Her equilibrium is broken on this afternoon. She has tried without success to reach Steven at work to discuss an error on a credit card statement. Busy at work, Steven has insisted on not having any interruptions. Michelle has already called four times and is still unable to "get through." After the fifth attempt at reaching Steven, Michelle is connected to her husband who says:

Steven: Hi! I've got to make it quick. Everything O.K.?

Michelle: Barely.

Steven: You sound awful. What's going on?

Michelle: I have been trying to reach you for the last two hours, Steven. All I got was one secretary after another!

Steven: You know how busy I am at this time of year. Sometimes, things have to wait. The sooner that you understand that I just can't drop everything and—

Michelle: But Steven, I just picked up the mail and got the credit card bill. The statement is wrong and I don't know who to call. There are some very large charges—and I thought for sure that you would know about them. I was so upset—I know that you're busy and all—but I just didn't know what to do.

Steven: I see.

Michelle: Well, is that all you are going to tell me? Do you realize what I'm saying or are you too busy for me?

Steven: I have an office full of people here, Michelle. Let me get back to you on this.

Michelle: When? You're always too busy for me.

Steven: Finished? (*Little is heard on the other end.*) I said that I'd discuss this with you later.

Michelle: Don't you realize that this cannot wait! I've been calling you all morning. I finally get through to you—and now, you're telling me that you can't talk to me. What am I supposed to do now?

Steven: If you don't stop harping on this—

Michelle: What'll you do? I suppose that because of this—you will never let me pay with the charge card again.

Steven: Now, why would you say something like that?

Michelle: Well, after this, maybe you think that I can't manage any of our credit cards.

Steven: Did you hear what I just said? I cannot spend the day on the phone with you rehashing this.

Michelle: What are you talking about? We didn't even discuss anything.

Steven: Why are you opening my mail anyhow?

Michelle: Since when is it "your" mail?

Steven: Since I pay the bills that come in that mail!

Michelle: Where does that put me?

Steven: Did I ever tell you to pay the bills?

Michelle: Well, not exactly—

Steven: You're damn right. So, take advantage of it and leave it to me. O.K.?

Michelle: No, it's not O.K.! There are all of these extra charges—

Steven: Did you hear me? I said that there is nothing wrong.

Michelle: I don't know what's going on, but I'm calling VISA and—
 Steven: Don't call VISA!—I'll take care of everything later.
Michelle: This is all very strange—you're scaring me.
 Steven: Well, that's just for openers if you keep interfering.
Michelle: I don't understand—
 Steven: Well, that's too bad. I have another call; I have to go.
Michelle: Not until I get some explanation.
 Steven: I don't want to tell you again. I will take care of it. Stay out of my affairs, Michelle. I don't tell you want to make for dinner, so don't tell me how to run my business!

CaseConcerns

1. What is Michelle's relationship level message to Steven? What is Steven's to her? Is this issue really over the bank account or something else?
2. Describe the type of relationship that Michelle and Steven have.
3. Describe the type of power that each character uses in this case. Does the type change during the situation?
4. Is Michelle taking the role of abdicrat or autocrat? Is the role appropriate? What about Steven's role?
5. Role play one of the characters and change something in their communication behavior that you didn't like.
6. Write the dialogue for the scene when Steven comes home from work.

ReflectiveResponses

1. Can you describe a power struggle in your life? How did you handle the situation? After understanding how power can be used unproductively, would you now handle the situation differently?
2. What happens when one person in a relationship is an abdicrat and the other person is a democrat? Can there ever be a balance in the relationship?
3. How does the balance of power in a relationship affect the way we communicate?

Case 41

TargetTerms

- parallel versus complementary relationships
- democratic control
- sources of power

PreviewNotes

This case illustrates what happens when neither person wishes to accept the decision-making role.

CaseParticipants

Don Matland—27 years old; quiet; thoughtful; reserved
Maddy Alpert—26 years old; quiet; thoughtful; reserved

"I'll do whatever you want to do."

Quite frequently, Saturday night finds Don and Maddy together. Having known each other for three years, the two have gone from a "platonic" to a more serious, intimate relationship. At the time of this conversation, Maddy and Don are trying to plan "what to do" on the upcoming Saturday night as Don suggests:

Don: You know, I can pick you up a little earlier tomorrow. What do you want to do?
Maddy: Well, I don't know exactly. What do you want to do?
Don: Dinner?
Maddy: I'm really trying to watch what I eat. I guess it depends on where we go.
Don: Well, then what else is there? What would you like to do?
Maddy: Oh, I don't really care.
Don: Well, then, how about a movie?
Maddy: After today, I'm not really sure if I can sit through anything that's too long. What's playing close by?

Don: I'd have to get the paper and check it out. Anything that you don't want to see?

Maddy: Nothing in particular.

Don: Well, that doesn't give me much of a clue. Let's see—what else can we do?

Maddy: I'm game for anything, I guess.

Don: Like what?

Maddy: Oh, I don't know.

Don: Want to go for a ride?

Maddy: Where?

Don: We'll find someplace.

Maddy: Well, that's just it. Where will we go?

Don: Can you try and help me think of someplace?

Maddy: Like where?

Don: If I knew where, I wouldn't be asking you to help me think of someplace.

Maddy: Well, I don't know. I'm thinking . . .

Don: And?

Maddy: Why don't you just think of something and we'll do it.

Don: Like what?

Maddy: I'll do anything that you want. I'm not that picky.

Don: Well, be "picky" and think about what would be fun to do.

Maddy: Anything, really, Don. I'd much rather that you surprise me.

Don: But, then, you might not like what I have planned.

Maddy: Well, let me be the judge of that.

Don: I'm just so surprised to hear you say that. None of this is really fitting in with what I think of our relationship.

Maddy: And what is that?

Don: I guess that what I'm saying is that I'm so caught up in trying to be the one who makes you contented in having a good time that I'm forgetting about what you might be feeling along the way. I never did think about how you might react to my constantly asking what you wanted to do and where you wanted to go.

Maddy: There you go again. You're so hard on yourself. Let's just have a good time and not think about . . .

Don: Each other?

Maddy: No, that was not what I was going to say at all. Just let me know where you're taking me. I'll go wherever you want.

CaseConcerns

1. Analyze this case in terms of Schutz's control/power needs (abdicrat, autocrat, democrat). Which role does each play? Are these roles symmetrical, complementary or parallel? Why?

2. Is Maddy's use of power appropriate? Typical? What about Don's use of power? Do females and males typically fall into these (Schutz's) categories? In the 90s, are these roles appropriate? Typical?

3. What is Don's source of power? How does he feel in the role in which this source forces him to be?

ReflectiveResponses

1. Why do you feel that we are sometimes prone to leave the decision making in a relationship to others?
2. Have you ever given power to a significant other in your life to accommodate his or her needs? How did this affect the communication in your relationship?

Case 42

- content versus relationship level of message
- source of power
- the need to be right
- type of power

When people are friends but they are also in positions which involve power, how do the roles affect the friendship? Here we see the effects of power on a friendship.

Scott Selby—21-year-old senior in college; "BMOC" (Big Man On Campus); newly elected president of "Beta," the hottest fraternity on campus; friend of Alex

Alex Gordon—20-year-old junior in college; self-confident; wants to be the best in whatever he does; newly appointed pledge master of "Beta"; friend of Scott

"You better watch it!"

Alex and Scott are busy making arrangements for "rush" week. One of the matters that need immediate attention is how the pledging process will take form. Alex and Scott find that they share some fairly different views on what should take place and how.

Scott: Think about how we sweated out "Hell Week!"
I am not going to tiptoe around with these guys just because the campus is toughening up with new rules.

Alex: I'm with you all the way. But we have to deal with the new required monitoring system.

Scott: You've got to be kidding. This fraternity's been around for fifty years with the same initiation for the guys to go through. No way I'm going to be the one to change it. It's my duty as president to continue the traditions set up before us.

Alex: Well, it's not like I'm not for tradition or anything—but remember what happened last semester at the "Beta" chapter down South. Those guys are going through indictment charges—well, doesn't that tell you something?

Scott: What are you—chicken or something?

Alex: Ahhh—get off it, Scott.

Scott: Listen, I was elected president of this fraternity and what I say goes. Remember that it was me who was elected to set the policies in "Beta." In case you forgot—I'll remind you that I was unanimously given this position. Now—to other business. Do you know how many guys are pledging this term?

Alex: A lot, I guess.

Scott: You bet! The reason guys wanna be with us is because we're the best. And don't forget it!

Alex: Hey, Scott—isn't there more to what keeps us together than ritual drinking marathons and hazing stuff? I mean, read our by-laws—we're the best on campus because of the stuff that we do—not because of our pledge week traditions. Who the hell really cares whether or not someone is capable of chugging down six cans of beer in three minutes!

Scott: Man, I can't believe I'm hearing you talk this way. Just keep in mind buddy, that you were on the council that initiated all of these "by-laws." And, one of them—Section Eight, to be exact—explains what's to be expected of new pledges. If you wimp out, that'll make great press for the *Beta Release* coming out next month. Headline: "ALEX GORDON—STATE UNIVERSITY BETA PLEDGE MASTER—SINGLEHANDEDLY DECIDES TO BREAK PLEDGE TRADITION." Everything in this fraternity needs council approval. Just keep remembering that I head the council. I was elected to veto what I felt was not in keeping with the "Beta" tradition.

Alex: Aren't you getting a little carried away with your power?

Scott: Aren't you forgetting who appointed you "pledge master?"

Alex: I'm not forgetting that. Seriously, do you really feel that pushing this hazing stuff this year is the right thing to do?

Scott: It's not what's right or wrong. We've done it for fifty years and we'll do it for another fifty. If you're having panic attacks about this, I'll tell you right now—get out. No one needs you. You know why—because I'm not going to stand behind you when you start on about how our hell night routine is "not in compliance" with the campus regulations. I'll tell you exactly what I think—that you're scared of your own shadow! And I don't want that kind of guy on my council—or in my fraternity.

Alex: I get the picture, Scott.

Scott: You haven't seen anything yet. Don't keep up with this goody two-shoes crap or you'll regret what happens if you turn your back on me!

CaseConcerns

1. Identify the specific source of power Scott thought he was using. What happens when legitimated power is misused?
2. Why is it so difficult to establish power over peers? How can this situation be made more positive and effective? Are there any types or sources of power that would be appropriate?
3. What need is motivating Scott to communicate as he does?
4. Analyze Scott's relationship-level messages to Alex. Do the same for Alex's messages to Scott.
5. As the recipient of Scott's messages of power, how does Alex react? What position is he taking? How does the need to be right enter into this case?

ReflectiveResponses

1. Describe what happens to people when elected to positions of power.
2. Sometimes people confuse leadership and power. Can you describe the differences? What types of power are appropriate for leaders to use? Which are most effective?

11
Chapter

Dealing with Conflict

TargetTerms

- conflict
- intrapersonal conflict
- interpersonal conflict
- conflict myths
- competing

- collaboration
- compromise
- avoidance
- accommodation

CoreConcepts

1 the definitions of conflict
2 the types of conflict
3 the myths about conflict
4 various conflict styles and strategies

"You make me so mad!"

Overview

Conflict in relationships is inevitable and necessary. We cannot avoid it, and without it we are unable to develop meaningful, in-depth relationships. So, as the saying goes, "if you can't beat 'em, join 'em!". While conflict can create an unpleasant environment, it is not always bad. If the above statements are true—conflict is bound to happen in our lives and it is essential for relationship development, then we had best know some things about conflict and how to deal with it effectively. Are there ways to confront difficult issues without all the screaming? Can we actually have discussions instead of arguments? Can conflict be productive? Well, the answer to these questions is "yes!" Conflict does not have to live out its negative reputation; it can be positive, productive, and helpful in maintaining the relationships we have worked so hard to develop.

In this chapter, we will investigate the impact of conflict upon our relationships. We will discover the various definitions of conflict, the types of conflict, the myths about conflict, and the various conflict styles and strategies. Understanding the underlying components that contribute to interpersonal conflict can facilitate learning how to manage conflict more effectively.

Definitions

People view conflict in many ways, but the fundamental elements necessary for a situation to be referred to as conflict are few. Morton Deutsch (1984, p. 26) explains that conflict is a pervasive aspect of existence. It occurs at all levels of social life: interpersonal, intergroup, interorganizational and international. Basically, **conflict** is "an expressed struggle between two interdependent parties who perceive incompatible goals, scarce rewards, and interference from the other party in achieving their goals" (Hocker and Wilmot, 1994, p. 23). Similarly, Charles Brown and Paul Keller define conflict as "differences involving real or perceived incompatible positions (1979, p. 243). R. Likert and J. G. Likert (1976) agree when they say,

"Conflict is viewed as the active striving for one's own preferred outcome, which, if attained, precludes the attainment by others of their preferred outcomes, thereby producing hostility" (p. 7). James McCroskey and Larry Wheeless (1976) view conflict as "the opposite of affinity . . . the dissolution of perceived homophily (similarity) and the increased perception of incompatible differences . . ." (p. 247). In the final analysis of understanding the basis of conflict, scholars concur that each party attempts to create an imbalance or relative favored position of power vis-à-vis the other. The definitions indicate that conflict is confrontation over incompatible or opposing needs.

According to Sarah Trenholm and Arthur Jensen (1992), there are several positive characteristics of conflict. They explain that conflict is a sign that two people are involved in each other's lives. If people were apathetic, they could not experience conflict. The fact that people do, in fact, have difficulties with each other may imply that they still care.

While these definitions display a variety of perspectives on what conflict is, we ought to also explain **what conflict is not**. Conflict is not simply disagreement; we all disagree on many pieces of information which does not necessarily lead us to conflict (McCroskey, Richmond, and Stewart, 1986, p. 202). Other incidental fights, arguments, and "blowups" should be considered as normal results of everyday stress—not conflict, for these minor events really have nothing to do with the relationship overall. These events happen quickly and spontaneously, and then they are over and done, only to be remembered in a humorous light, if at all. Remember the last time you thought you were really mad at someone and then the next day could not remember why? This is not conflict; it is one of those daily, minor explosions which relieve stress.

To be considered a conflict, the interaction must have certain elements present; some key words are differences, incompatibility, perceived and expressed struggle, interdependence of participants, and scarce rewards. However compatible one may feel with another person, there will come a time when one's respective needs, motives, thoughts, values, actions, or ownership of belongings may not exactly match. These issues will present the inevitable and pervasive nature of interpersonal conflict.

What Do You Think?

Kim: Terry, can we talk about our current project? I have some ideas, and I'm sensing a few problems which I think we could solve easily.

Terry: What's to talk about—my part is done and I think it turned out great.

Kim: Well, would you be willing to examine the document with me to discuss some possible changes?

Terry: Why?

Kim: Don't you think two heads are better than one? I mean, I know you have spent lots of time working on this project. I just thought we could combine forces and make both of our sections stronger—together.

Terry: Oh, I didn't know you thought that.

How would you describe the conflict in this example? Do you think Kim's approach is positive or negative? How do you think this conflict will be managed?

Types of Conflict

Conflict is a pervasive and inevitable part of our relationships. It can cause pain and frustration, but it can also lead to our growth as individuals as well as to our development in relationships with others. Let's first take a look at the types of conflict that exist in our lives.

Two important types of conflict deserve attention here. We can be mad at ourselves or we can be mad at our partners. **Intrapersonal conflict** is that conflict which is internal and deals with personal problems; it does not involve another person. Sometimes we use an intrapersonal "hang-up" to create a problem on the interpersonal level. For example, if I am compulsive about cleanliness and I get angry at you when you do not clean your half of the room as my roommate, then I am imposing my values on you by creating an interpersonal conflict out of an intrapersonal problem. To reduce intrapersonal conflict, try picturing your multiple "selves" as an orchestra. All of the "selves" represent your beliefs, attitudes and values. If one of those "selves" is out of tune or gets "plucked" at the wrong time, your internal balance and peace will be disturbed. This is no reason to get angry at someone else or to blame others for your internal "disharmony." The goal is to create internal "harmony" so that all of your "selves" will present a harmonious melody to others. Intrapersonal conflict should be dealt with on a personal, individual level.

On the other hand, **interpersonal conflict** is the type of conflict we have defined above as an expressed struggle between interdependent parties who perceive incompatible goals and scarce rewards. This becomes a relationship conflict, one which deals with and affects both parties in the relationship. First, we must identify which type of conflict we are experiencing. Quite often, we mistake intrapersonal conflict as a relationship issue which results in very unclear interpersonal conflict.

What Do You Think?

Kim: Stop playing your music so loud! I've got a terrible headache.

Terry: Oh, I'm sorry. I didn't even know you were home.

Kim: And while you're at it, why don't you finish the dishes like you promised.

Terry: Ok, Ok. Take it easy.

Kim: You never remember to do your share of the household duties. Why do I always have to remind you? It's not fair. I'm under enough pressure as it is.

Terry: I do them—just not at the exact time you want them done.

Kim: And another thing . . .

What type of conflict is this—intra- or interpersonal? What is the conflict about? Why is Kim so angry?

Special Note: While we have presented various definitions that deal with interpersonal communication conflict, we would be remiss if we did not acknowledge that both gender differences and culture differences can cause conflict and can affect the ways in which we deal with conflict. Therefore, we need to remember to assess how the variables of **gender** and **culture** may impact on our conflicts. See Chapter 9 in this book to identify sex and gender differences which may impact upon the causes and management of conflict. In addition, an important note is that our focus in this book has been on conflict in our North American culture only.

Myths About Conflict

As reflected in the preceding definitions, interpersonal conflict is an essential part of life; however, people have historically viewed it as negative. Hocker and Wilmot (1994) identify eight common images that people have about conflict. Most of these images are negative metaphors. These metaphors illustrate the **myths about conflict** which get us in trouble when confronted with conflict in an interpersonal relationship.

- **Conflict is War**—when conflict is characterized as an argument or a battle and words such as "victim" and "winner" are used
- **Conflict is Explosive**—the perception that conflict is made up of flammable materials (such as feelings) and that once it is started, it cannot be stopped
- **Conflict is an Upward Struggle**—the feeling that if we can get high enough, on top of things far enough, we can beat this battle and exercise control
- **Conflict is a Trial**—presenting evidence for our case and awaiting the impending verdict of right or wrong; relationship problems are seldom settled by trials—parties keep going back to court
- **Conflict is a Ball Game**—this assumes that there are rules and regulations which must be followed along with expected behaviors

- **Conflict Requires a Hero**—having a leader who will protect others; hero worship of the good guys and the bad guys; the myth that someone will help us win
- **Conflict is a Bargaining Table**—describes a collaborative approach involving meetings, negotiations, and parliamentary procedure (pp. 13–17)

Hocker and Wilmot (1994) also maintain that conflict can be seen as a natural process, inherent in the nature of all important relationships and amenable to constructive regulation through effective communication (p. 6). Because people view conflict in many different ways, the approaches to conflict vary as well. These different approaches cause much confusion and result in having each party play by different rules. Consequently, conflicts involve not only the content and relational issues but also the procedural ones. The questions that come up seem to be, "What is the conflict about?" "How does the conflict affect the relationship?" and "How do we go about dealing with the conflict?"

Communication theorists now suggest that the typical negative view of conflict is limited in scope (Borisoff and Victor 1989; Myers and Myers 1992). These theorists contend that studying the positive perceptions about conflict can make interpersonal conflict productive instead of destructive. Dispelling the myths we have about conflict can assist us in developing healthy, positive attitudes toward its resolution. When we come to grips with the fact that conflict *will* exist in our lives and that it *can* actually be helpful when approached positively, we can then begin to make conflict work *for* us instead of *against* us.

What Do You Think?

Kim: Terry, there's something we have to talk about.
Terry: Do we have to do it now? I'm really tired.
Kim: Yes, conflicts should always be handled immediately so you don't hold everything in and build up resentment.
Terry: OK, I'm listening (*continues to read the paper*).
Kim: You have to look at me when I'm talking.
Terry: Yes. (*turning to face Kim*)
Kim: First, I will explain the problem as I see it and then you can respond from your point of view.
Terry: No, wait a minute. I have to think about whatever you say for a day or two before I can react.
Kim: No, that's not how it's supposed to be done.

What myth about conflict does Kim believe in? How does that belief manifest itself in Kim's language? What do you do when someone views conflict from a different perspective?

Conflict Management Styles and Strategies

Brown and Keller (1979) discuss how conflict works in interpersonal communication:

- If feelings about the other person become indifferent, one begins to put less energy into maintenance of the relationship, and the relationship begins to become vulnerable
- As the feelings toward each other become more negative, one of the two people will become more self-assertive
- Assertive behavior arouses counterassertive behavior
- Thwarted assertive behavior arouses frustration
- Frustration arouses frustration
- The expression of frustration stimulates aggressive behavior
- Aggressive behavior arouses counteraggressive behavior (p. 245)

These steps demonstrate to us how initial feelings of indifference can develop into aggressive conflict behavior. Sometimes what starts as a misunderstanding of perceptions ends up as a major argument. As the conflict escalates, defensive behaviors create more defensive behaviors and the vicious circle begins. The more frustrated we become, the more aggressive we feel. At this stage, we are at a point of no return and intense conflict has emerged.

R. Kilmann and K. Thomas (1975) provide five **conflict styles** based on Robert Blake and Jane Mouton's (1964) strategies that describe how individuals approach conflict; all have advantages and disadvantages. These strategies illustrate the role or roles we take when we are involved in a conflict:

- **competing**—aggressive and uncooperative behavior; pursuing our own concerns at the expense of another; can be appropriate for quick decisions and creativity
- **collaboration**—highly assertive behavior aimed at reaching one's own goals mixed with a high concern for others; both parties work creatively to find new solutions that will maximize goals for both
- **compromise**—an intermediate style between assertiveness and cooperativeness; getting both parties to "split the difference" so that each gets something; unsatisfying resolutions resulting in another conflict; can take less time but may result in an easy way out without attention to the demands of the situation
- **avoidance**—nonassertive, passive behavior, refusing to participate in the conflict; provides time to think and plan but usually demonstrates an attitude of apathy
- **accommodation**—when a participant is nonassertive and cooperative; the opposite of competing, the person puts aside personal

concerns in order to satisfy the concerns of other participants; gains points with the other person but displays low level commitment to the relationship (pp. 971–980)

J. McCroskey, V. Richmond and R. A. Stewart (1986) maintain that the best way to manage conflict is to prevent it by:

- raising a person's level of tolerance for disagreement
- reducing the importance of the issue in our communication
- increasing the level of affinity between communicators (p. 212)

In addition, these same authors explain four **conflict management strategies** that provide strategic options of dealing with conflict that we cannot prevent:

- **leaving the field**—stopping the communication that is instigating the conflict by physically or psychologically leaving, or changing the topic; does not resolve the conflict but merely postpones it
- **restoring trust**—dealing with the suspicion and distrust that has initiated the conflict
- **reinstating communication**—an attempt to begin again by increasing the amount of communication; can backfire by actually increasing the amount of conflict; does not mean free ventilation and disclosure of feelings; a common, higher goal can facilitate conflict resolution; in a sense, directing the communication in the most effective direction
- **compromise and negotiation**—assumes strong mutual interests are at stake with a common goal established at the outset; process of discovering the range of acceptable solutions through cooperative communication (pp. 208–212)

Consequently, communication becomes necessary to clarify and express the conflict. Deborah Borisoff and David Victor (1989) have developed a five-step verbal and nonverbal conflict management strategy which encourages a flexible attitude toward managing differences.

Steps to integrative conflict management:

- **assessment** of the content
- **acknowledgment** through articulating and understanding both views
- developing and displaying an **attitude** conducive to productive interaction
- **action** through clear, empathic and accurate verbal and nonverbal communication
- **analysis** of the effectiveness of implementing the agreed-upon solution (p. 21)

There is not one precise way to handle conflict; we each have our own approach to dealing with conflict. In order to be effective, we need to investigate our personal conflict management style and select appropriate strategies for different situations. We may choose to integrate one or several conflict management strategies into our behavior in order to be effective in this process. Given the diversity of conflicts we typically encounter, what often is of most concern is how much is at stake in any conflict. We need to assess whether conflicts are pedestrian or profound, whether their effect on our lives will be trivial or tremendous, and whether they are major or minor maelstroms (Folger et al., 1993, p. 6).

Summary

Although conflict has a bad reputation, it can regain our respect when the myths surrounding it are removed. We are taught that conflict is bad and that we should always avoid it at all costs. Consequently, we develop strategies to ignore it, suppress it, and deny it. These strategies are unproductive and debilitating to the communication process. By reprogramming our old thought patterns to view conflict in a positive light, we can develop ways in which it can be used to our advantage and the advantage of our relationships. Collaborative, productive approaches to conflict management will enhance healthy growth in our relationships.

References

Blake, Robert and Jane Mouton Jr. *The Managerial Grid*. Houston: Gulf Publishing, 1964.

Borisoff, Deborah and David Victor. *Conflict Management: A Communication Skills Approach*. Englewood Cliffs, NJ: Prentice-Hall, 1989.

Brown, Charles T. and Paul W. Keller. *Monologue to Dialogue: An Exploration of Interpersonal Communication*, 2nd ed. Englewood Cliffs, NJ: Prentice-Hall, 1979.

Deutsch, M. "Subjective Features of Conflict Resolution: Psychological, Social, and Cultural Influences." In *New Directions in Conflict Theory: Conflict Resolution and Conflict Transformation*, R. Vayrynen, ed. London, England: Sage, 1984.

Folger, J., M. Poole, and R. Stutman. *Working Through Conflict*. New York: HarperCollins, 1993.

Hocker, Joyce and William W. Wilmot. *Interpersonal Conflict*, 4th ed. Dubuque, IA: Wm. C. Brown Publishers, 1994.

Kilmann, R. and K. Thomas. "Interpersonal Conflict-Handling Behavior as Reflections of Jungian Personality Dimensions." *Psychological Reports*, 37 (1975): 971–980.

Likert, Rensis and Jane Gibson Likert. *New Ways of Managing Conflict*. New York: McGraw-Hill, 1976.

McCroskey, James C., Virginia P. Richmond and Robert A. Stewart. *One on One: The Foundations of Interpersonal Communication.* Englewood Cliffs, NJ: Prentice-Hall, 1986.

McCroskey, James C. and Larry R. Wheeless. *Introduction to Human Communication.* Boston: Allyn and Bacon, 1976.

Myers, Gail E. and Michele Tolela Myers. *The Dynamics of Human Communication: A Laboratory Approach,* 6th ed. New York: McGraw-Hill, 1992.

Trenholm, Sarah and Arthur Jensen. *Interpersonal Communication,* 2nd ed. Belmont, CA: Wadsworth, 1992.

Case 43

TargetTerms

- intrapersonal conflict
- conflict is war
- competing versus compromising conflict style

PreviewNotes

Our view of conflict influences how we participate in it. Our participation is also influenced by our conflict style.

CaseParticipants

Kurt Hollins—51-year-old man; recently married for the second time to Angela Ripase

Amy Ripase—15-year-old daughter of Angela Ripase, who had divorced Amy's father two years ago; recently has become a stepdaughter to Kurt Hollins; very rebellious and self-centered

"Just hear me out . . ."

Amy has not accepted her new situation of having Kurt Hollins in her life, as both her stepfather and her mother's new husband. She has just moved into a new home close to where she lived earlier with her mother. Although she sees her real father often, she wishes that her life would be like when her parents were married. Her frustration has manifested itself by Amy's hanging out with the wrong crowd at school. Kurt and Angela are most concerned about her attitude change and have entertained the thought of presenting Amy with the option of going to a nearby private school. Angela persuades Kurt to bring this idea up to Amy.

Amy: I'm not listening to anyone who pretends to be my father!

Kurt: If I said it once, I must have said it a million times before. I promise, I'll never make you call me anything other than Kurt.

Amy: I had no intention—believe me.

Kurt: Do you think that you and I can have a little talk?

Amy: What about?

Kurt: Amy, I am not your enemy. I know that I can never be your Dad.

Amy: Well, we agree on that one!

Kurt: Your mother means the world to me and I want to give both of you everything I can.

Amy: Who said we didn't have what we needed before you took over?

Kurt: I am not taking over. I want you to share in the life that your mother and I have chosen. You know that I never had a daughter.

Amy: I'm not your daughter—and I don't want to be your daughter. And besides, what about your son?

Kurt: You know that he doesn't live with me and I miss that.

Amy: What makes you think that I'll be a good substitute?

Kurt: I don't want a substitute. I never said that. But, I will tell you that I want to be—

Amy: What about what I want?

Kurt: O.K.—I'll reword to make you feel better—to try to be—well, a parent to you. If you want Amy, I'll define that, too.

Amy: Finished?

Kurt: What are you being so difficult?

Amy: Because I don't want to go to that private school.

Kurt: So, that's it. I knew it had to be something. Well, I just want you to realize that I had nothing to do with that decision.

Amy: Sure!

Kurt: It just so happens that your mother talked to me about it and I said that I'd do whatever she wanted.

Amy: Bullshit!

Kurt: Amy, I will not have you talk to me like that!

Amy: Well, you're lying. My mother would never think about sending me to private school. She never wanted to before you came into the picture.

Kurt: She never had that option.

Amy: Oh, boy—now that you can buy her off with anything, I guess I have no choice. And stop putting down my father.

Kurt: I'm not. Please calm down for a second. O.K. If this makes any sense to you at all—I can't always do what's best for my son—although I sometimes wish that I could. Amy, the fact is that your current friends are holding you back.

Amy: By whose standards—yours? I grew up with these people.

Kurt: Breton Academy will offer you the finest education with the finest teachers.

Amy: And the finest friends for me? Is that it? You want me to change everything. You changed my house—you changed my mom and now you want to change me. Well, I hate you and I wish I never had to see you again!

CaseConcerns

1. What intrapersonal conflict is evident in Amy's behavior? How is this influencing the way she communicates with her stepfather?
2. Which participant views conflict as war? How does this myth about conflict influence the communication process in this case? In your life?
3. What strategy does Kurt use to reduce or avoid the conflict with his stepdaughter? Does this method work for him?
4. Does the source of the message in this case influence the potential for conflict? How? What if Amy's mother had initiated this conversation? Would the conflict be the same?
5. If you were the stepparent in this case, how would you role-play this scene? Do the same for Amy.

ReflectiveResponses

1. Identify an intrapersonal conflict that you have had involving an intimate relationship. Describe how this conflict affected your communication with the other person.
2. Describe your personal conflict management style. Do you usually handle conflicts in the same way? Explain your answer.

Case 44

TargetTerms

• conflict avoidance

PreviewNotes

Shakespeare once said, "Never a borrower nor a lender be." All too often, this advice is not heeded and thus conflicts arise.

CaseParticipants

Mary Conrad—sensitive, sweet, and vulnerable; too nice for her own good

Jan Nordstrom—level-headed friend of Mary; pragmatic

"Boy, have you got a problem!"

It's been seven months since Mary lent her friend Betty a considerable amount of money. Although Mary and Betty have continued to see each other socially, the borrowed money has never been repaid—nor has it been discussed. Mary feels uncomfortable reminding her friend about repayment, and at first just doesn't think about it . . . until the idea of losing the money starts to gnaw away at her. While trying to set aside some personal vacation funds, Mary realizes how low her reserve is getting. She decides to seek the advice of her friend Jan.

Mary: Got some bad news—I'm not gonna be in a position to take that long weekend that we planned.

Jan: Why not?

Mary: I'm low on funds.

Jan: But you said that you were gonna get some money that was owed you.

Mary: Well . . .

Jan: C'mon—out with it! I've been counting on this.

Mary: I don't have the money.

Jan: This makes no sense. You said you would have the money. What happened?

Mary: I lent it to Betty.

Jan: Why?

Mary: Well, she sounded—you know Betty—like she needed the money right away—so, I went to the bank—cashed a check and lent it to her.

Jan: How much money are we talking about?

Mary: Over five hundred bucks.

Jan: How much over?

Mary: Seven-fifty, to be exact.

Jan: Did you ask her for it back?

Mary: No.

Jan: Boy, you're a good friend to have. I wish you would be so nice to me!

Mary: C'mon, of course I want it back. But, Betty, well—she's raising that baby by herself—and you know—can't work because she can't get babysitting and all. I just feel funny asking her for the money.

Jan: Does she know you want it back? That you need it for a vacation?

Mary: I don't know. She keeps telling me that she has no money coming in from that idiot she divorced. And she's raising the baby herself, you know.

Jan: You said that twice, Mary. Guess you don't want that vacation or the money—otherwise, you'd ask her for it.

Mary: I'm telling you this knowing how stupid it must sound—but I just can't ask her for it. She's got so many—well—problems.

Jan: Well, so have I. Now I have no one to go away with.

Mary: I guess I could take a loan, if it means so much to you.

Jan: You jerk. I can't believe how dumb you sound—you want to take a loan because someone else owes you money. Tell Betty to take a loan—and pay you back. And then tell her to take a hike and never bother you again.

Mary: Oh, sure. I can jut picture me telling her that.

Jan: Well, if you won't tell her—get a lawyer to.

Mary: Nothing's in writing.

Jan: How dumb can you be?

Mary: You're not helping, you know. And what's more—a lawyer will cost a fortune and I'll end up owing money.

Jan: You know what?

Mary: What?

Jan: You've got yourself one big problem.

Mary: O.K.—you're right. I'll call her—so, quick—give me the phone before I lose my courage. (*She starts to dial and hears the ringing signal as Betty answers with a pleasant sounding "hello." Upon hearing her voice on the other end, Mary quickly hangs up the phone, and turns to Jan.*)

Jan: What happened?

Mary: She wasn't home. I'll try her later.

CaseConcerns

1. Describe the intrapersonal conflict in this case for Mary. How does she deal with it?
2. Why is it so difficult to confront others about money when it is owed to you? Have you ever had this happen to you? What did you do?
3. Why does Mary lie at the end of the case? Have you ever found yourself in a similar situation?
4. Describe Mary's conflict style in this case. How and why is her choice not effective?

ReflectiveResponses

1. Why do we avoid conflict? What are the fears that we feel?
2. How do you deal with lending money to friends? What are your rules?
3. Why is it harder to tell friends things?

Case 45

TargetTerms

- conflict styles
- conflict strategies

PreviewNotes

How we individually handle conflict may have an impact on how others respond to us.

CaseParticipants

Judy—34-year-old woman who is extremely confident, independent and assertive; involved in a consulting firm partnership with George and Rob

George—44-year-old divorced man who is a single parent of one child; goal-oriented and wants to expand the boundaries of his career

Rob—40-year-old happily married man with two children; suffered the premature loss of his father within the last year and now has been consumed with taking care of his mother

"Now, what do we do?"

Judy and George are in a conference room waiting for Rob to discuss the upcoming week's schedule. Another item on the agenda is to discuss consulting fees and allocations. Since Rob has been in and out of the office for the past two weeks attending to his mother's affairs, he has not participated in the last three client proposals and offerings.

Judy: So, where is he? Just another example of his irresponsibility, it seems to me.

George: Calm down—you know he's having some problems.

Judy: So do I, and I separate them from what I do here. He promised he was not going to pull this stuff anymore.

George: Maybe, you're right. I just want to hear what he has to say. (*enter Rob*)

Rob: Sorry I'm late. I've had to catch up on some personal business. I'm trying to get my mother on the waiting list for a nursing home. I must've spent an hour waiting for real people to replace voice mail at the Social Security offices. (*Sensing the strain in the room*) Speaking of real people—

Judy: Mmmm-hmmm. We realize you have a lot of problem, but we are here to discuss business now.

George: And our compensations for the Smith project.

Rob: "Our?" Don't tell me that you are still thinking of cutting my share. Without me, you wouldn't've gotten the entire project off the ground.

Judy: That's exactly what we are thinking.

George: Rob, hey, we are just feeling that we should get the benefits of doing most of the work on this account. You must agree that since Judy and I had to take the burden of your work we deserve some type of increase in remuneration.

Rob: You mean all the stress I've had finishing the preliminary contracts and dealing with my family problems is worth nothing!

George: Hey, pal, I understand where you're coming from. But, in order to accomplish what we want to, we have to focus on business—not on friendship. We busted our brains this week.

Rob: If this happened to either of you, I sure would not expect to take away your share of the fee.

George: I'm sorry, I—we—don't feel that way. If this happened to us, we would accept our losses.

Rob: It's pretty clear that I'm no longer appreciated around here. What about all the preliminary work I did?

George: You do have a point. Maybe you do deserve something, but not all of your share.

Judy: I was having personal problems at the time, too—but you two did not even hear about it and my work was not affected. Business is business.

George: C'mon, guys. This isn't getting us anywhere. No one's listening to anyone.

Rob: Fine, I'll solve the problem. Take the money—and your partnership . . . (*He storms out of the room, slamming the door.*)

George: (*looks at Judy with a sarcastic look on his face*) So, big shot! What do we do now? We still need him.

CaseConcerns

1. How did each of the case participants handle the conflict in this case. Describe each person's interpersonal conflict management strategy and whether you believe it was effective.

2. What were the underlying reasons for the conflict in this case? Do you believe that the conflict was inevitable or could the situation have been managed prior to this incident?

ReflectiveResponses

1. How do you handle conflict in your life? Do you have one predominant conflict handling strategy? Explain your answer.
2. When working in a group or professionally with others, how do you handle conflict which may occur?
3. How can conflict be productive in an organizational communication situation?

Case 46

TargetTerms

- conflict styles
- conflict strategies
- interpersonal conflict

PreviewNotes

Frustration can result when one person fails to recognize that a conflict may be brewing.

CaseParticipants

Nick—30 years old, hard working, has an associates degree; married with one child; experienced in his field and has an opportunity for a promotion

Rena—24 years old, single, college grad from a prestigious business school; has the potential to succeed and pursues that goal zealously

"Who said so?"

Rena and Nick work for the same company. After exiting a company business meeting, Nick signals to Rena and says:

Nick: C'mere. I want to talk to you—right NOW!

Rena: I really don't have time now. I'm in a hurry.

Nick: Well, you're gonna have to make time. (*He leads her into an office and slams the door*.) What on earth do you think you are doing—stealing the ideas I've worked on for months—and then presenting them as your own at the meeting?

Rena: It just so happens that I've had the same views you've had all along. You simply reinforced my ideas, and I simply expressed them before you did.

Nick: Oh yeah! You stole the ideas to get the promotion I told you I wanted.

You knew that I applied for the next level position.

Rena: Promotion? You never told me that you were interested in a promotion. If anyone deserves a promotion, I do—I—

Nick: (*interrupting*) You deserve a promotion? All you've done since you've been here is take credit for everyone else's ideas. I never thought you'd do this to me, though.

Rena: Try to prove it! How do you know they weren't my ideas? I may not have as much experience as you, but getting my degree in business administration certainly taught me a lot.

Nick: Not to mention teaching you how to steal.

Rena: I still don't see what the problem is and what I did wrong.

Nick: How can you be so blind?

Rena: What do you mean? (*She watches him storm out of the room as she repeats her question aloud.*)

CaseConcerns

1. In your opinion, does Rena really think that she is right in presenting what Nick believes to be his ideas. Defend your answer.

2. Can the conflict in this case be managed? If so, how? If not, why?

3. Imagine it is the next day in the office. Continue the dialogue in this case between Nick and Rena.

ReflectiveResponses

1. How can we as communicators protect ourselves from other people taking our ideas and getting credit for them?

Case 47

- conflict style
- conflict strategies
- cultural differences

PreviewNotes

Learning to manage conflicts in the age of diversity is extremely important

CaseParticipants

George—20-year-old immigrant from Russia who has lived in the United States for the past 17 years; he has been accepted in college and has registered for courses

Malcolm B.—Chair of the Foreign Language Department

"I thought the Cold War was over!"

During the first week of scheduled classes, George was informed by his Russian language teacher that he is not to take the class. Both angry and surprised, George promptly reports to the head of the Language Department.

George: . . . and after she called my name on the attendance list, I responded and she looked up. She walked toward me, stopped and said that I am not allowed to be in this class and that I should get my books and leave. I opened my mouth to speak, but she ignored me. I stood up then to leave. And that's when I headed to you.

Malcolm: The bottom line is that I cannot allow you to take the class. (*switching to the Russian language*) I have known students like you. People like you who speak Russian at home take these classes—and don't bother to show up, or disrupt the classes and the lectures. (*switching back to English*) However, I will allow you to take one of the advanced classes.

George: The problem is that if I could read or write in Russian, I would not have even signed for the first level class in the first place. I could never survive in an advanced level class. Second, no matter what kinds of experiences you might have had with other students, I am not the same. You cannot just place me in one category and assume everyone behaves the same. (*takes a transcript out of his notebook*) Here—look at my academic record as proof.

Malcolm: All I can do is offer you a placement test in Russian.

George: I would be glad to take it except that I don't know how I am going to answer those questions.

Malcolm: (*laughing*) Look, don't worry about this because I am not going to let you take these courses anyhow. Your knowledge of Russian would have an adverse effect on the class, and I just won't allow it.

George: Please, look at my record. I could easily take Hebrew or Spanish, which I read and write fluently, and receive an "A." What other possible reason could I have for taking Russian than wanting to learn about my cultural heritage and language?

Malcolm: Look, I'm really busy, and I suggest that you start thinking about picking up those extra credits elsewhere in the school.

George exits from the office, saying nothing as he thinks about what to do.

CaseConcerns

1. Describe some of the intercultural stereotypes that are indicated in this case. How do these stereotypes affect the conflict in this situation?

2. Is this case about cultural differences or academic procedures? Support your answer.

3. How would you remedy the problem in this case through more productive communication?

ReflectiveResponses

1. Have you had an opportunity to form a relationship with a person from a different culture or background? What were some of the considerations you dealt with in the relationship? Were you both receptive to understanding your respective differences? If applicable, explain some of the obstacles in your relationship.

12
Chapter

Relationship Stages

TargetTerms

- initiating
- experimenting
- intensifying
- integrating
- bonding

- differentiating
- circumscribing
- stagnating
- avoiding
- terminating

CoreConcepts

1. the interaction sequences for coming together
2. the interaction sequences for coming apart

From "Hi, what's your name?"
to "Can we still be friends?"

Overview

Meeting someone for the first time is one of the most difficult parts of the relationship process. "What do I say?" "What if we can't think of anything else to say after the first few minutes?" "How should I start out the conversation?" These and other questions crop up when trying to begin a new relationship. The standard lines of "new in town?" or "come here often?" are clichś used all too often. Authors have made millions selling books about "How to . . " do anything related to creating a relationship—from finding the right partner to selecting the right employer. Whatever the context, starting a new relationship is not easy.

Equally as difficult, if not more so, is ending a relationship. We fear the thought of having to end a relationship. Some of us were raised, for the most part, with the belief that commitment meant forever. Dealing with another type of relationship ending—death—is even more difficult. Frequently, we do not possess the knowledge to deal with change, let alone dissolution or completion. We do not know the words, we do not have the skills, and we simply do not want to do it. It is too painful. So, what do we do? We avoid change. We stay in bad relationships. We get stuck in debilitating grief. And we isolate and hibernate instead of taking risks after devastating breakups.

The coming together stages represent what over 90 percent of all Americans do at least once in their lifetimes—date, court, and marry. The coming apart stages represent what almost 60 percent of all married couples do—divorce. Whether coming together or coming apart, each person goes through a series of steps that are representative of building and/or tearing down a relationship. Ironically, however, each partner in the relationship does not necessarily go through the same steps at the same time. Herein lies the problem. Although we probably all go through similar steps, we do so at different times and different speeds—and not necessarily in order. This variation in sequencing causes confusion and conflict. With this knowledge under our belt, perhaps we can become more aware of how and why this process works.

Mark Knapp deserves special note here since this chapter focuses on his interaction sequences of relationship stages, as explained in *Interpersonal Communication and Human Relationships, 2/E* (Knapp and Vangelisti, 1992). In ten steps he describes the process that all relationships go through. Our focus will be on the effect that these stages have on relationships and the interpersonal communication process. Knapp divides the ten stages into two sections: interaction sequences for coming together and interaction sequences for coming apart.

Interaction Sequences for Coming Together

The first five stages contribute toward the initiation and development of the relationship foundation. When we first meet, we try to put our best foot forward, which often results in creating a facade. These are the times when we act like the "fake banana" (putting on a facade) instead of the "real plum" (being who we really are) (Buscaglia, 1972). Awkward situations in these new relationships are created through this uncertainty and insecurity. We are testing out the waters, so to speak, and we want to make sure we do not drown.

The first five stages described by Mark Knapp and Anita Vangelisti (1992) as interaction sequences for coming together are:

- **initiating**
- **experimenting**
- **intensifying**
- **integrating**
- **bonding**

Initiating

The first stage is **initiating**. During this stage we do all those foolish things that later we wish we had not done as we meet and greet people for the first time. Quite often we put on facades or masks so that others will see "our best side" when, in fact, this "side" does not even belong to us. Leo Buscaglia (1972) calls this process being a "fake banana" (wearing a mask) instead of being the "real plum" (letting your true personality show). We want to make a good first impression so we try to be "pleasant, likeable, appealing and socially aware" (Knapp and Vangelisti, 1992). These goals strongly affect the way we communicate during this stage. Basically, we are not being honest. Much caution is exercised during this stage while adhering to the rigid norms and expectations of conventional "first meeting" formulas.

Conversations are usually strained during the initiation stage and range from phatic communication mixed with cliches to minimal amounts of fact and information sharing (levels one and two of Powell's self-disclosure—see chapter 7). We are afraid to disclose too much information at this time, so we are cautious about what we say and how we say it. This unnatural, unspontaneous manner of communicating produces surface-level interaction; however, this process is actually necessary for the next stage to occur. Starting at this level puts us on firm ground for the risks we begin to take in the next step of relationship development, for we are trying to see if we do want to proceed to the next step.

What Do You Think?

Terry: Hi. Have I seen you here before?

Kelly: Gee, I don't know, have you?

Terry: (*laughs*) How silly of me. How would you know if I had seen you here before? I guess what I meant . . .

Kelly: I know what you meant. And, no, you haven't seen me here before—I'm from out of town.

Terry: Oh, really, so is my uncle, I mean . . .

Kelly: (*smiles*) So where is your uncle from?

Terry: Oh, I mean, where are you from?

Kelly: I'm visiting from out west.

Terry: I've been out west. Where about?

Kelly: Could you excuse me for a minute? I'll be right back.

Terry: (*mumbling*) Yeah, right! I really blew that one.

What characteristics of the initiating stage do Terry and Kelly demonstrate in this conversation?

Experimenting

Once the ice has been broken, the groundwork for more risky interactions is set. During the **experimenting** stage, we begin to put out bait to see if there are any bites. If we say what we do, then maybe they will say what they do. When the bait is taken, we continue; when it is not, we depart and the relationship probably ends or stays at a very superficial level. Searching for what Knapp calls "an integrating topic" is the key for this stage. For example, if you help me find a topic we can both discuss, I will assist you in the progress of the discussion. If I sense that you are not assisting in this search for a common ground of knowledge, then I will retreat.

Usually, a great deal of time is spent in this experimenting stage. For new relationships, the effort becomes a desire for more depth of information from the other person. As the relationship grows, the goal may stay the same or become an attempt to avoid awkward situations or conflicts. However, during this stage the communication is a continued effort to discover similarities within the relationship.

What Do You Think?

Terry: Oh, hi. I didn't think you would really come back.

Kelly: Why not?

Terry: Oh, I don't know. So where were we?

Kelly: I was trying to tell you that I am from San Francisco and that I am here for a computer convention.

Terry: Really? I'm into computers, too. What do you do with computers?

Kelly: I'm a graphic artist—you know desktop publishing. I work for an advertising agency.

Terry: Neat. I'm more in the programming end of it. MAC or PC?

Kelly: MAC, of course. And yourself?

Terry: Same. You can just do so much more with the MAC. Have you seen the PowerMAC?

At this point, what characteristics of the experimenting stage have Terry and Kelly demonstrated? What changed from the first encounter?

Intensifying

This stage is all that it implies in its name—**intensification**. Here we see new risks being taken in order to begin to cement the relationship and "rev" it up to a more committed stage. Although caution is exercised during each new risk taken, once approval is received, the new risk behavior is added to the repertoire of relationship behaviors to establish a large list of "things we can do together." Accepting an invitation to your friend's Thanksgiving family dinner is a risk that establishes a certain amount of commitment to your new friend and the relationship. Favors are used here to get the other person to commit to the relationship and to you, the person.

More intimate disclosures are offered during intensifying in an attempt to deepen the relationship. Other language usage differences include more informal forms of address (nicknames, terms of endearment), first person plural pronouns (we, us), and more direct expressions of commitment ("I really like you").

What Do You Think?

Terry: Hi, Hon. Are you ready for this week-end away together? It's our first!

Kelly: I sure am. I can't wait. Oh, could you stop on the way over here and pick up my dry cleaning so I will have it here Monday morning for work? I'd really appreciate it—I'll pay you when you get here.

Terry: Sure, no problem. I'll be there in about 30 minutes. Can you be ready by then?

Kelly: I'm always ready for you!

What changes have occurred at this intensifying stage? What differences in language do you notice? What risks have been taken?

Integrating

This is the stage where the word coupling can be used—the two people involved now become "an item." More time is spent together, you seldom see one without the other, and a fusion of personalities begins to develop. Although the intention is not complete loss of individual identity, there are times when this can happen if the intensifying and **integrating** stages are happening simultaneously. Usually some trace of self is left for each person, even though each may not admit it. Giving more and more of oneself is the focus in this stage and the result is the creation of a relationship that is distinguished by outward symbols of pairing (rings, pins), highly-intimate nonverbal communication, common property (joint checkbook, "our song"), and higher levels of empathy. The individual "I's" become a "we."

What Do You Think?

Kelly: Oh, turn it up. That's our song! (*Kelly sings along*)
Terry: (*singing too*) I love it! And I love you, too.
Kelly: (*grabbing Terry's hand*) I love you, too, doll face.
Terry: Tomorrow let's move the rest of your things into my apartment. I mean, we already live there most of the time anyway. How about it?
Kelly: I'd love to. Sounds like a good idea. I'm scared, but I trust our love.
Terry: Me too. (*They kiss.*)

What has happened in this integrating stage? How is the content and language different? What has changed?

Bonding

Bonding is the public ritual that announces to the world that commitments have been formally contracted. This stage can take many forms such as business contracts, marriage contracts, or performance contracts. This act, whatever the form or ritual may be, puts new light and dimension on the relationship. It is no longer an informal interaction with a wide range of choices; the contract *or* the institutionalization of the relationship establishes certain limitations and barriers which must be acknowledged. Although agreement with these stipulations has been made prior to the bonding commitment, much of the communication during the bonding stage is devoted toward defining, refining, and interpreting the terms of agreement.

What Do You Think?

Terry: After we have our commitment ceremony, do you think things will change between us? I always hear of couples separating or fighting more after they formalize their commitment.

Kelly: I hope not. All I know is that I love you more than I have ever loved anyone before.

Terry: We have so many things to talk about—handling finances, establishing roles, deciding on . . .

Kelly: Hold on, dear. We have plenty of time for that. Don't worry, we'll talk everything out—we always have, haven't we? Right now I want to bond with you in a different way. Take your clothes off, come on—you gorgeous . . .

What types of content and language are evident during this stage?

Interaction Sequences for Coming Apart

We are taught that relationships are forever, especially the committed ones. This myth creates a false perception of what relationships are really like. The reality of the situation is that relationships have a life which has a beginning and an ending—they are not immortal. Accepting this distasteful truth is difficult for most people; most of us think that we will fall in love and live happily ever after with the same person. Statistics indicate that this is not true for the majority of people. While the "coming together stages" are awkward but exciting, the "coming apart stages" are painful to the point of devastation. Learning how to deal with the end of a relationship greatly assists in the process of interpersonal growth.

These five stages from Knapp describe the process that relationships go through as they end. While some stages are characterized by conflict, others are riddled with pain and hurt. It is difficult to let go and to remove oneself from a relationship, for whatever reason. Whether the end of a relationship comes because of a death or because one partner wants out, the process of grief and hurt are basically the same. Time is the only healer.

Knapp's five stages that describe the coming apart process are:

- **differentiating**
- **circumscribing**
- **stagnating**
- **avoiding**
- **terminating**

Differentiating

At this point in a relationship, one or both of the partners are feeling a need to re-identify the self. As opposed to the stage of developing a "we," **differentiating** is a time when an "I" is needed. We feel lost in the "we-ness" of the relationship and cannot find ourselves. Individual differences become a major focus in creating some needed interpersonal distance. A great deal of time and energy are spent determining how we differ from our partner. This is a scary time because the need for the return of the "I" does not mean the need for the end of the relationship, but that is what it feels like. It just means you have probably overintegrated and now need some "I" time and identification.

When bonding takes place before sufficient depth develops in the relationship, differentiating can be an intense, expanded, revisited stage. Reactions in this stage may also be caused by adverse social conditions, catastrophes, or unexpected individual change and growth. Perhaps one person in the relationship is growing a great deal faster than the other which will cause the high need for differentiating. Although it is possible to differentiate without conflict, fighting and arguing usually become an uncomfortable focus of the relationship. Testing the other person to see how much they really care is a common occurrence.

Differentiating is the ego saying, "what about me?" It is a normal process of which we should not be afraid. However, if we give up who we are in a relationship, which is easy to do under the guise of being in love, we will feel this need very strongly at one time or another. It is neither healthy nor realistic to give up who we are to become part of a relationship—that is not what bonding is all about. The key is to realize that the relationship can still continue and will probably become stronger if the two individual people become stronger "I"s which in turn will make a stronger "we." Giving up control and letting the other person do what is necessary for them to grow is the greatest gift you can give to anyone—and that opportunity usually happens during this differentiating stage.

What Do You Think?

Terry: I really need some space, Kelly. I'm feeling suffocated.

Kelly: But, things are going so well, I don't understand what . . .

Terry: It's not about you. It's about me needing some breathing room. It doesn't mean I love you any less.

Kelly: You're scaring me.

Terry: I'm sorry, but I just want to see some of my friends once in awhile. We do everything together and I need a break.

Kelly: Do you want me to move out?

Terry: No, that's not what I said. Don't you understand?

Kelly: I guess I don't.

How has the language changed in the differentiating stage of this relationship? What about the content of the conversation? Why is Kelly feeling insecure? Why is Terry feeling the need to be alone or have more space?

Circumscribing

This stage is characterized by constricted or restrained communication which is decreasing both in quality and quantity. Certain topics are avoided, and communication is restricted to safe areas of discussion which results in talking for shorter time periods. Typical phrases such as "let's not talk about that anymore" indicate a change in ground rules and a reduction of spontaneity in the relationship.

In **circumscribing** we see the beginning of withdrawal from the previous commitment. We begin avoidance strategies—not only physically, but emotionally; we also avoid certain topics and issues. Communication time and amount are reduced. We begin to fear saying anything to the other person. Communication is much more contrived and intentional than spontaneous. A lot of unclear and misdirected fighting can occur here, as well. Both parties are frustrated and want to talk things over, but neither of them really know what to say or how to say it. This stage can be very long and reoccurring.

What Do You Think?

Kelly: Terry, can I talk to you?
Terry: Not right now; I'm busy.
Kelly: Well then, when?
Terry: I don't know. I don't have anything to say to you anyway. Besides, all we do is fight lately.
Kelly: I know. That's why I thought we could talk things over.
Terry: What else is there left to say?
Kelly: Well, I know my friendship with Kim bothers you, and so . . .
Terry: Stop. I don't want to talk about Kim. Just leave me alone.

What happened to Kelly and Terry's relationship? What kind of language is being used at this stage, and what about the content differences?

Stagnating

At this point the relationship stops moving—it merely marks time and goes nowhere—it's **stagnating**. Communication interaction is not only more substantially reduced than in the last stage, but it also takes different forms. Communication becomes a process of self-talk, rationalizing that "I might as well not bring up this topic because I know how it will end anyway." These covert discussions with the self are reflected in negative nonverbal behaviors exhibited to "let the other person know how I feel" without having to say anything. Communication becomes more rigid, shallow, and narrow.

Stagnating is sometimes extended due to the costs and reward structures of relationships. Each party may be receiving certain rewards from staying in the relationship, even though it becomes nearly unbearable. This stage is also extended sometimes because we do not really want to give up; we would rather endure than foreclose. In many ways, enduring is less painful, and there is always the possibility that the relationship might be saved. Others may spend time in this stage because of outside rewards (such as work or a new relationship) or the perverse pleasures of sado-masochism (punishing self or others). It is easier to stay in a bad relationship for a longer period of time when the power is in your pocket because you already have a new relationship or you have a new job just starting. This is the stage in which many marriages get stuck for years. Nothing new, nothing exciting, nothing at all. The partners become "strangers in the night" and really end up more like roommates than lovers or committed partners.

What Do You Think?

Terry: Hi.
Kelly: Hi.
Terry: How was your day?
Kelly: OK, and yours?
Terry: Fine.
Kelly: I'm going to a lecture tonight. I'll see you later.
Terry: OK. Ah, maybe we can talk then.
Kelly: Yeah, maybe.

What type of communication is characterized in this stage? What has happened to the content? What has changed about the language?

Avoiding

While stagnating can be tolerated while both partners are in the same environment, **avoiding** seeks to put physical distance between the partners. They avoid talking to and being in the same place as the other party. Antagonism or unfriendliness establishes the tone of relational messages; the communication also becomes more direct and to the point. Bluntness may occur when one person wants to pursue the relationship and the other person does not, so avoidance clues are presented. If physical distance is not possible, avoidance takes on serious disconfirmation signals such as imperviousness.

For Example

Terry: (*calling Kelly at work, hoping to get voicemail*) Hi. I'm not going to be home for dinner tonight. I'm going out with some friends.
Kelly: (*that same night at home, leaving a message for Terry on the table*) Terry—going to my parents' house for a few days.

Terry: (*arriving home late that night and reading Kelly's message*) What a relief!

What form does communication take during this stage? Describe the channels used. How does this stage differ in content and language?

Terminating

Terminating can happen at any stage in a relationship. It is the most uncomfortable stage to deal with, and all attempts are made to avoid having to go through this stage. **Terminating** is ending the relationship through death or dissolution. However, when it does occur, terminating is the result of many different reasons. The most common reason for termination is the psychological or social growth of two people at different rates and in different directions. While this change may take months or even years, other termination situations can occur abruptly, such as the death of one partner or involvement of a third party. Sometimes the termination is abrupt because one person just cannot stand it anymore and walks out. For whatever reason, ending a relationship is never easy.

Communication during this stage takes the path of distance and disassociation. Here we find one or both partners seeking to put psychological and physical distance between them or increasing the concern for one's self-interests in preparation for continued life without the other person. The language is usually selfish and egocentric in nature; sometimes it is sad and remorseful, and sometimes it is vicious and spiteful. Sometimes it is unrealistic, pledging future friendship and loyalty. Face-to-face confrontations are often too painful, so other channels of communication are employed.

What Do You Think?

Kelly: (*carrying a suitcase, leaving a good-bye letter for Terry but reading it aloud*) Well, Terry, this is it. I never thought it would end this way, but I must leave. I can't stand the silence anymore. What we had was great, but it's over. Maybe we can still be friends; let's wait and see. Thanks for everything and take care of yourself.

In this final stage, how does the language change? What about the content? What about the channel?

Summary

In the beginning of developing relationships, we follow cultural norms and expectations. We start with low-risk communication behaviors and increase the risks as we proceed through the steps. As we test the grounds for more solid footing, we become more confident as we receive positive reinforcement—confirmation begets confirmation—if you tell me, I will tell you. The first five stages somewhat follow Powell's five levels of self-disclosure, particularly the first four: cliche communication, facts and information, thoughts and ideas, and feelings. Each level of disclosure increases the amount, the depth, and the intimacy of information shared. Knapp's integration stages progress systematically but also allow each person to progress individually. During these first five stages, each party involved in the new relationship usually maintains a fairly even development.

While relationships come and go, we do not like to think of them in this way. We like to think that friendships, marriages, and agreements will last forever. Realizing that this myth is simply that—a myth—we discover that all relationships go through a series of stages that describe what is happening during different times in the life of those relationships. "Breaking up is hard to do" as the popular song claimed; many times we would rather stay in a bad relationship than end it. Although there are many different reasons why this might be done, it is the costs and rewards of a relationship that determine what we are willing and not willing to do about it. For whatever reason a relationship may end, we are never prepared for the pain and grief that follows. Realizing that life is a cycle and all things in life must go through this cycle—including relationships—allows us to bear the pain with a little more understanding.

Knapp's interaction sequences for coming together and coming apart reveal for us the stages our relationships will probably go through—not necessarily in that order and not necessarily at the same time as the other person. An understanding of what happens during these stages, and how we operate while we are in them, will provide rich information for us about how to deal with things that are happening in our relationships that we do not understand—namely when things change. What we are experiencing is the change of the stages from one level to another. When we begin to become comfortable with change, we then can participate in a relationship with more realistic expectations and fulfillment.

References

Buscaglia, Leo. *Love*. New York: Fawcett Crest, 1972.

Knapp, Mark L. *Social Intercourse: From Greeting to Goodbye*. Boston: Allyn and Bacon, 1978.

Knapp, Mark L. and Anita L. Vangelisti. *Interpersonal Communication and Human Relationships*, 2nd Edition. Boston: Allyn and Bacon, 1992.

Case 48

- appropriateness
- unmatched stages
- initiating
- intensify

PreviewNotes

Generally, when meeting new people, we try to be polite and friendly. Testing the waters in terms of how far the new relationship may go often makes for uncomfortable situations.

CaseParticipants

Bob O'Connell—44 years old; eyes exude both friendship and emptiness; a kind man

Diane Feil—34 years old; very friendly, but maintains her reserve

"See you later?"

On this early morning in a seaside resort, Diane has just had another disappointment with her newly-built summer house. This time— no water! After some reassurance by the builder, Diane can't help but notice that another neighbor is also dismayed by his circumstances. Smiling to herself, and knowing that misery loves company, she calls out to him:

Diane: Hi! I guess I better introduce myself to you.

Bob: So you're the new kid on the block!

Diane: That's me—just moved in yesterday.

Bob: I saw. How's everything going?

Diane: Well, my car just went in for repairs—so I can't go shopping to fill my refrigerator. And, I guess if I had water—I'd feel a little better.

(*embarrassed by her own tirade*) Listen to me—I guess what I'm saying is that I'm not doing real well without my first cup of coffee.

Bob: No, you're doing just fine. Keep going.

Diane: Thanks, but there's so much to be done on the house that I'm feeling very overwhelmed. Your house seems so complete compared to mine.

Bob: Don't let exteriors fool you. I have no kitchen.

Diane: You've got to be kidding!

Bob: I haven't known you long enough to start making things up.

Diane: That's a different way of putting it—so, if you knew me longer, I suppose you could tell me all kinds of lies!

Bob: Well, (*smiling*) not exactly. How long will you be here?

Diane: The whole week—through Sunday.

Bob: Hey, I'll tell you what. There's a coffee shop down the road. Since I have no kitchen and you have no water—and we both are in dire need of caffeine, can I offer you a ride? The coffee will be on me to welcome a new neighbor.

Diane: You know, that sounds great.

AT COFFEE

Diane: (*sipping coffee*) You'll go to heaven for this.

Bob: Would that it were so easy. (*pauses*) What's a nice lady like you doing in this secluded community?

Diane: There is a husband—absentee at the moment. (*warmly*) He had to return to the city for business, but my teaching schedule permits me the summer off.

Bob: Oh, you teach?

Diane: Yes, college. And you?

Bob: There was a wife. This was where she loved to be each and every free weekend, especially during the summer. She died here, four months ago.

Diane: (*honestly moved*) I am so sorry.

Bob: (*as if not to hear her*) So, now I've decided to try to gradually start doing things alone—things we always did together. (*realizing what he said*) I'm sorry, I'm making you feel uncomfortable.

Diane: No, no, not at all. I just feel so badly for what you must be going through.

Bob: Well, I do have a great support system from my four kids.

Diane: How old are they?

Bob: They range from age 9 to 22—boy—girl—boy—girl—from youngest to oldest.

Diane: And they're there for each other?

Bob: (*He nods.*) She was diagnosed in the fall of last year, so they were able to have some time to start dealing with this. But, no matter what, I guess we never know what it's going to be like. The kids are sort of taking care of me now.

Diane: Well, it's wonderful that you have so much support. (*finishing her coffee*)

Bob: They're great, my kids. And what about you? Any children?

Diane: None. (*starting to feel infringed upon*) Well I guess I better get back to . . .

Bob: Just a second—I ordered you a coffee to take out. I figured that you might need it if the going gets rough. What's on your agenda today?

Diane: Writing.

Bob: In the summer time?

Diane: It's my only real free time. I've been collaborating on a book to be completed in a few months.

Bob: On what?

Diane: Human relationships.

Bob: I could help write the introductory chapters after all of the calls I've been getting since my wife's death. I'm getting on-the-job training in trying to understand people—especially women.

Diane: Funny you should say that! If I had a dollar for every person who offered me their story—but, I'll remember your offer. (*looks impatiently at her watch*) This was nice, but I need to get back to the drawing board and get some writing in before it gets too hot. (*awkwardly holding the coffee cup and her handbag*).

Bob: Here—(*grabbing her hand*)—Let me help you with that.

Diane: (*very abruptly*) No, I'm O.K. (*almost stubbornly cradles both the cup and handbag closely as they enter the car*) And, by the way—thanks.

Bob: No, I should thank you. (*drops her at her house*) See you again, later? (*Diane opens the car door. Pretending not to hear him, she gets out—without ever looking back.*)

CaseConcerns

1. What happens in the initiating stage of this relationship? Are there any indications at this point that the relationship might develop into something meaningful?

2. Explain what transpires in the experimenting stage of this case. Think of an incident in your life where this type of experimentation took place in the development of a relationship.

3. Identify examples of intensifying in this case. Who is the initiator?

4. Identify the transitions in the various stages of initiating the relationship in this case. How does this happen in any of the relationships that you develop?

5. Will Bob pursue Diane's friendship? Will Diane accept any overtures of friendship from Bob? Why? Why not?

6. Evaluate the appropriateness of responses from both participants. What happens when two people who have just met are operating on different stages?

ReflectiveResponses

1. What happens in a real life situation when the initiating stages of a relationship do not match?
2. How is communication affected when one person is operating on a higher level of disclosure in an initiating phase than you are?

Case 49

TargetTerms

- initiating
- experimenting
- intensifying
- matching levels

PreviewNotes

Sometimes in an attempt to make a "good" impression on the job, we try too hard. This eagerness can backfire with both co-workers and supervisors. Even jobs have unspoken rules for beginning relationships.

CaseParticipants

Renee Ferguson—recent college graduate in the field of Public Relations; newly employed as an assistant account executive

Andrea Marks—Senior account executive who has worked in Public Relations for twenty years; trains new assistants in her company while overseeing their work

Mr. Henderson—gentle, older man, who has been a graphic artist for years; maintains a respectable but not too prestigious profile

"I thought we understood each other . . ."

Renee has just been hired by a reputable public relations firm. She is presently being trained by Andrea Marks. New to the company, Renee wants to please but just doesn't know quite how to act on the job. Prior to starting Renee's first assignment, Andrea issues some last-minute pointers.

Andrea: Finally, just remember not to clutter up this work area with any of your layouts or press releases. Otherwise, Henderson, who has been here longer than God, will blow his stack. And training rule number one—Henderson will be the best friend you'll have here. He's the finest graphic artist around.

Renee: So, in short, I'm supposed to stay on his good side.

Andrea: You got it, kid. You'll play the game very well, It's nice to know that you were hired at such a busy time in the firm. We need people like you. Now, what else do you need to know before you begin your first assignment?

Renee: Who will I report to for approval?

Andrea: Me—and only me. We have a written and unwritten chain of command. The only problem you'll encounter is when this code is broken. I'll give you all of the policy statements that relate to this.

Renee: That won't be a problem. In my communication studies program, there was a great emphasis placed on this area. Is that all, Andrea—I mean, that is, if it's O.K. to call you "Andrea?"

Andrea: Sure, we're all on a first name basis here . . . except for Henderson. Remember that I said that he's the senior member of our team. Although he's just about ripe for retirement and just does his own thing without getting in anyone's way—we are all hoping that he'll always be here in the company—and we know and respect him as "Mr." Henderson.

Renee: Thanks. I'm feeling very comfortable, and I know I'll like it here.

A WEEK LATER

Renee: Well, hello again, Mr. Henderson.

Mr. H: So good to see you on the job, Renee. Looks like you're a pretty busy woman.

Renee: You know, I must tell you how much I have admired your work. You really know your field.

Mr. H: Why, thank you Renee. That's very nice to hear.

Renee: You really seem to enjoy what you do. I'm hoping that I have the same type of confidence in my work.

Mr. H: Well, I don't know what to say—other than I'll always be around the corner if you need any assistance. Just call out—

Renee: You know, there is something. I can use your advice. Do you see these ad layouts? (*He nods.*) Well, I've been really working on them day and night and they're due on the thirteenth.

Mr. H: The day after tomorrow?

Renee: Yes. And, there's so much more to do. You know, it's my first assignment, not to mention my first job—and I'd like your opinion on what I've done. Would you look at them, please?

Mr. H: (*He studies them and makes the necessary comments in terms of constructive criticism.*) Well, young lady, looks like you need to focus on a few more areas, here. If I were you, I'd talk to your supervisor about this and check about making the changes. Perhaps you'll get an extension on the deadline. I know that with a little work, you'll do just fine.

Renee: How can I thank you? Well, my work's sure cut out for me.

THE FOLLOWING MORNING RENEE GOES INTO ANDREA'S OFFICE

Andrea: So, how's it going? Since I haven't heard from you all week, I'm assuming that the proposal for the account is ready to go.

Renee: Well, not exactly.

Andrea: Please explain this to me—immediately. The client is due here at 9:00 A.M. on the thirteenth. That's tomorrow, Renee!

Renee: (*squeamishly*) Mr. Henderson advised me to focus on some other areas, and I've been trying to . . .

Andrea: He, what?

Renee: He was critiquing my work—

Andrea: (*quick to interrupt*) And, why may I ask, was he doing my job?

Renee: I saw him yesterday. I never thought it would be a problem to receive additional input.

Andrea: Additional? You never asked me for the original.

Renee: I didn't want to bother you.

Andrea: That is my job. And **your** job, Renee, is to report directly to me. I left you alone because I wanted you to feel independent here— and not as if someone was breathing down your neck. Henderson is an artist—not a consultant!

Renee: I'm sorry. But I didn't know what else to do.

Andrea: Well, just have them on my desk tomorrow morning—9:00 sharp!

Renee: (*squirming*) I'm afraid that it's not as complete as I thought.

Andrea: And that's why you have a supervisor to help you, as well as direct you on such matters. (*She starts to go through other papers.*) On my desk, tomorrow, please. And I trust that it will be as thorough as we've discussed in our initial conference.

Renee: (*a bit unsure of herself*) If you don't mind my saying this, I think Mr. Henderson made some really crucial points—some of which were validated in my course work at State University. Can I discuss some of them with you?

Andrea: Let's get something straight right now. This is not State University— nor is this firm "Henderson and Company." You are in my charge. And this, my dear, is the way it will be—if—you are to remain with us. Understood?

CaseConcerns

1. What is revealed in the experimenting stage of the relationship in this case?

2. At what point is the relationship between Andrea and Renee intensified? How does this affect the development of the business working relationship?

3. What will be the outcome of the relationship between Renee and Andrea? Why? What will be the outcome of the relationship between Mr. Henderson and Renee? Why?

4. Who is at fault in this case? Explain your answer.

ReflectiveResponses

1. Describe an initial encounter in a business relationship that you have had. What problems can you identify?

2. Compare John Powell's levels of disclosure to Knapp and Vangelisti's integration stages. How are they the same? How are they different?

3. Should there be any guidelines in the development of a business relationship? If so, what would they be? How are they the same as or different from the relationship stages in this chapter?

Case 50

TargetTerms

- initiating
- experimenting

PreviewNotes

Starting out a new relationship is difficult. What do you say first? How much should you say? How far should you push? Not knowing the sex of the participants (as in this next case) will promote some interesting discussions about who says what to whom and why.

CaseParticipants

Participant One—26 years old, intelligent
Participant Two—26 years old, intelligent

"Hi—come here often?"

The scene: A singles bar at any time, in any place. Participant One ("1") approaches Participant Two ("2") with the ulterior motive of initiating a relationship.

1: Hi. Sorry to be staring. I couldn't help but notice you.
2: What am I supposed to say to that?
1: I guess what you want to say.
2: Tell me, is this a standard opening line for you?
1: Pretty analytical, huh? Next thing I know you'll expect me to ask you what sign you are.
2: On that note, you'll get an accurate answer. It just so happens that I like all that stuff.
1: So, what are you?
2: Aries! Creative, artistic—impetuous—
1: (*cuts off*) And very interesting. So, do you come here often?
2: Believe it or not, this is a first.

1: Really?

2: Honest!

1: How do you feel about being here?

2: You don't stop, do you?

1: Just curious, and the truth is that I'd like to get to know you.

2: Are you coming on to me?

1: Sounds as if you've played the game before. The next move is yours.

2: I like your style.

1: And I like yours. Wanna dance? (*"2" nods.*)

2: (*on the dance floor*) You move well, Nice rhythm!

1: We're pretty good together.

2: (*smiles*)

1: Where are you from?

2: The North End.

1: Me, too. North End High School?

2: Yes.

1: Me, too. When did you graduate?

2: Eight years ago. Seems like another lifetime.

1: I must have been there at the same time.

2: Hey, do you remember that crazy French teacher who must be about 97 years old by now?

1: Who could forget?

2: Those days seem so far away, don't they.

1: We're not that old!

2: Well . . .

1: So much has changed for me, anyway. (*pause*) What do you do?

2: I'm in Public Relations.

1: I'm in the same sort of business—I produce commercials.

(*"1" subconsciously lightly touches "2's" hand—and then as with a sudden abrupt reaction, quickly pulls away.*)

CaseConcerns

1. Identify the sex of Participant One and Participant Two. Was there a specific way in which he/she communicated in this initial stage that led to your conclusion? Explain.

2. Trace the initiating stage of coming together in this case. Do the same for the experimenting stage. What other stages are evident in this case?

ReflectiveResponses

1. What types of risks are involved in the initiation stage of a relationship when the meeting ground is in a bar? Are the risks different in other locations? How so? How does this affect the communication process? How is the communication process different from being introduced through a formal introduction?

2. Consider what will happen next in the case if you were to have the opportunity to create an ending. What stages of interaction would you choose to develop? Why?

3. Describe an initial relationship encounter, identify the location and explain your communication behaviors. Would you change anything in retrospect?

6. Why do people have a difficult time initiating relationships? What are some of the problem you have encountered?

Case 51

TargetTerms

- initiating
- experimenting
- intensifying

PreviewNotes

Dating creates all sort of superfluous communication.
Sometimes the levels of initiating relationships are condensed.

CaseParticipants

Kent Toal—divorced for the past six years; business friend and
associate of Martin Dwyer, who has given him the
name of an "eligible" co-worker

Sally Dawson—somewhat unsure of herself in her role as a
newly-divorced woman; mother of a three-year-
old daughter; co-worker in the same company
as Martin Dwyer, who arranges a date for her

"I think I'm going to like you . . ."

*Kent and Sally, both divorced, are going out for the first time. Both
seem to be relatively excited about the date because Martin has
spoken so highly about each of them. The time is 8:00 sharp, on a
very rainy Saturday night. The doorbell rings.*

Sally: (*opening door*) You must be Kent.
Kent: (*standing outside by the door*) And you're Sally.
Sally: I hope you didn't have any trouble finding the house.
Kent: No, to tell you the truth, my "ex" grew up in this neighborhood. I got
sort of nervous, in fact, when you gave me the address.
Sally: Still nervous?
Kent: No, let's just say—pleasantly surprised. (*He is a little awkward about
not being in the house at this point.*)

Sally: My God, you'll be drenched—I'm sorry, come in, please. Let me take your things.

Kent: (*A little girl peers out from the hallway.*) Thank you. (*turns to the little girl*) And—who are you?

Sally: (*The little girl whizzes away.*) That's Betsy, who is three years old going on thirty-three! I just need to wait for the sitter. While we're waiting, may I offer you a drink?

Kent: No thanks.

Sally: Nothing?

Kent: No—but, I hope that you're going to be hungry. I've picked out a great new surprise restaurant.

Sally: That reminds me—I hope it won't spoil the surprise, but I'll have to ask where. I must tell my sitter where I'll be.

Kent: Sebastiano's—it's a new Italian Restaurant.

Sally: Yes—I know. It's great.

Kent: Oh, you've been?

Sally: Wow—What a stupid start! I shouldn't have said that.

Kent: Hey—I can't help it if someone else beat me!

Sally: Yes—especially when that someone happened to be my mother! (*They both laugh.*)

Kent: So, Martin tells me that you've worked with City Bank for twelve years.

Sally: Martin's a wonderful, understanding man. He's made us have one thing in common—knowing him, that is. It's as if I've known Martin forever. He's in a tough position, too. Before I came into the picture, Martin knew my ex-husband. His allegiance is to both of us—which makes it hard. Hey, I must sound like a first class heel! Confession number two—and I better tell you now—you're my first date since the divorce.

Kent: I think I figured that out.

Sally: How are you so smart?

Kent: Rule number one from an old pro—we don't talk about "baggage."

Sally: Baggage?

Kent: That's the term that spells out what you're "carrying" from your past—like what habits you hated about your "ex," why you feel so hurt or deserted, and all the other stuff that goes with your previous married life.

Sally: Makes sense. So, I'll resolve to leave the "baggage" home tonight. Oh, there's the doorbell. That must be Jenny, the sitter. (*Sally ushers her in and Jenny makes herself at home, calling for Betsy.*)

Kent: Everything set? Ready to go?

Sally: Yes, just let me tell Jenny where I'll be. (*Sally goes to the hallway and calls to Jenny, who quickly comes to get her last-minute instructions.*)

Jenny: Anything else, Mrs. Dawson?

Sally: (*in a barely audible whisper—very nervously*) Well, yes there is. Do you suppose that—well, maybe, if I call later—if necessary—that you might be able to spend the entire night with Betsy?

CaseConcerns

1. How are the stages in initiating relationships condensed in this case? What impact does it have on the relationship?
2. How are Sally's initial feelings about Kent revealed? How are Kent's initial feelings about Sally revealed? Is the dialogue you identified typical?
3. How will the evening progress? What do you think the next stage will be?
4. What pressures from society influence "second-time-around" dating? How did these pressures impact on Sally and Kent?

ReflectiveResponses

1. Do you have evidence in your life that the coming together stages are not realistic? Explain. Do intimate relationships "side-step" these stages? How?
2. Have you had a first date where the initiation stages were mismatched?

Case 52

- terminating
- differentiating
- circumscribing

PreviewNotes

Divorces with children involved disallow the termination of a marriage to be final. Although the marital relationship is over—another type of involvement still exists between mother and father. Divorced couples are forced to go through several other interaction stages even though their marriage contract is terminated.

CaseParticipants

Jeremy Adelson—46-year-old, recently married a younger woman after his divorce; successful businessman; devoted father

Rosalie Adelson—40-year-old, having a difficult time entering the life of a suburban, single mother; bitter, but devoted to her daughters

"Whatever you want—I give up!"

Jeremy and Rosalie, married directly after college graduation, were originally the epitome of what a happy marriage could be. Fifteen years of misunderstanding each other changed that and led to divorce. Although the proceedings began amicably, dividing the assets accumulated during the years they spent together resulted in animosity and anger. After a settlement was finally reached, Jeremy met and fell in love with Sara, whom he later married. Following the divorce and Jeremy's marriage, Rosalie found it extremely difficult to re-enter the mainstream of life as a single parent. She bitterly fought joint custody, but the court ruled against her. The rift continued to grow between the parents. The first time that Rosalie has to send her two young girls off to their father and stepmother is very traumatic for her. Jeremy arrives at the house.

Jeremy: Kids ready?

Rosalie: I've had them packed and ready to go for forty-five minutes. I already called in late for work, you know.

Jeremy: No, I didn't know. Rosalie, the roads are a sheet of ice and I couldn't get here any sooner.

Rosalie: Back to your old excuses again. Can't you ever say that it was your fault—that you are sorry?

Jeremy: Let's try to be civil, Rose. This has been hard enough on the kids already. They don't have to hear us screaming on the front steps.

Rosalie: Well—it's about time you started feeling what they are going through, Jeremy. That's the one thing you are right about. Susie is in an absolute panic about having to share a home with a new "step" as she calls "her." If it was up to me, I wouldn't even have her stay with you—and that slut.

Jeremy: (*obviously incensed by this remark*) Her name is Sara. She is my wife. I have done everything you have asked me to do. I have given you everything I could. What else do you want? We can't go on like this . . .

Rosalie: Don't get so hot under the collar.

Jeremy: Let's get something straight right here and now. Leave Sara out of this. I never, ever, once, gave you any reason to feel that I was judging your new choices of friends.

Rosalie: Shouldn't you have added that I was forced into making those new friends?

Jeremy: Does being mean come naturally to you or is it something that you sit up nights thinking about?

Rosalie: Now, just a minute. Let's look at this a little more realistically. There you go in your brand new sports car while I have to make do with an old station wagon to carpool **your** children back and forth to wherever and whenever—and you're doing who-knows-what with a girl who's almost young enough to be your daughter. And you want me to talk like a normal person to you?

Jeremy: Look, Rosalie, we may have gone through a lot of mud-slinging, but I still know you better than you probably know yourself. And there's more to this than meets the eye. I am taking it for granted that you are not real fond of my wife—but, she is good to the girls. She's not pretending to be you, but she is trying real hard. And they seem to really like her. So, what is it? What's going on?

Rosalie: Look, you never offered **me** any emotional support in our marriage. To presume that you understand me **now** is the farthest thing from reality.

Jeremy: Just wait a minute. I know we didn't have a storybook marriage, but, don't tell me this garbage now about my not understanding you. We went through this a zillion times . . . I just could not be there for you when you needed me. We were and still are very different. But that is not to say that I don't respect you. I'm probably your biggest promoter when it comes to making a new life for yourself.

Rosalie: Sure, so that you will have less alimony to pay. Stop pretending to be sensitive. If you had any feelings before, we wouldn't be where we are now.

Jeremy: Why are you blaming me? Remember, it was you who served me with the divorce papers—and you always make it sound as if I'm the culprit.

Rosalie: What is this—a step-by-step instant replay? I'm not in the mood. The girls are waiting.

Jeremy: Do they have everything? Oh, wait, Sara wanted me to tell you that they didn't have enough clean socks last visit and she had to go out to buy new ones.

Rosalie: (*defensively*) So?

Jeremy: I don't know—she just told me to tell you that. Are the girls ready? (*He reaches out to touch her.*) Hey, are you crying?

Rosalie: No, it's nothing. (*with a broken voice*) Listen, what time are you going to bring them home on Sunday?

Jeremy: Are you sure you're O.K.?

Rosalie: I said—what time should I expect them? (*angrily*)

Jeremy: What time is good?

Rosalie: I want them home early enough to bathe and feed them dinner.

Jeremy: Don't worry. We can do that.

Rosalie: (*very distinctly*) Then, why did you ask me when?

Jeremy: No, I meant we'll do whatever you want.

Rosalie: Don't patronize me.

Jeremy: O.K.—whatever you want—I give up!

CaseConcerns

1. What coming apart stage is exhibited by Jeremy and Rosalie? Explain. Are there any examples of initiating a new relationship in the case? Explain.

2. What stages are used out of necessity even though the relationship in this case is terminated? Why does this occur?

3. Will Rosalie and Jeremy ever be able to have a civil conversation? Why or why not?

ReflectiveResponses

1. What are the problems created when a relationship is terminated but the participants must still communicate? Can you think of a situation other than divorce where this type of problem occurs?

2. Why can't people still be friends after "breaking up"? Should they have to be? What is it about terminated relationships that disallows "normal" conversation?

Case 53

TargetTerms

- stagnating
- terminating

PreviewNotes

"Closing the book" on past relationships is extremely difficult especially when it means tossing away memories. How often have we felt that we needed to "hold on" to just one more piece of memorabilia "just in case" . . .

CaseParticipants

Howard Benson—middle-aged husband of Patsy; quiet; unassuming and well-meaning; known to be personable and understanding of other people's shortcomings

Patsy Benson—middle-aged wife of Howard; overly enthusiastic about any project that she tackles; tends to take every project she undertakes too seriously; caring, overly considerate and very sentimental

"Just in case I need to call them . . ."

The leaves have turned brown. Howard and Patsy find themselves in the planning phases for the holiday season. Patsy is especially eager to start her Christmas card list before she gets too busy with other activities. Obviously excited yet anxious about "getting it all done on time," she begins to organize herself.

Patsy: It's that time again and I'm beginning to dread this whole procedure. I think I have a real "love-hate" relationship with this old rolodex file.

Howard: You always say the same thing every year at this time. What's with you and this address/phone file anyhow?

Patsy: I keep looking at the same names year after year, and I can't help wondering whether I should send a gift or a card or just not do anything at all.

Howard: You'd think it was something to worry about. You have two choices—one is to send a card—the other is not to send one. So, why the long face each year when we get to the card mailing?

Patsy: (*perusing the entries*) It's hard to explain. It's like this file holds everything we're all about—a listing of our whole past and present all linked together in names and addresses. Hey, how about this one? Look at this name, nearly faded with time.

Howard: Who?

Patsy: Ira Sedransk. How many years has it been?

Howard: How should I know? You were the one that knew him better than me. He was your boyfriend.

Patsy: That's just it. Wouldn't it be nice to send him a card—just to say hello, in a nice sort of way? (*starts to think aloud*) If I send him a card, he might not even remember me anyhow. And, then again, if I send him a card he might think it too presumptuous of me to be looking him up again in his "new" life with his maybe new, or old, for that matter, wife. But, then again, he might enjoy the attention. He always loved surprises. O.K.—Ira's card is settled. (*still looking through the file*) But what about this voice from the past?

Howard: Who's that?

Patsy: Bonnie.

Howard: How masochistic can you be, keeping her in the book in the first place? She never even acknowledged the fact that you and I had a child ten years ago. I don't want to say that I told you so—but, Bonnie only cared about one person—herself! Why keep her number?

Patsy: That's so unfair. She even introduced us. Don't you remember how inseparable we once were?

Howard: That's the word—"once." Not now—so wipe her off the list once and for all.

Patsy: I can't do that.

Howard: So, don't. Why are you asking me about these people? Don't make an issue out of something that doesn't need to be a big problem!

Patsy: You are right—(*almost questioning*)—I suppose.

Howard: Now, what?

Patsy: Well, they never remembered us in the last ten years. What good will it do except to unleash some memories that might be better left "unleashed."

Howard: If that will mean that you will honestly stop dwelling on your old boyfriend and your long, lost girlfriend every year—I won't hold you to making any other New Year's resolutions.

Patsy: It's a deal.

Howard: I'll even give you an early Christmas gift that I really thought carefully about selecting for you.

Patsy: I'm impressed that you shopped this early.

Howard: (*goes to the closet and gives Patsy a wrapped gift*) This ought to help you keep that New Year's resolution you made.

Patsy: (*cautiously opening the gift to find an attractive fabric-covered address book*) Were you that certain when you bought this that it would be so apropos?

Howard: I can only admit that I was positively certain that there would be an exact replay of discussing last year's Christmas card list—and the year before that—and probably, the next year. Before you agonize over one other name, let's go through the old list once and for all and start doing some soul-searching about who we really want to keep in our lives.

Patsy: Gosh, do you have to put it quite that way?

Howard: Patsy—do it cold turkey. Here's a big, fat, black magic marker. (*She resists taking it—while he places it in her hands.*) Start crossing out.

Patsy: I can't. How will I remember them ever again?

LATER

Patsy finishes the transfer of names from the rolodex file to the new address book. Pleased with her accomplishment of finally deleting some of the names, she tiptoes to the phone, almost as if she is doing something "naughty." With the old rolodex close at hand, she dials Bonnie's telephone number, only to hear an answering machine phone message. Patsy leaves word on the tape that she was just thinking of her old friend—all the time afraid to admit that the message might remain unanswered. Patsy then calls to her husband to announce that her triumphant task of transcribing and deleting names is complete. However, with second thoughts, and prior to throwing out the address/telephone rolodex file, she hurries to the top shelf of the laundry room closet (before Howard sees what she is doing) to quietly hide the last remains of the old addresses—just in case . . .

CaseConcerns

1. What is it that prevents us from terminating certain relationships in our lives? Have you ever thrown away an address book? Why? Why not? Why do you suppose we enjoy "saving memories?"

2. What is suggested about human nature in the conclusion of this case? Why is Patsy so secretive about hiding the old book?

ReflectiveResponses

1. Why do we become stuck and comfortable in the stagnating stage? Why do we hold on to the past? Why are we hesitant about losing track of certain friends?

2. Are women or men quicker to throw out nostalgia? Explain your answer.
3. Why do we fear "letting go?"
4. How does the fear of "letting go" affect the way we communicate?

Case 54

"I never said good-bye."

Roseanne and Alexis have known each other for fourteen years and have shared both happy and sad times. Roseanne's husband has died following a two year struggle with cancer. Widowed for one month, Roseanne is having tremendous difficulty adjusting to being alone. Her only comfort is the caring concern of her friend, Alexis, who has already weathered the adjustment to the loss of her own husband. Knowing how difficult it must be for Roseanne, Alexis tries to be available when Roseanne needs to talk.

Roseanne: The only hurt that won't go away is that I really don't know if I said everything I wanted to say to him.

Alexis: I'm sure you did.

Roseanne: I wish I could believe that. Even though I knew he had cancer and tried to be so strong—I never thought—that I'd actually see him die.

Alexis: And all the times we talked this through, you never gave up hope. There's nothing wrong with that. You gave him strength. You must believe that you did everything that you could.

Roseanne: Maybe. But maybe I should have faced reality more. You know—that he would not live forever.

Alexis: We never want to live our lives that way. It's what we don't want to think about when we care about or love someone.

Roseanne: I just wasn't prepared.

Alexis: Nor could you be. Just remember that you have so many people around you that care.

Roseanne: Oh, I know that. And I don't know what I would do if you weren't here—to listen—and to care. What I mean is that it doesn't help—what I'm saying is that everything has a connection with him. It's so hard.

Alexis: There's nothing wrong with that. You had a beautiful life together.

Roseanne: No, it's not just the nice parts; it's the other sides of our life together. Things like balancing a checkbook—or making car-buying decisions—or simply deciding what to have for dinner—I always relied on him. I'm feeling so insecure about everything now—as if I'm starting over.

Alexis: In a way, you are. Look at it as if there is a certain mystique about this time. You know, Rose, with time, you . . .

Roseanne: Don't say it, please.

Alexis: But, you need to hear it.

Roseanne: You can't tell me that it's going to get better. It never can.

Alexis: If you believe that, you won't be giving it a chance.

Roseanne: (*obviously shaken and distraught, tears streaming down her face*) I just can't shake this feeling. My world is crushed. (*trying to gain composure*) I held on to the thought that it would get better and that he'd be O.K.—and that didn't happen. It's not fair—it's just not fair. Now, there's nothing to believe in. No hope. (*sobbing*)

Alexis: I understand. Are you feeling as if an injustice was done to you?

Roseanne: I guess. And I'm not proud of that feeling either. But you know, he never stopped fighting, and I wish that we could control what happened. It's just that I'm totally obsessed with not knowing if he knew how I felt—(*She is obviously lost in these thoughts.*)

Alexis: (*lightly entering her thoughts—softly*) But, don't you think he did? You were always there for him.

Roseanne: But not enough.

Alexis: It never seems to be enough. But it is enough and we do go on.

Roseanne: Alexis, I never asked you this before—but how long did it take for you?

Alexis: It still hurts. I guess that it always will in different ways—some sharper than others. But that's what makes me who I am. With each new person I meet in my life now, I take and give back something of my past relationship with my husband.

Roseanne: You make it sound so easy. How can you make the memories go away?

Alexis: I don't think you have to make them disappear. That's part of who you are. Cherish them.

Roseanne: But no matter where I go in this house—he's there. And when I go to bed at night, I sit wide-eyed for hours thinking. I just feel so out of control—like I'm falling apart. Even when I turn on the radio, there's a song—or a cassette on the stereo—that brings it all back. Or when I open the master bedroom closet—how do I shut this out of my life? Do I throw all of the memories away?

Alexis: I don't know if I can answer that for you. There are no right or wrong answers, Roseanne. There's no rulebook on grief.

Roseanne: It just seems that with all that we've been through for the last two years, the pain would not be as great at this point. But it feels like it's getting worse.

Alexis: Then, give it time to get better. I'm not going to tell you that it is going to be easy—and even now, I'm biting my tongue not to tell you how extreme my ups and downs were. But I want you to know that whatever you feel is just that—and you're entitled to feel that way. The rest is up to time to heal. (*a long pause*) Any better?

Roseanne: Can you stay a little longer?

Alexis: I'm not going anywhere.

CaseConcerns

1. What makes "time being the only healer" difficult to swallow?
2. What can happen when the relationship is terminated by death and a partner still will not let go as in this case?
3. Describe the communication which takes place in this case as a result of empathic listening and caring. How do you relate to others in the event of a loss?

ReflectiveResponses

1. When the termination of a relationship occurs abruptly, how does the process of "letting go" change?
2. Does grieving still occur even when the termination of a relationship is not because of death? Why or why not? Can you explain the difference?
3. Describe some of your feelings as a result of a terminated relationship. How do you come to terms with these feelings?
4. Does the end of a relationship, regardless of the circumstances, necessarily mean that it is over? Can relationships ever end?

Case 55

TargetTerms

- terminating relationships
- aggressiveness

PreviewNotes

Heated arguments can be the cause of terminated relationships. Sometimes, we have just had enough, and we can't take it anymore. When it comes to this stage, sometimes we handle the end with aggressive emotions.

CaseParticipants

Francine Bennett—successful news reporter who is in the process of initiating divorce proceedings with her husband

Iris Cates—friend of Francine's who is having great trouble understanding her friend's preoccupation with her work

"I've had it!"

Francine and Iris have known each other for years. Iris never worked while raising her children. After hearing some rather distressing gossip concerning the divorce, Francine asks Iris to meet her at a restaurant after work.

Francine: I know you're just frantic to learn if the story going around is true—well, it is—I've decided to end that part of my life—yes—I've decided to divorce Gerald.

Iris: I think you're nuts! I can't believe that I'm listening to this. Did you talk to the children?

Francine: First, they're far from "children!" And since you've been eagerly questioning everyone you know about this—this is *my* concern—not yours and not theirs!

Iris: (*trying to quiet her*) Now, just calm down! You do know, of course, you're avoiding my question.

Francine: What's the question?

Iris: Why now? Being Mrs. Gerald Bennett always had a special—well, "ring" to it.

Francine: (*aggressively*) A ring that I bet you would love to be wearing as well—I'm sure.

Iris: What on earth is that supposed to mean?

Francine: I don't know—what does it mean? You tell me.

Iris: I know one thing. If Gerald were my husband I wouldn't be so quick to throw him out.

Francine: Throwing him out is hardly what is happening.

Iris: Then why is he feeling so dejected?

Francine: (*with an air of sarcasm*) Gee, I'm sure glad that he can open up with you. As I'm sure he has.

Iris: Well, the man hasn't had a decent meal in the last six months—you know, with all of your extra hours.

Francine: And you found it necessary to provide him with a home-cooked dinner—candlelight and all?

Iris: Save the editorial comments for your job. It was really not a big deal, Francine. I mean, I'm alone anyway. I cherish the company—and so does he.

Francine: I guess, then, that it hasn't been so lonely for you in the last few months. (*Iris turns away.*)

Iris: You know you've got this all wrong. (*There is no response.*) You are really overreacting to this. I mean, he's so special that it's hard to imagine what he would do if he knew you were carrying on like this.

Francine: (*starting to lean forward—almost face to face*) Well, and you would know all about "carrying on," wouldn't you?

Iris: Listen, all I am saying is that I would never leave a man like Gerald. If I'm so awful for saying that, then, well, too bad.

Francine: Bullshit!

Iris: Think about what you're saying.

Francine: As usual, you are taking Gerald's side. Why don't you come right out and say it? If you're so eager to add your two cents to what I'm going through start with the real facts about what you're really doing with my husband.

Iris: (*angry at the innuendo*) How would you know! You never gave your marriage a second thought since you became so wrapped up in your job.

Francine: You're not going to play these games with me—telling me for years to pursue my career full force—and then, when I turn my back, you're there to play Susie Homemaker for my poor, neglected husband.

Iris: What is that supposed to mean?

Francine: (*still charging at Iris*) If anyone would know—it would be you! (*dead silence*)

Iris: Gerald is a charming and handsome man. The fact that he is my friend should help me understand what you are both going through.

Francine: Spare me your definition of the word "friend."

Iris: Can't answer me—can you?

Francine: (*very emotionally charged*) I want **you** to answer **me**. And I want the answer, now. (*slowly and deliberately*) What are you doing with my husband?

Iris: (*smiling*) I really don't understand the question.

Francine: (*nearly screaming*) Well, let me help you. You will hear what I have to say just as I have heard everything that everyone has been saying about the two of you.

Iris: How can you believe any of those rumors?

Francine: Because I have these. (*She picks up her briefcase and takes out a folder of photos which she throws on the table directly in front of Iris.*) And these don't lie.

Iris: (*picking up the photos*) What can I say that will make you understand? (*Francine starts to leave.*) Come on, you're smarter than that, Francine. It really isn't what it appears to be. You're simply overreacting to something that is just not true.

Francine: I doubt it. Just for the record, it is time for **me** to start thinking of "me."

Iris: Just like that?

Francine: No, actually more like this. (*She takes a glass of red wine and throws it on Iris's white crepe suit, and she exits as Iris sits obviously humiliated.*)

CaseConcerns

1. Why did Francine stay in what she believed to be a stagnating relationship for as long as she did? Did this ever happen to you? Describe.

2. What developments led to the termination of Francine's relationship with her husband? With Iris?

3. Why is Francine mad at Iris? Does she have justification for her anger? How would you have handled this situation?

4. Is terminating a long-term relationship really the issue in this case?

5. What is the real cause of the termination of Francine's marriage?

ReflectiveResponses

1. Identify a time in your life when you terminated a relationship in a very distinctive manner which was, perhaps, not indicative of the right thing to do. What motivated you to act in this way?

2. Often we use the term "pushing buttons" to describe behavior that prompts us to do seemingly incorrect things. Has anyone ever "pushed your buttons" to the point of your doing the "unthinkable" while terminating a relationship?

13
Chapter

Characteristics of Relationships
Appreciating Differences

Specific Goals for Understanding Chapter Thirteen

TargetTerms

- intercultural communication
- ethnocentrism
- racism
- sexism
- heterosexism
- attraction-similarity thesis
- affinity
- similarity thesis
- needs fulfillment
- social exchange theory
- proximity

CoreConcepts

1 how we define relationships in various ways
2 the types of relationships and the communication problems inherent in the types
3 the reason we form relationships

"But we're so different . . ."

Overview

Basically, people are a lot more alike than they are different. We could seek to learn what similarities exist between us and others, but it seems we focus instead on differences. We crave contact and connection with another human being as much like us as possible. We form hundreds of relationships during our lifetimes, and yet seldom do we feel fulfilled and "really" connected. We keep trying and searching for just the right person. Along the way, we end up trying to change others to be more like us. In the end, we realize that the differences in others intrigue us and draw us closer to them—those very differences that cause us pain, make us crazy, and create all our frustration! Although we are similar in many ways, the appreciation of our differences becomes the glue of relationships.

We want to be different and unique, but yet not so different and unique that we feel weird or unusual. Different is good as long as it is not separate, for we long to be connected with others in relationships.

We begin this chapter by defining relationships in various ways. We continue by exploring the categories of relationships: strangers, acquaintances, colleagues, friends, intimates, and family. Each category presents its own individual communication problems. Finally, we will investigate the reasons we form relationships.

Defining Relationships

Relationships are defined in many ways by many people. The word covers all sorts of interactions—relationships with anyone we have ever met, or with a significant other in our lives. People's definition of the term depends on their particular need for connectedness. Identifying the existence of a relationship can be accomplished by using the following characteristics as **guides for relationship measurement** (Burgoon and Hale, 1984, 1987):

- **dominance-submission**—the degree to which each partner exerts control or uses power
- **emotional arousal**—the degree to which the parties are emotionally involved
- **composure-noncomposure**—the degree of conflict involved
- **similarity-dissimilarity**—the alikeness or differences between the partners
- **formality-informality**—whether the relationship is casual or contractual
- **task versus social orientation**—the degree to which either partner is concerned with getting things done versus focusing on feelings and relationship issues
- **intimacy**—the depth and breadth of the intimacy
- **depth or familiarity**—all relationships have a history that go with them and affect the interactions
- **affection, which includes attraction and liking**—the amount of attraction or liking which can develop into affection and even love; how much the partners like each other
- **inclusion-exclusion**—the amount of time spent together
- **trust**—the level of trust between partners
- **intensity of involvement**—the type of time spent together

Some relationships are casual, brief, transient, and basically nonrecurring. We often do not even qualify those types of encounters as relationships. A more informal list of **characteristics of relationships** would include such common-sense items as (Myers and Myers, 1992, pp. 241–242):

- relationships are relatively long-lasting
- persons in relationships spend time together and do things together
- persons in relationships share an important environment or setting
- relationships encourage and allow, if not require, the exchange of personal information and reports of feelings
- relationships are defined by those involved and others who see them relating

Although there are many dimensions and measurements we could use, the key **components to define our relationships** seem to be: context, degree of intimacy, and amount of time.

Context.   A major factor distinguishing one relationship from another is the context in which it takes place. Look at the primary setting of the relationship, and this picture will provide you with an excellent view of the relationship. Some contexts include work, home, social affairs, therapeutic, academic, religious, political, recreational and random.

Degree of intimacy.   A relationship can be measured by the degree of intimacy shared by the partners. While this level of intimacy is not always the same, an average will provide us with a realistic view of the closeness between the partners. Intimacy can be intellectual or platonic, emotional, or physical—or all three at the same time.

Amount of time.   The amount of time we are willing to spend with another person signifies the importance of the relationship. This measurement is about commitment to the other person to make him/her a significant part of our lives. While the exact amount of time is not necessarily directly proportional to the importance of the relationship (we do usually spend eight hours a day with people at work we sometimes hardly know), there is a general correlation.

What Do You Think?

Kelly: So, can you have that project done by tomorrow morning?

Terry: Yes, I think so.

Kelly: We can't just "think so" around here. I have to "know so" or I'll have to ask someone else to be in charge.

Terry: OK, no problem. I will have it done tomorrow.

Kelly: Morning, I said—tomorrow morning. Is that clear? I don't care if you have to work all night!

Terry: Yes. Tomorrow morning.

What is the context, the degree of intimacy, and the amount of time that characterizes this relationship. Which component would have to change the most in order for the relationship to be defined quite differently?

Categories of Relationships

All our relationships can probably be put into five general categories. While you may think of exceptions to this statement, for the most part these categories hold true. Although the categories may seem obvious and unimportant, they help us to understand how we relate to different people in different categories. We do not communicate in the same manner with everyone. We have different rules and roles for each category of person to whom we relate. These different rules and roles are not examples of hypocrisy or manipulation, rather they are important characteristics of a flexible, effective communicator. If we communicated in the same manner to our manager and our spouse, we would send very confusing messages. There are generally automatic and unspoken rules for each of the five relationship categories. As we will see, each category also carries some unique communication problems.

Strangers

The category of **strangers** includes people we do not know and people whom we are afraid to know because they are so different from us. Generally speaking, we are afraid of differences. When we investigate (in the next section) the reasons we form relationships, we will find that we are most attracted to people like us. This seems pretty normal. However, this also creates a fear of differences that disallows us from meeting people perceived as "too different." For some reason we are afraid we will either become like them and be "too different" too, or that we will be judged negatively by others for having them as friends. This fear is prevalent in prejudice, bigotry, racism, homophobia, and sexism.

Intercultural Relationships. A major type of relationship we will encounter more frequently in our "global village" is a cross-cultural relationship. We will be required to relate to many different cultures, particularly in the workplace. We are becoming increasingly mobile as people. In addition, most countries have become economically dependent on other countries, and there is a rapid development and use of communication technology. Thus, intercultural communication has become an important and necessary skill for effective communicators (DeVito, 1994; Dodd, 1991; Gudykunst and Kim, 1990, 1992). **Intercultural communication** refers to communication between persons who have different cultural beliefs, values, or ways of behaving (DeVito, 1994, p. 421). While it may seem more difficult to communicate with these types of strangers, the process is really no different than trying to communicate with anyone else by using the principles of effective communication—openness, empathy, positiveness, immediacy, expressiveness and other-orientation (p. 444). When we have to communicate with people from a different culture, we have many fears, but the major barrier to effective communication between cultures is **ethnocentrism**, or the tendency to evaluate the beliefs, attitudes, values, and behaviors of our own culture as being more positive, logical, and natural than those of other cultures (p. 426). This obviously does not promote effective interpersonal communication.

What Do You Think?

Kelly: What do you think of the new student, Tai?

Terry: Well, you know . . .

Kelly: No, I don't know. What do you mean?

Terry: Too weird. Maybe it's the strange clothing! I don't know—do you think Tai fits in?

Kelly: Well, of course not—that's the point. Tai is from another country—why do you think others should "fit in?"

Terry: Well, when they come to America—you know, when in Rome . . .

Kelly: Terry, I can't believe you! Get a grip!

What barriers was Terry putting up to decrease effective communication with Tai? How and why did Terry do this? What did Kelly think?

Racism, Sexism and Heterosexism.   Other strangers with whom it is sometimes difficult to communicate include people of different races, the opposite sex, and gay men and lesbians. We become afraid of the differences we perceive in a person's skin color, biological sex, or sexual orientation. Usually without intention, we may communicate offensive messages when we are insensitive to other people's differences regarding race, sex and sexual orientation. Any language, conscious or unconscious, that places any person in an inferior position can be considered **racist, sexist, or heterosexist** (Rich, 1974). Examples might include language referring to an African-American doctor (as an exceptional occurrence), discussions about how *men* are created equal (as if there were no women), or asking John if he has met the right girl yet (when John may be a gay male who does not intend to "meet the right girl"). This type of insensitive language does not take into consideration the differences in people— and results in severe communication problems.

What Do You Think?

Alan: Did you see that babe over there?
Kent: Where? (*looks—then whistles*) Wowie!
Alan: Get a load of that body, would ya!
Kent: Pretty hot! What I wouldn't like to do to her!
Alan: I saw her first, sleazeball. Find your own chicks.
Kent: Get a life!

How did Alan and Kent treat this stranger? What category of offensive language did they use? Why do you think they are unaware of their offensive language?

Acquaintances and Colleagues

Acquaintances and colleagues include people whom you have met and people with whom you work in various capacities (job, committees, civic organizations, clubs). While many times we do not consider these people as friends, we do have a closer and more intimate affiliation with them than we do with strangers. Although the intimacy level may be low, the amount of time spent together could be high (for example, at work). The context highly influences these types of relationships. A relationship with a massage therapist is quite different from a relationship with a manager at work. A relationship with a professor is quite different from a relationship with a dentist. The place where the relationship primarily occurs strongly affects the nature of the relationship. When discussing a problem, are you as honest with your manager (afraid of losing your job) as you are with your doctor (afraid of losing your life)? On the other hand, there are some acquaintance relationships that allow more honesty because you do not care what the other person thinks. I may not tell someone I work with how I really feel about them and their work because I still have to deal with them day in and day out. I might even lie in these types of relationships, depending upon the need, the consequences, and the probability of personal benefit.

What Do You Think?

Kim: Hi, Dr. Higgins.

Dr.: Hi, Kim. How are you feeling today? What seems to be the problem?

Kim: It really hurts when I go to the bathroom.

Dr.: Do you mean during urination?

Kim: Yes . . .

Dr.: Is there any blood?

Kim: Yes . . .

Dr.: Well, before you panic, if you haven't already, let's run a couple of tests. We'll start with some blood work. Meanwhile, it sounds to me like a urinary tract infection, so start with this antibiotic.

Kim: Thanks, Dr. Higgins. I was really scared.

Dr.: I don't think it's anything to worry about. We can take care of it pretty easily.

In this professional acquaintance relationship, what was the level of intimacy? What distinguishes the relationship as acquaintance rather than friend or intimate?

Friends

In the category of **friends** are people we consider important in our lives; people we can count on, and people who like us and we like them. Having good friends is the goal of everyone. People say you can measure your wealth by the number of good friends you have. We pride ourselves in having good friends. While we will meet many people throughout our lives, we will most likely only form relatively few important friendships. No matter what the number, the significance is high; we place friendships near the top of our importance list.

Most of us would claim that we know the most important characteristics of good friendships. Many lists have also been created by theorists and philosophers. One profile of **friends** includes enjoyment, acceptance, mutual assistance, confiding, understanding, trust, respect and spontaneity (David, 1985) while another list characterizes the **nature of friendships** as falling into the three categories of:

- **reciprocal**—each individual shares equally in the relationship
- **receptive**—one person is always the primary giver and one is always the primary receiver

- **associative**—giving or receiving that occurs is minimal, and the association between the friends is superficial rather than intense (Reisman, 1979 and 1981)

No matter how we define the word friendship or who we call our friends, we can be sure that the term is used for a broad spectrum of relationships. **Friendships** are interpersonal relationships in which people voluntarily intertwine—enjoying others for their own sake and for the rewarding feelings they provide about themselves (Weaver, 1993). Friends are people we like and who like us; friends actively seek each other out because they enjoy each other's company (Verderber, 1993). Unlike other relationships, the key element in forming friendships is choice. We are hired into job situations, we are born into certain families, but we ultimately choose our friends. There are four suggested **ingredients for a good friendship**:

- **reciprocity**—liking each other, giving and receiving
- **similarity**—being alike in attitudes and/or activities
- **availability**—we are more likely to create and maintain relationships with people we see more frequently
- **disclosure**—sharing information about the self builds and develops the relationship bond (Adler and Rodman, 1991).

What Do You Think?

Terry: Hi—Kelly?
Kelly: Yeah—is this Terry?
Terry: Yeah—how are you?
Kelly: Fine. What's up?
Terry: Well, dear friend I need a favor.
Kelly: I'll help if I can, but . . .
Terry: You're such a doll, I know you'll lend me your car while mine is getting fixed. Thanks, hon.
Kelly: Ah, Terry, I don't think so. I don't even know you that well, I mean, we only met last week in speech class. I don't even lend my car to my mother.

According to the nature of relationships, what category of friendship did Terry think existed with Kelly? What type of friendship did Kelly think existed with Terry? What was missing in this friendship?

Intimates

In the category of **intimates** are different types of close relationships such as close friends and intimate partners (but not necessarily synonymous with love)—the step we can choose to take after friendship.

Intimate relationships are those in which there is repeated interaction, high self-disclosure, high interdependence with mutual influence and high emotional involvement (Sillars and Scott, 1983). The degree to which these factors are present is directly proportional to the intimacy of the relationship, ranging from close friends to intimate partners. Intimate relationships are marked by high degrees of warmth and affection, trust, self-disclosure, commitment, and expectation that the relationship will grow and endure (Prisbell and Andersen, 1980). Although we may have countless acquaintances and a number of friends, we will probably only have very few close, truly intimate friends. These relationships are rare. While it is with our intimate friends that we usually share our deepest feelings and thoughts, ironically it is also these same people that we take for granted. Sometimes we forget to use our effective communication skills and strategies with our intimate relationships, but it is exactly these relationships that deserve this level of commitment to communication effectiveness. Three categories can describe the various **types of intimate relationships:**

- **intimate friends**—people you know you can count on who are mutually concerned for each other's welfare and stand by each other no matter what the circumstances; these friends can be same-sex or opposite sex
- **loving relationships**—while intimacy is not love, loving relationships require intimacy in addition to the characteristics of caring, mutual attachment or commitment, and passion but not necessarily sex or marriage
- **spouses**—the ultimate relationship which involves all of the above in addition to a contractual agreement (Verderber and Verderber, 1992)

With intimacy sometimes comes jealousy and the difficulty of communicating effectively with a person when you are emotionally involved. At this point, unfortunately, sometimes all that we know about effective communication strategies and communication competence goes right out the window with our logic and reasoning. For some reason, our emotions become very powerful in intimate relationships, and the communication becomes difficult. Jealousy, the suspicion of rivalry or unfaithfulness, is one of the major destructive forces in intimate relationships. Jealousy is triggered by low self-esteem (women and men), lack of attention (women), and positive attention paid to another person (men). Male-female communication differences include different communication styles (especially in content), different emotional needs, and different modes of behavior (Gray, 1992). John Gray (1992) characterizes male-female differences through metaphors such as "men are like rubber bands and women are like waves" (p. vii).

What Do You Think?

Betsy: John, we need to talk. I'm frantic with fear.
John: Good heavens, what about?

Betsy: Well, maybe it's not fear. I don't know, maybe I'm jealous.

John: Jealous of what or who?

Betsy: It seems like I see less and less or you and that scares me. You're gone all the time.

John: Betsy, stop this right now.

Betsy: But, John, I really need you right now.

John: I am standing right here.

Betsy: I mean NEED you—don't you understand?

John: I guess not. I have to go. Try to focus on what you mean.

Betsy: Oh, God. I'm losing you.

What is causing Betsy's fear and/or jealousy? What does Betsy really want from John? Why can't she express it? Describe John's point of view.

Family

Defining the term family has become increasingly difficult these days with the proliferation of many different family types. Traditional households (meaning working father, stay-at-home mother and some children) represented only 7% of the American population in 1983 (Blumstein and Schwartz, 1983). This means that we need new and revised definitions of what a family is today. It could be a single parent raising one or more children. It could be opposite-sex partners living together, with or without children. It could be second-marriage partners who have joined their children. It could be same-sex commitments between gays or lesbians. So **family** can be defined as a system where individuals have ongoing relationships with one another that have existed for some time and are expected to continue to exist; intimacy is regulated through communication and the relationships are able to change with time (Verderber and Verderber, 1992, p. 321). ''A family is a group of people with a past history, a present reality, and a future expectation of interconnected transactional relationships'' (Kramer, 1980, p. 43). The following list of various **types of families** (Gavin and Brommel, 1986, pp. 3–4) provides us with a clearer picture:

- **two-parent biological family**—a husband and wife with children from the union of their marriage
- **single-parent family**—one parent with children
- **blended family**—two adults with children who may have not come from the union of their marriage
- **extended family**—collection of blood relatives (grandparents)
- **communal family**—unrelated people who share a commitment to each other, live together and consider themselves a family

Other theorists (Fitzpatrick, 1977) describe three relational types in family communication. These types influence and impact the nature and amount of communication that occurs in the family unit. The three **family relational definitions** include:

- **traditionalists**—conventional ideas about marital roles which expect the male to be dominant and the female to be submissive
- **independents**—less conventional ideas about marital roles with a focus on equality, informality, high-level self-disclosure, and independence with commitment and connectedness
- **separates**—less of everything related to marital roles such as less intimacy, less sharing, less emotional involvement, less certainty and rigidity concerning relational expectations

While the functions of family communication are important and even crucial to individual development, the execution of effective family communication seems to fall short of its intentions. While our primary source of learning effective communication patterns comes from our family, the fact remains that often family communication is dysfunctional. A family provides several **communication functions** for its members (Adler and Rodman, 1991, pp. 202–206; Verderber and Verderber, 1992, pp. 324–327):

- convenience of information and sharing
- self-concept formation and identity
- recognition and social support
- models of communication behavior

It might also be a goal for a family to provide more effective communication role models for its members to follow such as role flexibility, shared power, unconditional positive regard for family members, and confirming communication feedback (Verderber and Verderber, 1992).

What Do You Think?

Grace: Honey, is that you?

Tim: Yes, Mom.

Grace: Oh, good. How was school today?

Tim: Mom, I think I got accepted in the honor society. They called me in for an interview next week. I'm really nervous.

Grace: Oh, Tim. I'm so proud of you. That's wonderful. What must you do to get accepted?

Tim: Well, I guess my grades count the most, but you have to pass the interview too. What should I say? What should I wear? I never did this before.

Grace: OK, now, let's see. Let's start by getting you a new suit. You could use one anyway. And then . . .

What function of family communication is Grace providing for Tim?

Why We Form Relationships

Erich Fromm (1956) talks about the dichotomous feeling of finally realizing you are an individual but fearing that you are too different. We struggle to be unique, but when we obtain that status, we fear that we are TOO different and will be rejected. We love our uniqueness and independence but we fear it at the same time; basically, we need other people and are afraid that our uniqueness separates us from the norm. We try to connect but not to conform. We try to join but not to blend into anonymity. We try all these different things to deal with this confusing dichotomy of wants and needs as human beings. "So at a very basic level, we are motivated to communicate by our awareness that we are unique" (Stewart, 1990, p. 252).

Fromm (1956) says we do four things to reduce our feelings of separateness in an attempt to overcome it: participate in orgiastic states (sex, drugs, cheap thrills), seek to conform, engage in creative activities, and learn to love. While the first three are unsatisfying and unfulfilling, it is only the last activity, love, which has the potential to satisfy our fear of separateness. So, the reason we form relationships and seek to give and receive love is to reduce our feelings of separateness.

Theorists over the years have developed many constructs which explain the reasons we form relationships. Below we will investigate four reasons for relationship formation.

Similarity and Attraction

One of the major reasons we form relationships is because we are generally attracted to people with similar BAVs, appearance, interests, and/or goals. It seems only natural that we are motivated to connect with people who are most like us in various ways. Since we both seek to distinguish ourselves and to mask our differences, it stands to reason that we would be more highly attracted to people who are more like we are. We also gravitate toward people who like or appreciate us. Thus, we like people who are similar to us and who like us—two very important elements in attraction.

The similarities need only be in one area. We can like someone because they support the same sports team, even if they are different from us in every other way. **Affinity** is the degree to which partners like or appreciate each other. We can develop an affinity for someone merely by working out at the same gym. However, a more intense affinity can be developed for someone we have started to date. Affinity for others can be developed for many different reasons, and these reasons do not have to be based on logic. They are based entirely on emerging personal preferences.

Our preferences related to personal appearance are also based on personal choice. While we are primarily a culture which judges others on first impressions and physical attractiveness, we do not actually form relationships of any importance or longevity merely on the way a person looks. While the physical attraction may be the initial connection, it is the degree of similarity that cements the connection. **Similarity thesis** states that a strong basis for relationship formation is the comfort of knowing someone who likes the things we like, who has similar values, and who may be of the same economic class or education status. This similarity thesis is the most well substantiated of all the reasons for forming relationships. The **attraction-similarity thesis** states that when we like a person, we perceive that similarities exist with that person (Adler, Rosenfeld, and Towne, 1992, p. 259). So similar attitudes attract and attraction creates perceived similarity.

What Do You Think?

Terry: You know, I am really getting to like you, Kim.

Kim: Well, I like you too.

Terry: We're so much alike, it's unbelievable.

Kim: I know. Isn't it amazing!

Terry: We like all the same things, our values are the same, we have the same goals . . .

Kim: Yeah, isn't it great. It makes me feel so much closer to you.

Terry: Let's test this out. What's your favorite type of music? Mine's techno.

Kim: Yeah, mine too, but more contemporary pop.

Terry: OK, and your favorite type of food? French, I bet.

Kim: Right—except for all those heavy sauces and small portions.

How are Kim and Terry demonstrating the attraction-similarity thesis? Is there any danger here?

Need Fulfillment

We communicate with others in hopes of getting our needs met, which is referred to as **needs fulfillment**. As we discussed in chapter 5 on interpersonal needs, we are motivated by the needs we have that must be met by someone. We have many interpersonal needs as suggested by Maslow (1970) and Schutz (1980): control or power; belonging, inclusion; love, intimacy, and affection; and self-esteem and pride. We also have needs to share and self-disclose our hopes, fears, dreams, and successes. These needs are met primarily through relationships, so we seek to find others who can meet these needs.

Needs are also met by the type of relationship we choose to enter. In chapter 10, we investigated symmetrical and complementary relationships based on needs. In the symmetrical relationship, both partners want the same thing and are almost too much alike. They are both vying for the same rewards, which results in a "one-upmanship attitude" where no one gets his/her need met. Complementary relationships, however, are based on the acceptance and enjoyment of difference. The differences complement each other and their individual needs.

What Do You Think?

Kelly: Terry? This is Kelly. I have to talk to you right away.
Terry: What's the matter? You sound frantic!
Kelly: Well, not frantic, but certainly crazed.
Terry: So, what is it?
Kelly: I got two job offers and I don't know which one to take. I'm really confused because I like both of them.
Terry: I should have such problems, but why the confusion?
Kelly: One offers great benefits with a lower salary while the other one has a really high salary with no benefits.
Terry: Well, what are your thoughts? You have a level head on your shoulders. What sounds the best to you?
Kelly: I'm attracted to the high salary, but I know that benefits are a must.
Terry: Sounds like you've made your decision.
Kelly: Gee, Terry, thanks! I knew you'd help.
Terry: Hey, what did I do? I just listened.
Kelly: And that's why I like you . . .

What needs of Kelly's did Terry fulfill by just listening? What is the reason they have formed a relationship?

Costs and Rewards

We frequently form relationships in order to get something—some reward or special benefit. While we like to think that we do not do this—that we are altruistic rather than self-serving—the reverse is usually true. We do things for others and they do things for us. This is a common circumstance in our society and a normal sort of expectation in relationships. Hallmark cards has built an entire industry on the belief that people feel obligated to reciprocate or hope that others will. If I send you a birthday card, I am really quite upset if you do not return the gesture. My cost (effort and expense to send the card) is rewarded (I get a card back from you). Although this seems like a very cold and calculating way of describing relationships, most of our relationships are structured on this cost and reward approach.

The **social exchange theory** (Homans, 1961; Thibaut and Kelley, 1959) is an economic model built on the premise that we seek out people who can give us **rewards** (physical, emotional, monetary, spiritual) that are greater than or at least equal to the **costs** (what we have to give) involved in being in the relationship. Business partners support each other through helping one another and filling in when necessary for each other. Marriages tolerate quirks and idiosyncracies because the good times, the contentment, and the love outweigh the problems or negative aspects of the relationship. When the costs become higher than the rewards, we begin thinking about changing the relationship in some way. Some friendships become more of a burden than a benefit—we get tired of listening to constant problems and negativity. The basic rule is that we must get out as much or more than we put in—put another way, the rewards must balance the costs. The arrangements must benefit both parties in order for the relationship to be satisfying and mutually acceptable.

What Do You Think?

Kim: Thanks for the card, Terry. How did you know I was feeling down?

Terry: I can read you like a book. It's been written all over your face for the last few weeks.

Kim: I guess I don't hide my feelings very well, do I?

Terry: Guess not.

Kim: Well, anyway, thanks again. Let me know if I can ever help you.

Terry: Sure. (*walks away to celebrate a birthday alone*)

What are Terry's costs in this relationship? What are Terry's rewards? What are Kim's costs? What are Kim's rewards? Will this relationship last?

Proximity

Common sense tells us that we are likely to develop relationships with people we interact with frequently. The more we see people, the greater the possibility that a relationship can form. These elements of **proximity** (being in the same physical location) and chance are the unexplainable situations where we met someone on the train or subway and they become a best friend or even a lover. We may become very attracted to someone in one of our classes at school. We see this person three to four times a week, and there are sufficient opportunities for a relationship to develop. Proximity can lead to liking.

The opposite can also be true. You can develop intense dislike for people you see all the time. A common saying that is generally supported is that familiarity breeds contempt. So, basically, you can develop strong personal feelings of either like or dislike toward others you encounter frequently (Adler, Rosenfeld, and Towne, 1992).

What Do You Think?

Terry: Did you see that new worker—Kim?

Kelly: No, why?

> Terry: I don't know. It seems as though Kim is always around—
> you know, just there when you look up.
> Kelly: So? What's the problem?
> Terry: Well . . . I don't know . . . but . . .
> Kelly: Come on, Terry, be honest.
> Terry: Well, I can't tell if I'm attracted or annoyed. I haven't
> decided yet.
> Kelly: Give me a call when you decide!

*Which side of the proximity connection is Terry feeling? Why?
What is Terry's uncertainty?*

Summary

We can define relationships through many different measurements,
but the key components are context, degree of intimacy, and amount
of time spent together. After defining our relationships, we can
categorize them into five general categories: strangers, acquaintances
and colleagues, friends, intimates, and family. Each of these categories
brings different communication issues and problems with which we
must deal. While the reasons we form these relationships in our lives
are many, there are four primary reasons: similarity and attraction,
need fulfillment, costs and rewards, and proximity.

References

Adler, Ronald B. and George Rodman. *Understanding Human Communication*, 4th ed. Ft. Worth, TX: Holt, Rinehart, and Winston, 1991.

Adler, Ronald B., Lawrence B. Rosenfeld, and Neil Towne. *Interplay: The Process of Interpersonal Communication*, 5th ed. Ft. Worth, TX: Harcourt, Brace, Jovanovich College, 1992.

Blumstein, Philip and Pepper Schwartz. *American Couples*. New York: William Morrow, 1983.

Burgoon, J. K. and J. J. Hale. "Validation and Measurement of the Fundamental Themes of Relational Communication," *Communication Monographs*, vol. 54 (March 1987): 19.

_____. "The Fundamental Topoi of Relational Communication," *Communication Monographs*, vol. 51 (June 1984): 193.

David, Keith E. "Near and Dear: Friendship and Love Compared." *Psychology Today*, 19 (1985): 22–30.

DeVito, Joseph A. *Human Communication: The Basic Course*, 6th ed. New York: HarperCollins, 1994.

Dodd, Carley H. *Dynamics of Intercultural Communication*, 3rd ed. Dubuque, IA: Wm. C. Brown, 1991.

Fitzpatrick, Mary Anne. *Between Husbands and Wives: Communication in Marriage*. Beverly Hills: Sage, 1988.

Fromm, Erich. "The Theory of Love," in *The Art of Loving* by Erich Fromm. New York: HarperCollins, 1956.

Gavin, K. M. and B. J. Brommel. *Family Communication: Cohesion and Change*, 2nd ed. Glenview, IL: Scott, Foresman, 1986.

Gray, John. *Men are from Mars, Women are from Venus*. New York: HarperCollins, 1992.

Gudykunst, William B. and Y. Y. Kim. *Communicating with Strangers: An Approach to Intercultural Communication*, 2nd ed. New York: McGraw-Hill, 1990.

Gudykunst, William B. and Y. Y. Kim, eds. *Readings on Communication with Strangers: An Approach to Intercultural Communication*. New York: McGraw-Hill, 1992.

Homans, G. C. *Social Behavior: Its Elementary Form*. New York: Harcourt, Brace, 1961.

Kramer, C. H. *Becoming a Family Therapist*. New York: Human Science Press, 1980.

Maslow, Abraham. *Motivation and Personality*. New York: HarperCollins, 1970.

Myers, Gail E. and Michele Tolela Myers. *The Dynamics of Human Communication: A Laboratory Approach*, 6th ed. New York: McGraw-Hill, 1992.

Prisbell, M. and J. F. Andersen. "The Importance of Perceived Homophily, Level of Uncertainty, Feeling Good, Safety, and Self-Disclosure in Interpersonal Relationships," *Communication Quarterly*, 28 (Summer 1980): 22–23.

Reisman, John. *Anatomy of Friendship*. Lexington, MA: Lewis, 1979.

_____. "Adult Friendships. In *Personal Relationships 2: Developing Personal Relationships*, Steve Duck and Robin Gilmour, eds. New York: Academic Press (1981): 205–230.

Rich, Andrea L. *Interracial Communication*. New York: HarperCollins, 1974.

Schutz, William C. *FIRO: A Three Dimensional Theory of Interpersonal Behavior*. New York: Holt, Rinehart and Winston, 1980.

Sillars, Alan L. and Michael D. Scott. *Interpersonal Perception Between Intimates: An Integrative Review*, 10 (1983): 153–176.

Stewart, John, ed. *Bridges Not Walls: A Book Abut Interpersonal Communication*, 5th ed. New York: McGraw-Hill, 1990.

Thibaut, J. W. and H. H. Kelley. *The Social Psychology of Groups*. New York: Wiley, 1959.

Verderber, Rudolph F. *Communicate!* Belmont, CA: Wadsworth, 1993.

Verderber, Rudolph F. and Kathleen S. Verderber. *Inter-Act: Using Interpersonal Communication Skills*, 6th ed. Belmont, CA: Wadsworth, 1992.

Weaver, Richard L. II. *Understanding Interpersonal Communication*, 6th ed. New York: HarperCollins, 1993.

Case 56

TargetTerms

- interpersonal attraction
- degree of intimacy

PreviewNotes

Close friends sometimes have problems with amount of time spent together.

CaseParticipants

Karen—44-year-old working woman who has just recently married; enrolled in an accelerated college program to gain promotion at work; childhood friend of Inga

Inga—43-year-old, successful, single woman; longtime friend of Karen; presently owns and operates a company she founded

"Do you remember when we . . ."

Karen and Inga have not spoken to each other during the past two and a half weeks. Inga, sensing a problem, calls Karen at work.

Karen: Oh, hi! Glad you called, but I'm in a hurry right now. I'm just going over some notes for class this evening. I'll have to call you later.

Inga: When's later? It's been over two weeks since I heard from you.

Karen: Yeah, I know. But I have to clean up the house before I leave for work, so I can't seem to get around to those early A.M. phone calls like we used to.

Inga: When did you become such a cleaner? You never even made a bed in the morning since I've known you.

Karen: Ugh—I guess it's the domesticated side of me showing up late in life!

Inga: Well, I suppose you better be going now, or you'll be late.

Karen: Yeah, OK, but I'll try to call you tomorrow—or you call me, OK?

Inga: How about you call me. (*She hangs up the phone.*)

At this point, Karen is feeling guilty for ignoring Inga over the past two weeks. She wonders if Inga realizes how much marriage, work and school have affected her life. As late as it is, she decides that when she goes home, she will call Inga and explain. Late that evening, Inga answers Karen's phone call.

Inga: (*surprised*) Hi—I didn't expect you to squeeze me in so soon.

Karen: Uh-oh! We are touchy, aren't we? I feel bad enough as it is. Please don't make it worse.

Inga: You feel bad! You get married and I'm left without my friend. Whew—lis—ten to me! Sounds like I'm a regular wallflower, feeling sorry for myself.

Karen: What's the matter with you anyway?

Inga: Since you got married, *you* are not the same. I mean, when you were dating, you were the same old Karen. But now—look at you. You're running home from work to wash floors and set the table. Remember when McDonald's french fries and a coke meant going out to dinner—or calling in for pizza. And you're wondering what's the matter with me!!?

Karen: Just because I don't see you as much doesn't mean that I'm not thinking of you. I probably think of you even more now because I have so little time. I get nervous about not calling—and then I just get side-tracked. I promise—when school's over, I'll be back to normal. Give me a little time to adjust to all of these changes.

CaseConcerns

1. There are many different responses that Inga may offer. In order to continue the amicable relationship the two women once shared, what can Inga suggest or say to her friend?

2. Describe Inga's definition of the relationship in this case. Do the same for Karen.

ReflectiveResponses

1. Describe some of your feelings about a time when your friend did not give you the attention you wanted. How did this affect your communication with this person?

2. Reflect on a period in your life when you needed to respect the differences in a changing relationship.

Case 57

TargetTerms

- categories of relationships
- defining relationships
- nature of friendships

PreviewNotes

Relationships in the workplace have many diverse dimensions. See what can happen when a worker perceives that the company president does not appreciate or understand the work being done.

CaseParticipants

Dave Jenkins—President of a major corporation where Jeri works
Jeri Wilks—worker in Dave's company

"I'll be back in a minute."

Dave likes to think of himself as being open to hearing what his employees have to say. In fact, he tells his employees that his door is literally "always open." When Jeri felt that she needed to make a job change, she felt very comfortable walking into Dave's office to say:

Jeri: You've probably been expecting this—but I wanted to tell you that after a great deal of thought, I'm giving you and the company notice.

Dave: This is a surprise. What's going on?

Jeri: I'm just not feeling challenged, and I'm ready for a change.

Dave: How is it that you never told me? You've got a great benefit package and an excellent salary, and your commissions reflect your hard work.

Jeri: Financial rewards are not everything. I just need a change so that I can feel more productive.

Dave: But you are productive. Everyone here is crazy about you, too.

Jeri: I know, and I really enjoy the people. Is there a possibility of transferring me to a different position in the company? Something that would give me more of a challenge?

Dave: Not right now. However, I will keep you first in my thoughts if something does come up.

Jeri: Could you be a little more specific? Do you anticipate any openings that might be of interest to me?

Dave: I really can't, Jeri. You know how it is—business can change in a minute. There might be several openings or several cutbacks. I don't have to tell you . . .

Jeri: I appreciate your honesty, but that does not give me any real hope for a new position. I just can't sit and wait for a transfer to just happen.

Dave: Just be patient, Jeri. You've put in so many years already and you know as well as anyone here, new jobs open almost monthly. Just hang on a little longer. I've got your number, and I'll keep my ears open for anything of interest here in the company, OK? (*starts to shuffle some papers while getting ready to make a call*) Thanks for stopping by, Jeri. I appreciate your honesty. Listen, I've got to make some calls, so I'll get back to you . . . Can you please close the door as you leave?

Jeri decides not to say anything else and walks out. Three weeks later, Mr. Jenkins calls Jeri's department and asks for her to come to his office. He is told that according to the Personnel Department, she quit last week. Mr. Jenkins thinks how odd this is as he just spent so much time listening to Jeri's concerns. Rather surprised, he wonders why she didn't wait for him to get back to her.

CaseConcerns

1. Describe the relationship between Jeri and Mr. Jenkins.
2. Identify the level of relationship characterized in this case.
3. What do you believe went wrong in this case? How would you have used your communication skills to deal productively with the issues in this situation?

ReflectiveResponses

1. Think of a time in a working relationship when you felt that a person you worked with did not understand your needs. Were you able to communicate your dissatisfaction? Did the other person comply with your concerns? Why or why not?
2. What do you believe to be one of the most important elements of communication in your relationship with significant others in your life? You might begin to think back on some of the most effective interpersonal communication skills you have learned and applied so far this semester.

Case 58

"I'm not paid to do this!"

Herb, chair of an upcoming dinner dance fundraiser to raise money for building expansion, informally meets with Marilyn, another program planner, to discuss a major upcoming event.

Herb: I'm really glad that you agreed to work on the dinner dance. Now, this is what I want to do . . .

Marilyn: Well, I really didn't want to get involved in this, but I've got to admit that after the problems we had last year, we really do need to look long and hard at this year's planning. I thought that you wanted me to take care of all of the arrangements for the entire event.

Herb: I take care of all that. And, well, frankly, I thought last year's event was really well run, didn't you?

Marilyn: There were some ups and downs. But, before we go any further—what is my job?

Herb: To make some phone calls and send out the invitations.

Marilyn: Listen, I'll have you know that I have run about seven dinner dances in the last few years. I'm not going to just address invitations and make follow-up phone calls. That's garbage work.

Herb: Don't you realize that every job is important to this volunteer effort? We need you, Marilyn.

Marilyn: I know, but you are not giving me the opportunity to serve the organization to the best of my ability. Last year there were so many foul-ups, and I want to do a little more trouble-shooting in this year's event if I can.

Herb: I respect what you are saying, and—there's always room for improvement, I suppose. But, we need our volunteers to do what they can to raise money. Higher numbers—that's the name of the game.

Marilyn: That's the problem around here—everyone looks only at the bottom line.

Herb: I don't understand.

Marilyn: Doesn't anyone realize that there were plenty of people who felt very left out of last year's dinner? It was much too expensive, and only a select few were able to attend.

Herb: Not so at all. Why, there were all sorts of ways that people could work toward attending the dinner dance. And besides—why didn't those that felt left out bother to say something? Everyone loves to complain, and no one ever does anything about it. That's why we need people like you.

Marilyn: That's what I'm here for—to speak up for the rest of the people who can't voice their own ideas. (*She takes out her notepad and opens to a prepared agenda.*) So, let's begin our meeting. I have a whole bunch of ideas to present to you. Ready?

Herb: (*Smiling, he glances at her list of considerations for the meeting as he takes out another agenda from his portfolio.*) And here's my list of things that we need to accomplish this morning. (*They both smile as they put their agendas side by side.*) Yes—I think that this is all going to work very well, and we're going to make this whole event a fine success. You certainly seem to know what you are doing. We need more volunteers like you!

Marilyn: And—if I don't pass the test—you'll just have to fire me!

CaseConcerns

1. Identify the role of each participant in this relationship. Are the respective roles clear?

2. Explain the context of the relationship in this case. How does the type of relationship affect the degree of intimacy in the participant's interactions with each other?

ReflectiveResponses

1. Describe a volunteer position in which you have been involved? Was your role defined? If so, how? If not, how did you know what to do?

2. How do you personally respond to acquaintances on committees when you do not agree with them? Can you effectively communicate your difference in opinions so as not to offend the others on the committee? How so?

Case 59

TargetTerms

- social exchange theory
- defining relationships
- characteristics of relationships

PreviewNotes

Sometimes when we give, we want something back. If the costs outweigh the rewards in relationships, we get angry. There are two short cases below focusing on the same issue. Try both Case A and Case B.

CASE A

CaseParticipants

Tim Roberts—28-year-old executive, expects what is due him
Ray Wiess—29-year-old executive, focuses on self-responsibility

"You owe me one!"

Tim and Ray have been friends since college. Lately, they have sort of lost contact with each other. Tim tries to rekindle the friendship.

Tim: Ray, how are you? This is Tim. I haven't talked to you for ages.
Ray: Why—Tim, I haven't heard from you since you helped me get this job. What's up?
Tim: Well, nothing really. I just thought I would give you a call to touch base and see what's going on in your life.
Ray: I'm glad you called. How's it going at work?
Tim: Great. I have a lot of autonomy here which gives me a lot of freedom.
Ray: And how's the family?
Tim: Well, actually Janet and I just split up. We just weren't getting along, I guess. She threw me out last night.
Ray: I'm sorry to hear that. Everything OK?

Tim: Well, that's one of the reasons I called. I need your help. Hey, I figure you owe me one—right?

Ray: Well, a . . . what do you mean?

Tim: You said it yourself—I did help you get the job you're enjoying—right?

Ray: You sure did, and I really appreciated your help back then. Boy, we were both struggling, weren't we?!

Tim: (*sarcastically*) Well, maybe you more than me! Anyway, I need the favor returned now.

Ray: Explain. I guess I don't understand.

Tim: Well, I figure that I helped you get your current job, so I thought you could help me with a place to live—just temporarily, you understand.

Ray: Gee, Tim, I don't know. I'd have to talk this over with Lisa and the kids. It's not just my decision.

Tim: Aw, come on. Can't you help out an old friend? Don't you figure you owe me?

Ray: I never thought of it that way, Tim.

Tim: Well, I did, and I think it's about time you paid me back. But if it's too much to ask, don't bother. I'll find another friend who knows how to pay his dues. (*Tim hangs up*)

CaseConcerns

1. Why does Tim feel that Ray owes him something? Is this feeling legitimate?
2. Why doesn't Ray seem receptive to Tim's request—or does he?
3. What would you do if you were Tim? Would you have handled things differently if you were Ray? Did Tim have a right to expect reciprocity in their relationship? Do friends have a right to expect reciprocity?

ReflectiveResponses

1. Did you ever feel that someone "owed" you something because of something you did for them? Did you ever get paid back? How did you respond?
2. Where do you stand on the social exchange theory? How does it impact on your life?
3. Select a current relationship in which you are involved and analyze the costs and rewards you give and receive.

CASE B

CaseParticipants

Chris—a close friend of Kim

Kim—a close friend of Chris

Chris and Kim have known each other for a long time and consider themselves best friends.

Chris: Hi, Kim. It's Chris.

Kim: (*angrily*) Oh, hi. What do you want?

Chris: Well, I haven't heard from you lately and I wondered what was going on.

Kim: Nothing is going on. Why would anything be going on?

Chris: I just wondered why you haven't returned my calls.

Kim: Why bother?

Chris: What do you mean? I thought we were such good friends.

Kim: (*long silence and then slowly*) The good friends I have send me birthday cards on my birthday.

Chris: (*another pause*) Oh, Kim, I'm so sorry. did I forget your birthday?

Kim: Yeah, and it's not the first time. That just goes to show you how important I am in your life—you can't even remember my birthday—especially since I never forget to send you a card for your birthday—for the past five years.

Chris: I guess I have just been so busy at work, and what with starting this new relationship with Terry—I guess I am just overwhelmed by my life right now and forgot about my best friend.

Kim: You can't spend five minutes in a card store?

Chris: Is it too late for me to make it up to you?

Kim: How?

Chris: How about dinner and a movie tomorrow night?

Kim: Call me tomorrow. I have to decide if it's worth it.

CaseConcerns

1. Why was Kim angry with Chris? Did Kim have a right to be so upset?
2. Does Chris view the friendship in the same light as Kim? Explain.
3. Do friends have a right to expect reciprocity?

ReflectiveResponses

1. Do you send birthday cards? Do you send any cards? Do you ever expect one in return? Why or why not.

2. What do you do when someone forgets your birthday? Does it depend on who it is?

3. How do you deal with reciprocity in relationships? Describe a way in which you showed reciprocity in a relationship.

14
Chapter

Communication Competence and Effectiveness

Specific Goals for Understanding Chapter Fourteen

TargetTerms

- communication competence
- pragmatics
- communication style
- impression management
- communication effectiveness
- adaptability
- humanistic model
- pragmatic model

CoreConcepts

1. the background and importance of communication competence
2. the definitions of communication competence and similar terms
3. the characteristics of competent communication through various perspectives
4. the specifics of the humanistic model and the pragmatic model of communication effectiveness

"Let's try it this way . . ."

Overview

Why is it that some people seem to say all the right things at the right time to the right people? Is it that some people are born as good communicators? Are others doomed to be social misfits because of their poor communication skills? According to researchers, the desire to communicate effectively is innately human, but the ability to do so is a skill which must be acquired and developed.

For example, when students are asked why they are taking a particular communication course, the answer most often focuses on the desire to express to others what they really think and feel. Students proclaim an inability to say what they mean clearly, to say what they feel at the right time, or to express these ideas and feelings effectively. "I feel so incompetent," and "I would like to learn how to communicate more effectively so people understand me," students say.

As we have discussed throughout this book, we all have a strong desire and need to be understood as human beings. We want to communicate, and we want to do it effectively. From the statements expressed above, it would seem that these speakers realize that being understood depends on their ability to communicate effectively. While we do not always put the burden of that goal where it belongs (on ourselves), the strength of the desire to be understood eventually outweighs our need to blame the other person for the ineffective communication we experience. Eventually we learn that effective communication begins at home—with ourselves.

Identifying the key components of effective communication skills can assist us in developing what researchers call communication competence or effectiveness. While theorists may not agree precisely on what communication competence is, they certainly do agree that it is a necessary ingredient in the interpersonal communication success formula.

After reviewing the background and some definitions of communication competence, we will examine several models or approaches to becoming competent in our communicative behaviors. Identifying specific communication skills that promote or enhance communication competence will help us in our quest to become more effective interpersonal communicators.

Background and Definitions

Background

Determining what elements contribute to communication competence has required considerable time and energy by communication scholars over the years (Bostrom, 1984; Cegala, 1984; Duran, 1983; McCroskey, 1982; Parks, 1985; Rubin, 1985; Spitzberg and Cupach, 1984, 1989; Wiemann and Backlund, 1980). "This research suggests that communication competence is determined by both conversational partners, involves knowing how to communicate, references actual communication behavior, and reflects the communicator's success at achieving his or her goals" (Canary and Cody, 1994, p. 380).

In their research, B. H. Spitzberg and W. R. Cupach (1989) found that communication competence is positively correlated to having friends and with the ability to function personally. For example, married couples who were identified as effective communicators reported happier relationships than less skilled couples (Kirchler, 1988). Conversely, a lack of communication competence is associated with mental illness, depression, anxiety, shyness, loneliness, academic problems, and other malfunctions of social behavior (Canary and Cody, 1994, p. 380).

The criteria for communication competence may differ from culture to culture. A society's beliefs and values affect its standards of communication. Because Americans tend to believe that individuals should have control over what happens to relationships, our culture decides for us that communication competence is important and necessary. It is also true that each relationship, as well as the individuals within the relationship, will probably develop and establish specific and unique criteria for communication competence. The various criteria established by society, the relationship, and the individuals may not quite match. The discrepancies create a problem when attempting to measure competence (Knapp and Vangelisti, 1992, p. 354).

Definitions

Most communication scholars agree that "**communication competence** is the ability to obtain what you are seeking from others in a manner that maintains the relationship on terms that are acceptable to both you and the other person" (Adler, Rosenfeld, and Towne, 1992, p. 21). According to this definition, **four factors characterize communication competence**:

- there is no single "ideal" or "effective" way to communicate (*variety and flexibility are necessary ingredients*)

- competence is situational not universal in nature
- competence has a relational dimension (*it takes two*)
- competence can be learned (pp. 21–22)

W. B. Pearce and V. Cronen (1980) view communication competence "as a person's ability to move within and among the various systems he or she is co-creating and co-managing" (p. 187). Sometimes the word **pragmatics** is substituted for the term communication competence to mean the ability to understand and use constitutive and regulative rules (Caputo, Hazel, and McMahon, 1994, p. 131).

Other theorists refer to **communication style** as competence in the selection and use of verbal and nonverbal language which enables people to create, maintain, and/or improve their relationships with one another (Wheeless and Lashbrook, 1987; Norton, 1983). According to M. R. Parks (1985, pp. 192–194), if others evaluate our communication style as being both appropriate and effective, these receivers will attribute communication competence to us. Eric Goffman (1959, pp. 209–237), noted anthropologist, uses the term **impression management** to describe how we manipulate our image through what we choose to say or not say. (*This term can also apply to the nonverbal aspects of our messages such as the way we dress, the way we walk, and the way we look at others*). Both of these terms can be referred to as a form of communication competence in that they can both change the receiver's perception of the sender which is the basis for measuring communication effectiveness. Joseph DeVito (1995) provides a perspective on what he calls communication effectiveness through a list of humanistic and pragmatic characteristics which, to be considered effective, should be monitored through mindfulness, flexibility, and metacommunication awareness (see Unit 6).

Mark Knapp and Anita Vangelisti (1992) offer a composite of these definitions. "Communication behavior is evaluated as effective when a person or persons is perceived as having appropriately adapted to the self-other-topic-situation interface in order to achieve a desired response or responses" (p. 362). So, if a person is perceived to exhibit effective communication behaviors in a variety of situations involving different people, topics, and goals, he or she is likely to be called an effective communicator (p. 362).

No matter which definition we use to measure our communication competence or our communication effectiveness, we can be sure that the final determination of success rests in the receiver's perception. Competence and effectiveness are receiver-based perceptions. What we can do to influence those perceptions is to present ourselves in the most competent and effective style we are capable of exhibiting. In changing ourselves through personal growth and development, we influence and impact our relationships more positively.

Characteristics of Communication Competence and Effectiveness

The skills used to demonstrate competence from one situation to another can very greatly, but theorists have identified several common denominators that characterize effective communication in most contexts. Let us take a look at how various scholars characterize the terms communication competence and communication effectiveness (used here as interchangeable terms for the same skill).

Communication competence can be described by the specific characteristics a person exhibits in his or her communication behavior (Adler, Rosenfeld, and Towne, 1992) such as:

- **a large repertoire of skills**—the number of options we have about how to communicate
- **adaptability**—choosing the right behavior for a particular situation
- **ability to perform skillfully**—successfully performing the behavior we have selected as appropriate
- **involvement**—caring about the other person and the topic at hand
- **empathy/perspective taking**—understanding the other person's point of view
- **cognitive complexity**—the ability to construct a variety of different frameworks for viewing an issue
- **self-monitoring**—the process of paying close attention to one's own behavior and using these observations to change the way one behaves (pp. 22-24)

Six commonly-researched criteria which characterize communication competence are (Canary and Cody, 1994):

- **adaptability or flexibility** (*identified as the most commonly cited standard for judging competence*)—the ability to change behaviors and goals to meet the needs of the interaction
- **conversational involvement** (*labeled as a critically essential criterion*)—cognitive involvement in the conversation demonstrated through nonverbal interaction behaviors (*head nods, vocal cues*)
- **conversational management**—how smoothly communicators regulate and control their interactions
- **empathy** (*identified for years as an important skill in interpersonal communication*)—the ability to show our conversational partner that we understand his or her situation and that we share his or her emotional reactions to the situation; it is not feeling sorry for another person

- **effectiveness**—achieving the objectives we have for our conversations
- **appropriateness**—upholding the goal expectations for a given situation (pp. 382–384)

Another perspective on communication competence offers two models: a humanistic model and a pragmatic model (DeVito, 1995). Again, specific characteristics are endorsed as contributing to more effective interactions. Adaptability and empathy appear on both lists. Involvement is defined somewhat differently but the term also appears on both lists. Conversational management could be one aspect of self-monitoring. Effectiveness and appropriateness could be viewed as examples of the ability to perform skillfully. Comparing the two sets of characteristics gives you a sense of what researchers confront when trying to quantify or measure a concept which varies (however imperceptibly) with each example.

The **humanistic approach**, which follows humanistic psychology, is gleaned from the writings of Abraham Maslow (1970), Gordon Allport (1937), Carl Rogers (1972), and many others. Joseph DeVito (1995) claims that these qualities foster meaningful, honest, and satisfying interactions. The five general qualities are:

- **openness**—willingness to disclose honest and responsible feelings and thoughts
- **empathy**—to feel as the other person feels, to experience what the other is experiencing from that person's point of view without losing our own identity
- **supportiveness**—when our communication is descriptive rather than evaluative; provisional rather than certain (see Gibb, 1961)
- **equality**—acceptance and approval of a person through "unconditional positive regard" (see Rogers, 1972)
- **positiveness**—stating positive attitudes and verbally stroking the person with whom we interact (DeVito, 1995, pp. 92–99)

The **pragmatic or behavioral approach** focuses on specific behaviors that a speaker or listener should use to gain his or her desired outcome (DeVito, 1995). This approach has been derived from the work of scholars such as Paul Watzlawick (Watzlawick, Beavin, and Jackson, 1967; Watzlawick, 1977), William Lederer (1984), Don Jackson (Lederer and Jackson, 1968), and others (Spitzberg and Hecht, 1984). The five qualities of effectiveness are:

- **confidence**—an exhibited ease with the other person and with the communication situation in general
- **immediacy**—conveying a sense of interest and attention, a liking for and an attraction to the other person which results in a joining of the speaker and the listener
- **interaction management**—effectively controlling the interaction to the satisfaction of both parties through self-monitoring or manipulating the image we present to others

- **expressiveness**—the skill of communicating genuine involvement in the interaction with demonstrated responsibility for thoughts and feelings expressed
- **other-orientation**—the ability to adapt to the other person during the interpersonal encounter by communicating attentiveness and interest in the other person and in what is being said (DeVito, 1995, pp. 99–105)

While the characteristics offered in this section may use different terminology, the advice seems rather universal. Effectiveness in communication is based on our ability to relate to the other person in a positive, responsible, and respectful manner. The importance of adaptability and flexibility is continually stressed as a means of applying the prescriptive characteristics of these models in a descriptive way which adapts to the situation, the person, and the message. Communication competence and effectiveness are two terms which are meant to have broad definitions with some universal applications—all of which are intended to improve our interpersonal interactions.

Summary

Interpersonal communication competence has been identified as an important concept by communication scholars over the years. While this term has been difficult to define and has created some disagreement among researchers, some basic characteristics have emerged which have some universal applications. Communication competence has no single ideal approach, is situational in nature, has a relational dimension and can be learned. Communication competence can be demonstrated by the sender through such characteristics as appropriateness, flexibility, empathy, positiveness, respect, involvement, and responsibility. Most importantly, communication competence is measured through the perceptions of the receiver. While exhibiting the characteristics of communication competence is no guarantee that we will be viewed as effective communicators, using these characteristics as a goal can certainly enhance our ability to become more effective in our interpersonal relationships.

References

Adler, Ronald B., Lawrence B. Rosenfeld, and Neil Towne. *Interplay: The Process of Interpersonal Communication*, 5th ed. New York: Holt, Rinehart and Winston, 1992.

Allport, G. W. *Personality: A Psychological Interpretation*. New York: Holt, Rinehart, and Winston, 1937.

Bostrom, R. N. *Communication in Competence: A Multidisciplinary Approach*. Newbury Park, CA: Sage, 1984.

Canary, Daniel J. and Michael J. Cody. *Interpersonal Communication: A Goals-Based Approach*. New York: St. Martin's Press, 1994.

Caputo, John S., Harry C. Hazel, and Colleen McMahan. *Interpersonal Communication: Competency Through Critical Thinking*. Boston: Allyn and Bacon, 1994.

Cegala, D. H. "Affective and Cognitive Manifestations of Interaction Involvement During Unstructured and Competitive Interactions," *Communication Monographs*, 51(1984): 320–326.

DeVito, Joseph A. *The Interpersonal Communication Book*, 7th ed. New York: HarperCollins, 1995.

Gibb, Jack. "Defensive Communication," *Journal of Communication*, 11(1961): 141–148.

Goffman, Eric. *The Presentation of Self in Everyday Life*. Garden City, NY: Doubleday Anchor Books, 1959.

Kirchler, E. "Material Happiness and Interaction in Everyday Surroundings: A Time-Sample Diary Approach for Couples." *Journal of Social and Personal Relationships*, 5(1988): 375–382.

Knapp, Mark L. and Anita L. Vangelisti. *Interpersonal Communication and Human Relationships*, 2nd ed. Boston: Allyn and Bacon, 1992.

Lederer, William J. *Creating a Good Relationship*. New York: W. W. Norton, 1984.

Lederer, William J.and D. D. Jackson. *The Mirages of Marriage*. New York: W. W. Norton, 1968.

Maslow, Abraham. *Motivation and Personality*. New York: HarperCollins, 1970.

McCroskey, J. C. "Communication Competence and Performance: A Research and Pedagological Perspective." *Communication Education*, 31(1982): 1–8.

Norton, R. *Communicator Style*. Beverly Hills: Sage, 1983.

Parks, M. R. "Interpersonal Competence and the Quest for Personal Competence." In *Handbook of Interpersonal Communication*, M. L. Knapp and G. R. Miller, eds., pp. 171–201. Newbury Park, CA: Sage, 1985.

Pearce, W. B. and Cronen, V. *Communication, Action and Meaning: The Creation of Social Realities*. New York: Praeger, 1980.

Rogers, Carl R. *On Becoming A Person*. Boston: Houghton Mifflin, 1972.

Rubin, R. B. "The Validity of the Communication Competence Assessment Instrument," *Communication Monographs*, 52(1985): 173–185.

Spitzberg, Brian H. and W. R. Cupach. *Interpersonal Communication Competence*. Newbury Park, CA: Sage, 1984.

_____. *Handbook in Interpersonal Communication Competence*. New York: Springer-Verlag, 1989.

Spitzberg, Brian H. and Michael L. Hecht. "A Component Model of Relational Competence." *Human Communication Research*, 10(1984): 575–599.

Watzlawick, Paul. *How Real Is Real: Confusion, Disinformation, Communications Theory*. New York: Vintage, 1977.

Watzlawick, Paul, Janet Helmick Beavin, and Don D. Jackson. *Pragmatics of Human Communication: A Study of Interactional Patterns, Pathologies, and Paradoxes*. New York: W. W. Norton, 1967.

Wheeless, V. E. and W. B. Lashbrook. "Style," in *Personality and Interpersonal Communication*, ed. by J. C. McCroskey and J. A. Daly. Newbury Park, CA: Sage, 1987.

Wiemann, J. M. and P. Backlund. "Current Theory and Research in Communicative Competence," *Review of Educational Research*, 50(1980): 185–199.

Case 60

TargetTerms

- communication competence
- conversational management
- adaptability/flexibility
- other-orientation

PreviewNotes

Sometimes we wish our significant others knew how to say just the right words. Both Jen and Henry may need some assistance in this case.

CaseParticipants

Jen—middle-aged, married woman with two school-age children, who has just prepared and eaten dinner

Henry—Middle-aged, married man with two school-age children, who has just eaten dinner

"The Bickersons"

The following conversation takes place in the kitchen. Henry is busy reading a newspaper when Jen says:

Jen: What makes you so busy now that you can't give me a hand with this garbage?

Henry: Jeez—I had a hard day, ya know.

Jen: What do you think I was doing? Eating bon-bons at three in the afternoon?

Henry: Look, you're the one who brought up the topic.

Jen: What topic?

Henry: The one you're so edgy about.

Jen: Hey, it's not a topic. It's the garbage—and the stench is smelling up the entire kitchen. Can't you get it out of here?

Henry: You see that I'm reading.

Jen: So big deal—you can't take one second to help out?

Henry: C'mon—why can't I get one second of peace and quiet?

Jen: You bring this on yourself. You'd save so much time if you just did what I asked.

Henry: Always you—never me.

Jen: Don't you think that we oughta sit down—like now—and talk about it.

Henry: About what . . . the garbage?

Jen: You know that's not what I meant!

Henry: So what do you mean?

Jen: I want you to start thinking about what needs to be done around here.

Henry: Like I never do that?

Jen: Not really . . . look at that leak in the ceiling.

Henry: It can all wait, I'm sure.

Jen: Till when? Will you please look at me when I talk to you?

Henry: It's the same old thing every night. Speaking of ideas—I got one. Let's go out to dinner for a change, tomorrow night.

Jen: Sure—that's great! I have to help the kids with their homework—and I'm sitting here arguing with someone who could've taken out the garbage three times already.

Henry: Got any better ideas?

Jen: Nope—just that I'll take out the garbage myself!

CaseConcerns

1. Describe Henry's communication style. Do the same for Jen. How do they differ? How are they the same?

2. What advice would you give to Jen and Henry to enhance their communication competencies? Be specific in your answer and be sure to give practical examples of how they can develop more effective communication competence.

3. Using Canary and Cody's criteria for communication competence, analyze the communication that takes place in this case by focusing on the six areas researched by the authors.

ReflectiveResponses

1. Describe how you use the humanistic approach and/or the pragmatic approach in your communication behavior. Do you tend to use one approach more than the other? Explain your answer.

2. Develop your own definition of communication competence.

Case 61

TargetTerms

- adaptability
- flexibility
- empathy
- supportiveness
- positiveness

PreviewNotes

When communication competence operates at its best, very effective results can occur. Is it just luck? Is this case realistic?

CaseParticipants

Tom—best friend of David, university senior
David—best friend of Tom, university senior

"Saying the right things"

David is sitting in the university student center rereading his recently received "Dear John" letter from his girlfriend, who lives in another town. Although David believes he is masking his hurt emotions, his friend Tom notices and says:

Tom: Why the long face?

David: Oh, it's nothing.

Tom: (*sits down next to his friend*) Hey, I've known you for a long time. I know when something is bothering you. Anything I can do?

David: Thanks, I'm not ready to talk about it.

Tom: I understand. Can I get you a cup of coffee or something?

David: No, thanks. (*hesitant before he speaks*) Have you ever been dumped by a girlfriend?

> Tom: So that's it. Sure—and if it makes you feel any better, I was wild for about a week.
>
> David: Only a week—I thought that this would go on for about a year! (*They both smile.*)
>
> Tom: Listen, it's not the end of the world. I know the last thing you want to hear now is that there are other fish in the sea . . . but there are. In fact, I am having a little party tonight. Why don't you come?
>
> David: Ahhh . . . I'm not really up to seeing people yet.
>
> Tom: Don't think of it like that. You can have something to eat and if you want to stay, you'll stay. If not, eat and run. (*Waits for an answer and sensing none, he continues.*) There could be some interesting people there—including two women who just moved in the apartment down the hall.
>
> David: Nice try!
>
> Tom: I'm not kidding! There will be about eleven people and I hate odd numbers—so please come. The new neighbors need to meet people and I want to play the perfect host and introduce them to my friends. Please come.
>
> David: You always know just what to say and when to say it, don't you?
>
> Tom: Just lucky, I guess. (*They both smile.*)

CaseConcerns

1. How is communication competence evidenced in this case? Give specific examples.
2. Describe how empathy is used in this case.
3. Do you think David felt that Tom was empathic?
4. If you were David in this case, how would you have responded to Tom's conversation?
5. Do you think Tom illustrated adaptability or flexibility as a communicator? If so, how?

ReflectiveResponses

1. When you are feeling down and out, how do you want others to respond to your needs? Do you feel that you make those needs clear? If so, how?
2. Identify two or three characteristics of communication competence that you have used in your conversations.

TargetTerms

Abdicrat   William Schutz's (1958) description of a person who feels that he or she is not responsible or capable, so they allow others to make decisions for them; a "go-along-with-the-crowd" type person.

Ability to cope   A reward of self-disclosure that allows us to stay in the mainstream so we can continue to participate in our growth and development of our self-concept and our relationships.

Accommodation   A style of conflict that occurs when a participant is nonassertive and cooperative; the person puts aside personal concerns in order to satisfy the concerns of other participants.

Adaptability   The ability to change behaviors and goals to meet the needs of the interaction.

Affection   According to William Schutz (1960), the need for respect, confirmation, empathy, and love.

Affinity   The degree to which partners like or appreciate each other.

Agreement about content   Supporting or reinforcing information expressed by the sender; one of the Sieburg/Larson (1971) confirming responses.

Androgyny   The integration and utilization of masculine and feminine behaviors within a single individual, regardless of sex.

Anger   A result of our need to be right that takes a great deal of energy to control and direct into a positive path; a debilitating emotion.

Appreciative listening   The process of gratifying our senses and tastes while striving for maximum pleasure through listening.

Assimilating   A listening process whereby new experiences and concepts are incorporated into existing cognitive structures and are used in a meaningful way.

Attraction-similarity theory   When we like a person, we perceive that similarities exist with that person.

Attitudes   Our predispositions toward action based on what we like or do not like.

Attraction theory   People are attracted to people who share the same values.

Attribution   The process in which we attach meaning to behavior—verbal or nonverbal.

Autocrat   William Schutz's (1958) description of a person who is competitive and exercises power any chance he or she gets; a strong need for control.

Avoidance   A style of conflict that involves nonassertive, passive behavior refusing to participate in the conflict.

Avoiding   Mark Knapp's (1978) fourth stage in the relationship deterioration process that involves physical distance between the partners and an air of imperviousness.

Barriers to growth of self-concept   Certain barriers or things that we view as deficiencies in the self-concept that impair or impede the communication process and the growth of the self-concept; includes physical image, intelligence, social self, moral/ethical self.

BAVs   Our beliefs, attitudes, and values that are obtained through socialization and are influenced through various types of relationships; they strongly affect the way we communicate.

Beliefs Our individual perceptions of what is and what is not, based on our idea of truth and falsity.

Benefits of expressing emotions According to Adler et al. (1986), the advantages of expressing emotions are **physical health, increased intimacy**, and **conflict resolution** (see individual definitions).

Black and white perspective Seeing things only as one way or the other — opposites.

Blurting Communication that is inappropriate, untimely, overdone, and usually out of context.

Bonding Mark Knapp's (1978) fifth stage of developing relationships that involves the public ritual of announcing to the world that commitments have been formally contracted (business, marriage, performance).

Brain power The ability to remain open-minded, avoid making assumptions about stimuli we receive, and seek to maintain a clear, nonjudgmental vision; clear and accurate perceptions (Albrecht, 1980).

Bull's-eye theory Communication that removes the necessity of providing or allowing feedback making the communication process very one-sided. Myers and Myers (1975) refer to this type of communication as a one-way act, like shooting an arrow into a target (see also **conveyor-belt theory**).

Caring-too-much syndrome Overcompensating for times when we did not feel like satisfying a need of the other person; doing what we think represents caring and loving behaviors, which end up suffocating the receiver.

Certainty One of Gibb's (1961) six defensive climates that refers to a person feeling as if the sender is being dogmatic.

Circumscribing Mark Knapp's (1978) second stage in the relationship deterioration process that is characterized by constricted or restrained communication which begins decreasing both in quality and quantity.

Clarifying response Trying to clarify the response of the sender; eliciting more information; to repeat (in an inquiring way) what was understood; one of the Sieburg/Larson (1971) confirming responses.

Cliché conversation The lowest level of self-disclosure that takes the form of meaningless interaction; empty cocktail gibberish; phatic communication.

Co-dependency Giving up a part of who we are to "help" someone, although that person does not respect us and manipulates us into performing unhealthy behaviors.

Coercive power The ability to punish another person. Punishment includes removal of rewards which the person presently enjoys.

Cognitive dissonance Leon Festinger's (1957) concept of a state of discomfort created by two items of knowledge that are psychologically inconsistent (i.e., wanting to smoke but knowing it is unhealthy).

Cognitive interpretations The cognitive label that we put on emotions that establishes their meaning; one of the four components of emotion (Adler et al., 1986).

Collaboration A style of conflict that involves highly assertive behavior aimed at reaching one's own goals mixed with a high concern for others; both parties work creatively to find new solutions that will maximize goals for both.

Communication The process of transmitting and interpreting messages (Weaver, 1993).

Communication competence The ability to obtain what you are seeking from others in a manner that maintains the relationship on terms that are acceptable to both you and the other person (Adler, Rosenfeld, and Towne, 1992).

Communication effectiveness Achieving the objectives we have for our conversations.

Communication style Competence in the selection and use of verbal and nonverbal language which enables people to create, maintain, and/or improve their relationships with one another (Wheeless and Lashbrook, 1987; Norton, 1983).

Community values The importance of adopting the central values of the groups with which we associate; socialization values of society.

Competing A style of conflict that involves aggressive and uncooperative behavior; pursuing your own concerns at the expense of another.

Complementary relationship A relationship based on acceptance of each other, and enjoyment of each other's differences; opposites attract.

Components of emotion The four basic elements that describe our emotions (Adler et al., 1986): **physiological change, nonverbal manifestations, cognitive interpretations**, and **verbal expression** (see individual definitions).

Compromise An intermediate style of conflict between assertiveness and cooperativeness; getting both parties to "split the difference" so that each gets something; unsatisfying solutions obtained which usually result in another conflict.

Compromise and negotiation A conflict strategy that involves the process of discovering the range of acceptable solutions through cooperative communication.

Confirming responses Messages which make the other person feel good about himself/herself (Sieburg and Larson, 1971). The five behaviors include **direct acknowledgement, agreement about content, supportive, clarifying**, and **expression of positive feeling** (see individual definitions).

Conflict An expressed struggle between two interdependent parties who perceive incompatible goals, scarce rewards, and interference from the other party in achieving their goals; the bringing out of differences between us and the other party.

Conflict is a ball game The conflict myth that assumes that there are rules and regulations which must be followed along with expected behaviors; (Hocker and Wilmot, 1985).

Conflict is a bargaining table The conflict myth that describes a collaborative approach with implied meetings, negotiations, and parliamentary procedure; (Hocker and Wilmot, 1985).

Conflict is a trial The conflict myth that is characterized by presenting evidence for your case and awaiting the impending verdict of right or wrong; relationship problems are seldom settled by these trials, parties keep going back to court; (Hocker and Wilmot, 1985).

Conflict is an upward struggle The conflict myth that is characterized by the feeling that if you can get high enough, on top of things far enough, that you can beat this battle and exercise control; (Hocker and Wilmot, 1985).

Conflict is explosive The conflict myth which perceives that conflict is made up of flammable materials (such as feelings) and that once it is started, it cannot be stopped; (Hocker and Wilmot, 1985).

Conflict is war A conflict myth that characterizes conflict as an argument or a battle and words such as "victim" and "winner" are used; (Hocker and Wilmot, 1985).

Conflict myths Hocker and Wilmot (1985) present eight common images that people have about conflict, most of which are descriptions of negative metaphors and describe our myths about conflict: **conflict is war, conflict is explosive, conflict is an upward struggle, conflict is a trial, conflict is a ball game, conflict requires a hero**, and **conflict is a bargaining table** (see individual definitions).

Conflict requires a hero The conflict myth that is characterized by having a leader who will protect others; hero worship of the good guys and the bad guys; the myth that someone will help us win; (Hocker and Wilmot, 1985).

Conflict resolution A major benefit of expressing emotion (Adler et al., 1986).

Conflict strategies Four conflict-management techniques that provide strategic options for dealing with conflict that we can not prevent (McCroskey et al., 1986): **leaving the field, restoring trust, reinstating communication**, and **compromise and negotiation** (see individual definitions).

Conflict styles   Kilmann and Thomas (1975) provide five descriptions of how individuals approach conflict: **competing, collaboration, compromise, avoidance**, and **accommodation** (see individual definitions).

Consensual validation   The search for mutual agreement and the need to receive positive feedback of our perceptions.

Content level   The part of the message which involves the verbal aspect of a message; the words chosen.

Control   One of Gibb's (1961) defensive climates in which the receiver feels like he or she is being controlled or manipulated in conversation.

Control   William Schutz (1960) defines this as the desire to influence others and/or to feel some sense of power over our own lives.

Control values   The importance of making an effort to persuade others or to control others in a situation; treasuring of one's own power in interaction.

Covert response   The process of preparing within how we will overtly respond to the speaker.

Crazymaking   The use of indirect, double-speak language that sends unclear, confusing messages. George Bach and Ronald Deutsch (1979) highlight four rights that satisfy our needs: **the right to know, the right to feel, the right to impact**, and **the right to space** (see individual definitions).

Conveyor-belt theory   The model or view of the process of communication that causes us to assume that others understand our meaning which then absolves us from any responsibility beyond sending the message; one-way communication, similar to the bull's-eye theory by Myers and Myers (1975); the person who views communication in this way does not understand the importance of feedback (Berlo, 1960).

Dance's Helix   A model of communication that describes how we are influenced by every single person with whom we come into contact; described as a spiral, similar to that of a "slinky" toy (Dance and Larson, 1972).

Debilitative emotions   Feelings or sensations which are unmanaged and usually disallow effective communication.

Decentering   A process where we begin to become aware of other people's needs and learn sharing, caring, and giving.

Defense mechanisms   Four common "filters" (Festinger, 1957) that we create in order to combat differences in perception: **selective exposure, selective attention, selective perception**, and **selective retention** (see individual definitions).

Defensive climates   Gibb's (1961) six distinct communication behaviors that promote a defensive climate: **evaluative, control, strategy, neutrality, superiority**, and **certainty** (see individual definitions).

Democrat   William Schutz's (1958) description of a person who sees power as an equal exchange, and uses it appropriately; the most desired response to power.

Description   Nonjudgmental presentation of feelings, events, perceptions, or processes which do not ask or imply that the receiver change a behavior or attitude; one of Gibb's (1961) supportive climate responses.

Detachment   The fourth phase of empathy (Weaver, 1987) that involves pulling back and maintaining objectivity, having successfully engaged in the first three phases (feeling, incorporation, reverberation).

Differentiating   Mark Knapp's (1978) first stage in the relationship deterioration process that involves one or both partners feeling a need to re-identify the self after having bonded.

Direct acknowledgement   Reacting directly and verbally; acknowledging the other person's communication; one of the Sieburg/Larson (1971) confirming responses.

Disconfirming responses   Messages that tell the other person that you (the sender) do not like anything about him/her (Sieburg and Larson, 1971). The seven behaviors are **impervious, interrupting, irrelevant, tangential, impersonal, incoherent, incongruous** (see individual definitions).

Discriminating listening   The process whereby we consciously acquire material that will be of future value to us or that we deem to be of future value; learning to perceive, identify, and obtain information and ideas to store for use at a later time.

Dispute your irrational beliefs   A step in Rational Emotive Therapy that is characterized by using the list of irrational beliefs that lead to debilitative feelings, and identify which of these internal statements are based on irrational thinking (Ellis and Harper, 1977).

Dogmatism   An unwillingness or inability to consider opposing points of view or ideas contrary to existing attitudes; closed-mindedness; also disallowing others to have opposing views by strongly defending your own.

Drives   The physiological needs generated by our bodies that create the desire for action (i.e., hunger).

Duration   The length of time an emotion is felt; usually the more intense, the longer the duration.

Egospeak   Addeo and Burger (1973) refer to this when the process of covert response preparation occurs too soon or requires too much involvement on the part of the preparer; this process can be very negative when it becomes waiting to speak instead of listening.

Emotion is a means for self-understanding, self-control, and security   One of Weaver's (1987) reasons of why it is important to understand the term emotion.

Emotion is a supplement to reason   One of Weaver's (1987) reasons why it is important to understand the term emotion.

Emotion is an aspect of individual uniqueness   One of Weaver's (1987) reasons why it is important to understand the term emotion.

Emotion is an element of empathy   One of Weaver's (1987) reasons why it is important to understand the term emotion.

Emotion is part of the human condition   One of Weaver's (1987) reasons why it is important to understand the term emotion.

Empathic listening   Listening to someone's problems with an open ear and an open heart. The goal of empathic listening is to help the speaker understand his or her feelings.

Empathy   A person feels a high degree of caring from the sender; one of Gibb's (1961) supportive climates.

Entropy   A chaotic state caused by **cognitive dissonance** (see individual definition) which measures the degree of uncertainty.

Equality   Occurs when one person tries to keep the roles within the transaction on an even level; a person feels equal to the sender; one of Gibb's (1961) supportive climate responses.

Ethnocentrism   The tendency to evaluate the beliefs, attitudes, values, and behaviors of our own culture as being more positive, logical, and natural than those of other cultures (DeVito, 1994).

Evaluative climate   One of Gibb's (1961) defensive climates in which the receiver feels like he or she is being judged.

Expectation   The perception process of avoiding the set up of desired outcomes through predisposed visions.

Experimenting   Mark Knapp's (1978) second stage of a relationship that involves more risky interaction and integrating topics; a long amount of time is spent in this stage.

Expert power   The ability to deliver some special service because you have special knowledge or abilities.

Expression of positive feeling Demonstrating support and agreement; expressing personal, positive feelings about the sender's message; one of Sieburg and Larson's (1971) confirming responses.

Expressive orientation The traditional stereotype of females as non-aggressive, illogical, emotional, subjective, and dependent.

Exterior locus of control A frame of mind where a person perceives that reward for actions stems from outside forces.

Evaluative listening The process illustrated as we weigh evidence or reason presented in an argument.

Facilitative emotions Feelings or sensations which are managed into effective functioning in conflict.

Fallacy of approval One of the seven irrational beliefs which assumes that it is vital to obtain everyone's approval (Adler et al., 1986).

Fallacy of catastrophic expectations Operating on the assumption that if something bad can happen, it will; one of the seven irrational belief fallacies (Adler et al., 1986).

Fallacy of causation One of the seven irrational beliefs that suggests you can cause others to feel in a certain way (Adler et al., 1986).

Fallacy of helplessness One of the seven irrational beliefs that assumes satisfaction in life is determined by forces beyond control (Adler et al., 1986).

Fallacy of overgeneralization One of the seven irrational beliefs which communicates by making statements which are based on inadequate information and are usually phrased as absolutes which are almost always false (Adler et al., 1986).

Fallacy of perfection One of the seven irrational beliefs which believes that we can be perfect if we just try hard enough (Adler et al., 1986).

Fallacy of shoulds The inability to distinguish between what "is" and what "should be"; operating from the perspective that everything should be the way you want it; one of the seven irrational beliefs (Adler et al., 1986).

Fear A debilitating emotion that restricts our freedom and can control our lives; clouds our logic, immobilizes us, and restricts us from taking necessary actions.

Fear of punishment A fear of being rejected that leads to a resistance to self-disclosure.

Fear of self-knowledge The fear that sharing information about ourselves will lead to learning about ourselves which causes a resistance to self-disclosure.

Feedback The preparation of a message to send back to the original sender of a message.

Feeling The first stage of empathy (Weaver, 1987) which involves letting the other's feelings act on us.

F.O.R. (frame of reference) Our personal view of reality; an aspect of communication that influences our message and includes the impact of ALL our experiences; understanding these influences can increase our clarity in message dissemination.

Four phases of empathy Richard Weaver's (1987) concept that describes four steps which lead to a clearer understanding of emotion: **feeling, incorporation, reverberation**, and **detachment** (see individual definitions).

Four ultimate values Four main value clusters through which we establish relationships (Bales and Couch, 1969): **community values, other person's unique values, control values**, and **our own unique values** (see individual definitions).

Functional value Values which influence our day-to-day communication behaviors such as cleanliness and friendliness (Rokeach, 1973).

Gender A psychological and cultural term that refers to our subjective feelings of maleness or femaleness and provides each person with a gender identity or role; not related to sex.

Gender role An evaluation of an individual's behaviors as masculine or feminine; unrelated to biological sex behaviors.

Gender-role stereotype The socialized oversimplified conceptions of our behaviors as males and females through stereotyped masculine and feminine roles.

Goblet issues Empty cocktail gibberish such as "Hi, how are you?"; usually occurs during Powell's (1969) **cliché conversation**.

Hearing The physiological part of the listening process when receiving oral stimuli. We hear the message, but if we do not process it, consequently, the message is lost.

Heterosexism Any language, conscious or unconscious, that places any person in an inferior position relating to sexuality or orientation.

Hierarchy of needs Developed by Maslow (1970), a triangle of building blocks used to establish a systematic list of needs for human potentiation. The five levels of needs are **physical, safety/self-preservation, love and belonging, self-esteem and pride**, and **self-actualization** (see individual definitions).

Honesty A value that is based on the whole truth.

Imagined vs. real self We can develop either a "real" image of our self-concept (one which is housed in reality and honesty), or an "imagined" self-concept (one which is housed in self deceit, ignorance, and fantasy).

Impersonal response Not acknowledging that the other person is present; speaking in generalized terms ("one" or clichés); conducting a monologue; one of the Sieburg/Larson (1971) disconfirming responses.

Impervious response Ignoring the speaker; denying the sender any feedback; failure to acknowledge; one of the Sieburg/Larson (1971) disconfirming responses.

Improvement of communication effectiveness and clarity A reward of self-disclosure which allows us to create trust and develop a satisfying, close relationship with another person.

Inclusion According to William Schutz (1960), the need to feel a sense of belonging (personal relationship, group, club, ethnic identity).

Incoherent response Not making sense; responses that are not understandable; rambling and difficult to follow; one of the Sieburg/Larson (1971) disconfirming responses.

Incongruous response Nonvocal and verbal disagreement in the message; when what you say is not reinforced by your behavior; incongruity between verbal intent and nonvocal/nonverbal behavior; one of the Sieburg/Larson (1971) disconfirming responses.

Incorporation The second stage of empathy (Weaver, 1987) which involves merging the other's feelings with our own.

Increased intimacy A major benefit of expressing emotion (Adler et al., 1986).

Indirect communication Sending messages that do not deal directly with the issue or problem; not saying what we really mean.

Initiating Mark Knapp's (1978) first stage of developing relationships when we try to make a good first impression and tend to put on a facade; minimal amounts of fact and information sharing.

Instrumental orientation The traditional stereotype of males as aggressive, logical, unemotional, objective, and independent.

Integrating Mark Knapp's (1978) fourth stage of developing relationships where the word "coupling" can be used; more time is spent together, and a fusion of personalities begins to develop.

Intensity The depth of our feelings that can keep us from thinking clearly and often leads to an urge to act on the feeling.

Intercultural communication Communication between persons who have different cultural beliefs, values, or ways of behaving (DeVito, 1994).

Interior locus of control A frame of mind where a person perceives that reward for actions follows from an individual's behavior.

Intensifying   Mark Knapp's (1978) third step of developing relationships which involves more commitment and more intimate disclosure to deepen the relationship.

Interpersonal conflict   An expressed struggle between interdependent parties who perceive incompatible goals and scarce rewards.

Interpretation   The perception process of attaching meaning and identification to the recognized stimuli while tolerating some ambiguity.

Interrupting response   Breaking into the conversation before the other person is finished; cutting off the speaker; to begin speaking while the sender is still speaking; one of the Sieburg/Larson (1971) disconfirming responses.

Intrapersonal conflict   A struggle which is internal and deals with personal problems, not relational issues.

Intimacy   A reward of self-disclosure that leads to private and personal relationships.

Irrational beliefs   Seven fallacies (Adler et al., 1986) which lead to illogical conclusions and result in debilitative emotions in relationships: **fallacy of perfection, fallacy of approval, fallacy of shoulds, fallacy of overgeneralization, fallacy of causation, fallacy of helplessness**, and **fallacy of catastrophic expectations** (see individual definitions).

Irrelevant response   Introducing a new topic without warning; disregarding what the speaker just said; one of the Sieburg/Larson (1971) disconfirming responses.

Jealousy   An intense feeling of loneliness, suspicion, or insecurity; a debilitating emotion.

Johari window   A model of how we present ourselves to others which also gives us an idea of the image we project to others.

Leaving the field   A conflict strategy that involves stopping the communication that is instigating the conflict by leaving physically or psychologically, or changing the topic; merely postpones the conflict.

Legitimate power   A matter of obeying tradition and the norms which we have been taught in our society; our legal and social structure; parents, police officers, and employers have this power.

Levels of self-disclosure   John Powell (1969) gives us five levels that describe the type and depth of self-disclosure: **cliché conversation** or **phatic communication; reporting the facts about others; my ideas and judgments; personal feelings and emotions; peak communication** (see individual definitions).

Listening   The conscious, active process of eliciting information, ideas, attitudes, and emotions during interpersonal oral exchange for the purpose of increasing the listener's capacity for understanding and using what he or she is told.

Listening as understanding   The process of trying to be understood. We spend the majority of our lives trying to make others understand who we are, what we mean, and why we do what we do; stresses the importance of listening.

Locus of control   A person's orientation toward the sources of rewards for his/her actions. A person can have an **interior locus of control** or an **exterior locus of control** (see individual definitions).

Looking-glass self   Our picture of our uniqueness that comes when we explore our own personal world with self-contemplation and discovery through images we receive from others; Cooley (1956).

Love and belonging needs   The human need for friendship, affectionate relationships, and interpersonal acceptance; the third step in Maslow's (1970) hierarchy of needs.

Mental health   A reward of self-disclosure that leads to a sound mind and freedom from mental diseases.

Mirror image   The picture we have of ourselves that comes from other people or the image we get about ourselves from others.

Monitor your emotional reactions A step in Rational Emotive Therapy that is characterized by recording and registering debilitative emotions and recognizing what emotion you are feeling (Ellis and Harper, 1977).

Motives Learned behaviors of action which satisfy our drives.

My ideas and judgments Level three of self-disclosure when we begin to break down with caution, the communication barriers we have erected (Powell, 1969).

Needs deprivation We cannot really exist if we are deprived of our emotional and psychological needs; verbal and nonverbal communication are the means by which our interpersonal needs can be met; severe needs deprivation can cause mental illness and damages the self-concept.

Needs fulfillment Communicating with others in hopes of getting our needs met.

Needs suffocation The act of giving the other person what *we* need instead of what *they* need.

Neutrality One of Gibb's (1961) defensive climates that refers to a person feeling apathy from the sender.

Noise The distortion of our message that may lead to us being only partially heard and/or misunderstood; can be physical (a bell) or psychological (nerves).

Nonverbal manifestations The concept that feelings are usually demonstrated nonverbally; one of the four components of emotion (Adler et al., 1986).

Organizing A listening process that involves organizing a spoken message in our mind so that it is decipherable.

Other person's unique values The importance of appreciating the unique values of the individuals we are related to; treasuring of other people as unique individuals.

Our own unique values The importance of asserting one's own individual and unique values; treasuring of one's own individuality.

Overt response A verbal or nonverbal response which is a result of the listening process that can be observed by others. An overt response becomes feedback only when it is received and interpreted by a receiver.

Parallel relationship A balanced relationship where partners share power and fulfill each other's needs; mutual acceptance and respect by both parties; (same as symmetrical-complementary compromise).

Peak communication The highest level of self-disclosure when true understanding and empathy are equally felt (Powell, 1969).

Perceived vs. ideal self Our perceived self is our self-concept that tends to come from other people, while our ideal self is our self-concept that tends to come from ourselves; the ideal self tends to win in the long run (Rogers, 1961).

Perception The process of becoming aware of objects and events from our senses (DeVito, 1986).

Perception process Three key **principles of perception** presented in Karl Albrecht's *Brain Power* (1980): **recognition, interpretation**, and **expectation** (see individual definitions).

Perceptual checking Assists in increasing the accuracy of our perceptions about the communication behaviors of self and others.

Perceptual framework Our frame of reference that we create from our awareness of objects and events as perceived from the senses; developed through our experiences.

Personal feelings and emotions Level two of self-disclosure that requires total honesty; we begin to take the chance on whether or not others will accept us for what we really are (Powell, 1969).

Personal growth and commitment A reward of self-disclosure that leads to a clearer understanding of ourselves and the ability to maintain that understanding.

Phatic communication A level of self-disclosure that breaks the ice and allows us time to decide if we want to continue the conversation (Powell, 1969); occurs during **cliché conversation** (see individual definition).

Physical health   A major benefit of expressing emotion (Adler et al., 1986).

Physical needs   The human need for food, water, sex, and air; the first step in Maslow's (1970) hierarchy of needs.

Physiological change   Changes in the body that occur when strong emotions are felt; one of the four components of emotion (Adler et al., 1986).

Platonic relationship   A friendship between a man and a woman that is purely spiritual or intellectual and is void of sexual activity.

Powell's rules for disclosing "gut level" feelings   John Powell's (1974) five guidelines for peak communication: Emotional openness and honesty must never imply a judgment of the other, emotions are not moral, feelings and emotions must be integrated with the intellect and the will, emotions must be reported, and emotions must be reported at the time that they are being experienced.

Pragmatics   The ability to understand and use constitutive and regulative rules in a practical manner (Caputo, Hazel, and McMahon, 1994).

Principle of consistency   The strong human desire to keep things basically the same. We like to keep things stable, in order, and visually definite.

Problem orientation   Communication designed to assure the other person that he/she is not being controlled or manipulated; both persons are engaged in mutual definition of the problem; one of Gibb's (1961) supportive climate responses.

Proximity   The physical distance between two people in terms of location.

Provisionalism   A willingness to be open to a person's views; when a person does not feel the effects of dogmatism; one of Gibb's (1961) supportive climate responses.

Punctuation of communication events   The phenomenon that occurs when the differences in people's frames of reference create a proportionally larger gap in the semantic differential scale and reduce overall message clarity and accuracy (DeVito, 1986); when we interpret events differently.

Racism   Any language, conscious or unconscious, that places any person in an inferior position because of race.

Rational Emotive Therapy (RET)   A four-step therapeutic approach (Ellis and Harper, 1977) to emotional control pioneered by Albert Ellis that assumes people make irrational assumptions that create emotional and behavioral problems; a technique which substitutes   logical and rational premises for irrational ones: **monitor your emotional reactions, notice the activating event, record your self-talk**, and **dispute your irrational beliefs** (see individual definitions).

Reasons for understanding emotion   Richard Weaver (1978) identifies five reasons why it is important to understand the term emotion. **Emotion is part of the human condition, an element of empathy, an aspect of individual uniqueness, a supplement to reason**, and **a means for self-understanding, self-control, and security** (see individual definitions).

Reciprocity   A condition which exists when each person in an interpersonal relationship satisfies the other person's preferences; sharing of intimate information from each person in the relationship; allows the relationship to grow and intensify.

Recognition   The perception process of deciding which stimuli deserve our attention and paying attention to those details.

Record your self-talk   A step in Rational Emotive Therapy that analyzes the thoughts that link the activating event to the feeling (Ellis and Harper, 1977).

Referent power   Exercised over someone when the other person wants to be like us.

Reinstating communication   A conflict strategy that is an attempt to begin again by increasing the amount of communication.

Relationship level   The part of a message involving the implied status and metacommunication message about how the sender views the receiver.

Reporting the facts about others   Level four of self-disclosure where we maintain our protective shield by not revealing anything about ourselves, but by sharing what others have said (Powell, 1969).

Resistance to self-disclosure   Factors based primarily in fear that influence our choice of the level of self-disclosure in which we will participate (DeVito, 1986): **societal bias, fear of punishment**, and **fear of self knowledge** (see individual definitions).

Restoring trust   A conflict strategy that deals with the suspicion and distrust that has initiated the conflict.

Retaining   A listening process that involves retaining data in our short-term memory.

Reverberation   The third phase of empathy (Weaver, 1987) which involves interacting with the feelings experienced by the other person.

Rewards of self-disclosure   The advantages and benefits of self-disclosure identified by DeVito (1986): **mental health, intimacy, personal growth and commitment, ability to cope**, and **improvement of communication effectiveness and clarity** (see individual definitions).

Reward power   The ability to deliver something of value which another person wants.

Right of impact   The crazymaking theory (Bach and Deutsch, 1979) that refers to our need to know that we matter and that we have an impact on others.

Role   A cluster of socially or culturally defined expectations that individuals in a given situation are expected to fulfil (Chafetz, 1978).

Safety/self-preservation needs   The human need for security, stability, protection, law, order, freedom from fear, freedom from anxiety, and freedom from chaos; the second step in Maslow's (1970) hierarchy of needs.

Selecting   The listening process in which we select the message stimuli as one to which we will attend.

Selective attention   One of the four defense mechanisms that involves listening only to those messages which reinforce our current frame of reference (Festinger, 1957).

Selective exposure   One of the four defense mechanisms that allows us to be exposed only to those messages which reinforce our current frame of reference (Festinger, 1957).

Selective perception   One of the four defense mechanisms which allows us to perceive and decipher messages only through our current frame of reference to the point of changing the intent (Festinger, 1957).

Selective retention   One of the four defense mechanisms that causes us to remember only those parts of the message that reinforce our current frame of reference (Festinger, 1957).

Self-actualization   The fifth and final step in Maslow's (1970) hierarchy of needs; doing what one is fitted for doing, self-fulfillment, and actualizing to one's highest human potential.

Self-concept   The relatively stable image or perception we hold of ourselves including physical features, emotional states, talents, dislikes, values, roles, and needs; includes multiple images and multiple selves blending together to form a unique personality with a unique frame of reference.

Self-disclosure   The act of sharing information about the self that will assist others in understanding a current behavior.

Self-esteem and pride needs   The human need for high self-evaluation, self-respect, self-esteem, esteem of others, strength, achievement, competency, reputation, prestige, status, fame, and glory; the fourth step in Maslow's (1970) hierarchy of needs.

Self-honesty   Being willing to tell yourself the truth about who you are.

Semantic differential   A scale used to measure latitudes of meaning that words can have. The scale displays visually the differences in meaning that one word can have (Osgood et al., 1957).

Sex   A biological term that categorizes people as being either male or female according to their sex organs and genes.

Sexism   Any language, conscious or unconscious, that places any person in an inferior position because of sex.

Sex role   Conceptions of our behaviors as males and females, many times mistakenly based on masculine and feminine gender-role stereotypes.

Sex-role stereotype   The oversimplified conceptions of our behaviors as stereotyped males and females; many assumptions are made here about behaviors which are not linked to one's biological sex but rather to our psychological gender orientation.

Sexual harassment   A negative form of interpersonal communication; defined through a description of the actions taken against a person and the feelings that person has about those actions (Neher and Waite, 1993).

Shoulding   The act of telling ourselves that we *have* to do something; being dominated by guilt, rules, and "shoulds"; a Wayne Dyer (1979) concept.

Similarity   A strong basis for relationship formation is the comfort of knowing someone who likes the things we like, who has similar values, and who may be of the same economic class or education status.

SMCR model of communication   David Berlo (1960) developed this process model that involves a sender who sends a message through various channels to a receiver who then provides feedback as the process begins again (see page 32).

Social exchange theory   An economic model built on the premise that we seek out people who can give us rewards that are greater than or at least equal to the costs involved in being in the relationship.

Societal bias   A fear of labels and stereotypes that leads to a resistance to self-disclosure.

Spontaneity   Behavior that is free, open, honest, and appropriate to the situation; one of Gibb's (1961) supportive climate responses.

Stagnating   Mark Knapp's (1978) third stage in the relationship deterioration process where the relationship stops moving—it merely marks time and goes nowhere; communication becomes more stylized, difficult, rigid, hesitant, awkward, and narrow.

Stereotype   A relatively rigid and oversimplified conception of a group of people in which all individuals in the group are labeled with the so-called group characteristics.

Strategy   One of Gibb's (1961) defensive climates in which the receiver detects a hidden motive or feels like a pawn in a game rather than like an individual.

Supportive climates   Six counterparts to Gibb's (1961) **defensive climates** that promote a positive communication atmosphere: **descriptive, problem orientation, spontaneity, empathy, equality**, and **provisionalism** (see individual definitions).

Supportive response   Expressing an understanding of the sender's message; reassuring and attempting to make the sender feel better; one of the Sieburg/Larson (1971) confirming respnses.

Superiority   One of Gibb's (1961) defensive climates that refers to a person feeling inadequate and subordinate to the sender.

Symmetrical-complementary compromise relationship   A pattern of balance that develops in relationships where partners agree upon sharing power; mutual acceptance and respect by both parties; (same as parallel).

Symmetrical relationship   A relationship based on a subtle struggle to establish or maintain equality; birds of a feather, flock together.

Tangential response   Acknowledging the original message but immediately taking the conversation in a different direction; "Yes, but I . . ."; one of the Sieburg/Larson (1971) disconfirming responses.

Terminal values   Values which influence our long-range, delayed gratification decisions such as successful life and a world at peace (Rokeach, 1973).

Terminating   The final (fifth) stage in Mark Knapp's (1978) relationship deterioration process that is characterized by one or both partners seeking to put psychological and physical distance between them or increasing the concern for one's own self-interests in preparation for continued life without the other person.

The right to feel   The right to have and express your own feelings and emotions without having a significant other tell you what those feelings and emotions are (Bach and Deutsch, 1979).

The right to impact   The right to have demonstrated to you that you mean something to a significant other (Bach and Deutsch, 1979).

The right to know   The right to clear and direct information about a significant other (Bach and Deutsch, 1979).

The right to space   The right to have a separate physical space or to have physical or emotional distance from a significant other (Bach and Deutsch, 1979).

Transactional communication   The view or model of the communication process which implies interdependency and mutual reciprocal causality between sender and receiver (Myers and Myers, 1975).

Trust   The ability to have faith in the behavior of another person; based on integrity of words and actions; a core value.

Tunnel vision   The inability to understand other people's points of view; **dogmatism** (see individual definition); seeing only one path; closed-minded.

Unitary receptive oral-aural communication   This system refers to the continuous and somewhat simultaneous process that occurs when we receive oral messages through the aural (ear) channel involving six intricate physical and mental activities: **hearing, selecting, assimilating, organizing, retaining**, and **covertly responding to aural and nonverbal stimuli** (see individual definitions).

Values   Things which we hold very dear that have a strong influence on our communication behaviors; our judgment of good and bad.

Verbal expression   One of the necessary and difficult components of emotion that vocally expresses the emotional meaning of a feeling (Adler et al., 1986).

AuthorIndex

TopicIndex